Praise for *American Mafia*

"Scholarly, well-written and perhaps one of the best of the literary genre, [*American Mafia*] delves in readable fashion into what brought the Mafia to power in the United States, what sustained it and what led to its downfall. . . . Reppetto does a masterful job of detailing the Mafia in America. It's probably a book Tony Soprano should read."
—*The Buffalo News*

"A smart, reasoned study of the ascendancy of Italian-American organized crime . . . Reppetto's book earns its place among the best, in part because he rarely lapses into belly-full-of-lead prose. And by narrowing his focus, he brings fresh context to a familiar story worth retelling. . . . [Reppetto] has navigated a world of wacky nicknames and Machiavellian alliances—of false romance and cold-blooded greed—to provide a lucid history of the American Mafia for those of us who would not know what else to say after greeting Sammy the Bull."
—*The New York Times Book Review*

"America's fascination with organized crime is seemingly endless . . . but how much of what we know of the Mafia is actually grounded in fact? It is a question that former Chicago detective Thomas Reppetto attempts to answer in his estimable *American Mafia*. . . . Mr. Reppetto's history is richly detailed. (Ken Burns would have a field day turning his book into a documentary.) . . . But *American Mafia* isn't all names, prosecutions and rub-outs. Mr. Reppetto addresses larger concerns, like the connection between the Sicilian Mafia and the American Mafia, arguing that they are in fact separate entities."
—*The Wall Street Journal*

"Reppetto adopts an appropriate tone of contempt for characters familiar from the lore. . . . He separates the savviest among them from the merely thuggish. . . . [He] duly recounts sensational incidents but embeds them within an analytical framework. . . . The mordantly humorous Reppetto makes a perfect guide to Mob history."
—*Booklist*

"A particularly well-qualified reporter . . . Reppetto's reporting touches all bases . . . vividly and authoritatively." —*Kirkus Reviews*

"Reppetto is well-qualified to analyze the mob. . . . *American Mafia* is a solid survey of the rise and fall of Mafia mayhem."
—*Richmond Times-Dispatch*

THOMAS REPPETTO

AMERICAN MAFIA

A History of Its Rise to Power

A HOLT PAPERBACK
John Macrae / Henry Holt and Company
New York

Holt Paperbacks
Henry Holt and Company, LLC
Publishers since 1866
175 Fifth Avenue
New York, New York 10010
www.henryholt.com

Library of Congress Cataloging-in-Publication Data
Reppetto, Thomas A.
    American Mafia : a history of its rise to power / Thomas Reppetto.—1st ed.
      p. cm.
    Includes bibliographical references and index.
    ISBN-13: 978-0-8050-7798-8
    ISBN-10: 0-8050-7798-7
      1. Mafia—United States—History. 2. Organized crime—United States—
    History. 3. Italian American criminals—United States—History. I. Title.
    HV6446R47 2004
    364.1'06'0973—dc22   2003056736

Henry Holt books are available for special promotions
and premiums. For details contact: Director, Special Markets.

Originally published in hardcover in 2004 by John Macrae / Henry Holt and Company
First Holt Paperbacks Edition 2005

Designed by Michelle McMillian
Printed in the United States of America

    9 8 7 6 5 4

In memory of
Lieutenant Joseph Petrosino, NYPD,
murdered while in the performance of his duty,
Palermo, Sicily, March 12, 1909

Contents

Introduction:
"The Most Secret and Terrible
Organization in the World"

It was the surprise television hit of the year. In the spring of 1951, the normally dull proceedings of a congressional investigation suddenly turned into a fascinating drama that gripped the country. Over eight days in March, a U.S. Senate committee chaired by Estes Kefauver of Tennessee held hearings on organized crime in New York City. All three major networks interrupted their regularly scheduled programming to carry the proceedings live. Household chores, office work, and factory schedules were put aside as people became glued to the TV. The New York sessions were the climax to nine months of hearings in fourteen cities. During the course of the investigation, witnesses were murdered and public officials were disgraced. Most important, shadowy underworld figures were made highly visible.

Throughout the Kefauver Committee proceedings, there was constant reference to a sinister, little-known group that played a major role in American life, including handing out death sentences to those who displeased it. Many of its leaders were men of Italian heritage, and the committee in its final report declared that, in its opinion, an organization known as "the Mafia," descended from the Sicilian original, controlled the most lucrative rackets in many major cities and tied together criminal groups throughout the country. Americans had heard tales about the Mafia for over sixty years.

Seemingly, the most prestigious legislative body in the country had finally confirmed its existence and its menace.

A generation earlier, Italian gangsters had been largely confined to preying on their countrymen in the Italian districts of big cities and mill and mining towns. Now, in New York, they controlled the country's largest port and the garment industry that produced most of America's clothing. Gangsters owned oil wells and premium liquor distributorships. In the 1930s their influence in Hollywood almost led to the takeover of the movie business. For a time the mob played a significant role in the automotive industry. In Chicago, the majority of unions were either run by gangsters or paid tribute to them. Even small cities like Tampa, Florida, and Covington, Kentucky, or tiny resort towns such as Saratoga, New York, and Hot Springs, Arkansas, were held in their grip. It was estimated that the wealth of the national syndicate was greater than that of the richest Fortune 500 corporation.

How had the mobs gained so much power in so short a time? If the Kefauver Committee's assertion was to be taken at face value, it was largely the result of the work of a group of ruthless foreigners. Yet many knowledgeable individuals who had worked to bring about the investigation and provided it with valuable counsel did not agree. From their standpoint, such a conclusion was not only wrong but would lead both the public and government down the wrong path. In the aftermath of Kefauver there was a flood of books, movies, television series, and official pronouncements about the "menace of the Mafia."

This book details the rise of the Mafia in America, from the 1880s to the 1950s. For much of the twentieth century, the American public, led by the press and movies, has used the word *Mafia* as shorthand for the Italian-dominated organized crime groups, but it is a misleading term. It places too much emphasis on foreign organizations and alien conspiracies. A more accurate label is "American Mafia," which conveys the reality that Italian-dominated gangs arose primarily out of socioeconomic conditions in this country and often worked in partnership with mobsters from other ethnic backgrounds. While never comprising the totality of organized crime, the American Mafia formed the most influential and cohesive element in the loosely organized national crime syndicate that emerged in the 1930s.

The use of the "Mafia" term is also seen as demeaning to a particular ethnic group. Tragically, during the period under study a hardworking, law-abiding, and patriotic people were frequently stigmatized by the sins of a few of their members. Yet many of those who fought the hardest against the American Mafia were themselves of Italian heritage.

Various reasons have been offered for the American Mafia's swift ascent to power. One of the most popular arises from a long history of anti-immigrant sentiment. Early in the twentieth century, newspapers used such phrases as "cruel, treacherous, vindictive, and violent" to describe Italians. In 1903, a U.S. Secret Service chief called the Mafia "the most secret and terrible organization in the world." Such declarations fostered the belief that Italians succeeded because they were a unique group of super-criminals. But powerful, well-entrenched organized crime groups were in existence long before the waves of Italians arrived. Early in the nineteenth century Ike Rynders, an ex–Mississippi riverboat gambler, controlled both Tammany Hall and the gangs of New York. After the Civil War, boss gambler Mike McDonald was the czar of Chicago politics, and at the turn of the century, Jerry Bassity was the vice lord of San Francisco.

A more benign, ethnically based explanation of the American Mafia's success holds that it was a combination of two factors: natural succession and luck. According to this theory, as the Irish and other groups moved into the middle class they were less likely to be represented in criminal activity, so the late-arriving Italians filled the void, just at the time when Prohibition was adding vast revenues to organized crime's coffers.

The ethnic succession argument can be overstated, since it was not universal. The idea that it happened everywhere comes from the common mistake of assuming that whatever took place in New York and Chicago also occurred in the rest of the country, though even in those cities, gangsters of other nationalities worked with Italian bosses. In Cleveland, the premier organized crime group continued to be a Jewish gang. In some other cities, Italian criminal incursions were repulsed. In places like New Orleans, Italians were invited in and allowed to remain as long as they accepted a subordinate role.

One element of the culture of southern Italian criminals did equip its members for success in American organized crime—their businesslike approach. Non-Italian gangs grew mostly out of neighborhood bonds formed by young men who committed ordinary crimes such as robbery, burglary, or assault. Even as Prohibition transformed these gangs into powerful mobs, they continued to operate much as they had in their wild early days, shooting at the drop of an insult; their organizations were largely extensions of street gangs. When death or imprisonment removed leaders of Irish, Jewish, or Polish gangs, their organizations usually collapsed. In contrast, despite their reputation for violence and ruthlessness, Italian leaders eschewed senseless mayhem in favor of more rational methods. Men like Chicago's Johnny Torrio and New York's Lucky Luciano displayed remarkable organizational skills. Torrio was a quiet little opera-loving family man and Luciano a tough drug dealer who squired Broadway and Hollywood beauties, but both built their mobs along corporate lines. They parceled out territories and adopted rules to provide for the arbitration of disputes. In the mold of Rockefeller or Morgan, they formed syndicates to end wasteful competition. Like other businessmen, they established national associations to promote common interests. When they passed from the scene, their organizations remained, lasting to the present. Thus while Prohibition was a lucky break for all gangsters, the Italians were better able to profit from it.

Unlike conventional entrepreneurs who sometimes bent or broke the law, the business of the American Mafia was fundamentally illegal, and its success also involved law enforcement's failures. To a certain extent the Mafia ascendancy was facilitated by the long-established corrupt alliances between politicians, racketeers, and cops, but that is not the whole story. Government was not always corrupt; sometimes its anticrime strategies were flawed. From the 1880s on, New York police policies on Italian gang crimes shifted from "let them kill each other" to ghettoizing the problem by exclusively assigning it to a small Italian squad.

At the federal level, law enforcement was fragmented among a plethora of agencies, each with its own narrow focus and unique operational strategy. In 1920, the Treasury Department created a national version of the Keystone Cops, the Prohibition Bureau. Given the impossible task of drying up America, its agents were easily bribed and prone to engage in reckless gunplay, to the detriment of innocent bystanders, leaving a legacy of disrespect for the law that has persisted to the present day. In 1929 the crack Treasury intelligence unit used the income tax laws to bring down Al Capone. Lacking jurisdiction to follow up with a broader drive against Chicago crime and corrupt politics, the agents could only watch while Capone's successors reestablished the gang's power. Law enforcement also drew the wrong lessons from the event. After Capone's fall there were a number of "Get Mr. Big" drives against men like Luciano and Frank Costello, which resulted in their imprisonment but left their organizations intact.

Often law enforcers failed to understand the nature and relationships of the American Mafia. Under Commissioner Harry Anslinger, the Treasury Department's Federal Bureau of Narcotics adopted the broad view that it was an extension of the Sicilian Mafia, rather than an independent American entity. In contrast, FBI director J. Edgar Hoover of the Justice Department saw Italian-dominated gangs as purely local problems to be dealt with by local police, ignoring the interstate ties between various mobs and the existence of a national control commission. Hoover's purported views were disingenuous. The real reason he chose to stay aloof from the battle was his fear that if the FBI became involved, the Mafia's ability to corrupt law enforcement would lead to scandal, and its political power would bring retaliation against his Bureau. Instead, he concentrated on relatively unimportant criminals like John Dillinger or "Ma" Barker, who were built up as major public enemies by his Bureau.

An account of the rise of the American Mafia is more than just a crime story. It is a window into American society illustrating the workings of political, governmental, bureaucratic, and economic forces. It is a story that is often ignored in texts on American government. Yet as this book reveals, men like Torrio, Capone, Luciano, and Costello had a great deal to say about how America was governed.

The rise of the American Mafia is an account of how groups of criminals achieved, enhanced, and maintained their power, in large part because they were more skilled, better organized, and better managed than their rivals or the law enforcement agencies that opposed them.

AMERICAN MAFIA

1: "We Must Teach These People a Lesson": A Murder and Lynching in New Orleans

One drizzly night in October of 1890, New Orleans police chief David Hennessy was walking home late with his friend William O'Connor. Threats had been made against Hennessy, and O'Connor, the captain of a private guard force, had volunteered to accompany him. The chief didn't appear to be too worried, however. They still had a block to go when Hennessy urged O'Connor to split off toward his own nearby residence. Continuing on alone, the chief may have been too absorbed in thought to hear a teenage boy whistling across the street. The tune was "La Marcia Reale"—the Italian "Royal March." It was a signal to ambushers, who emerged from a shed and let loose a blast of shotgun pellets. Hennessy managed to fire his revolver three times before staggering to the steps of a nearby porch. Taken to a local hospital, he died the next day.

At the murder scene near the corner of Basin and Girod Streets, the police found four luparas. A double-barreled, sawed-off shotgun with a retractable stock, the lupara folded up like a jackknife and could be carried on a hook under a coat. It was known as a "Mafia gun," and Hennessy had been investigating a case that involved two families of Sicilians vying for a contract to unload ships. Captain O'Connor's testimony was even more damning: On hearing the shots he ran back to his friend and knelt down beside him. "Who gave it to you, Dave?" he asked.

"The dagos did it," Hennessy whispered back.

His assassination sparked a firestorm of anti-Italian feeling, which the city's reform mayor, Joseph Shakespeare, did nothing to restrain. "Heretofore, the scoundrels have confined their murderings among themselves," the mayor declared. Now they had claimed "their first American victim," and "we owe it to ourselves and to everything that we hold sacred in this life to see to it that this blow is the last. We must teach these people a lesson they will not forget for all times." While Hennessy's body lay in state at City Hall—in the very chamber where former Confederate president Jefferson Davis had reposed a year earlier—police swept the streets, on mayoral orders to "arrest every Italian you come across." Soon the jails held a hundred of them—"Sicilians," as one newspaper put it, "whose low, receding foreheads, repulsive countenances and slovenly attire proclaimed their brutal natures." Other Italians were attacked by mobs or hid in their homes.

Mayor Shakespeare was understandably emotional about the loss of the police chief he had appointed two years earlier. He also had reason to be uneasy about the growing number of Italians in New Orleans, since they generally favored the Irish leaders who were his political opponents in the local Democratic Party. Whether through official laxity or (as some alleged) connivance, an eighteen-year-old boy who had delivered newspapers to Hennessy managed to slip into the jailhouse with a gun and wound one of the prisoners. "ASSASSINATION ATTEMPT OF ONE OF THE ACCUSED DAGOS," a local paper proclaimed.[1] Many readers regretted that this act of vigilantism had not been more successful.

The case made national as well as local headlines. Across the country, newspapers warned of a sinister criminal organization whose members would strike down anyone attempting to enforce the law against them. In truth, the story revealed at least as much about the shortcomings of American law enforcement as it did about the power of the Italian-American

---

[1] "Dago" was a corruption of the Spanish name "Diego." It had originated as a collective slur on all people from Latin countries.

underworld. It also showed how little anyone in or out of law enforcement understood an important new group of European immigrants. But then, not even many Europeans knew much about the out-of-the-way island that would, in time, be perceived as a major source of lawlessness and violence in the United States.

For centuries, Sicily had been governed—or misgoverned—by far-off foreigners: Arabs, French, Austrians, and Spaniards. From the early eighteenth century until the mid-nineteenth, Sicily, along with Naples and Calabria on the mainland, fell under the dominion of the Spanish Bourbons—incompetent cousins of the family that had ruled France for two centuries.[2] Contact between the Bourbon officers and ordinary citizens usually involved the collection of taxes or extortion of bribes, and the policy of most Sicilians toward the Bourbons was similar to what it had been toward their predecessors: avoid them as much as possible. In Sicily, as in southern Italy, people had long been taught not to rely on the law or government for assistance. ("The law courts are for fools," the saying went.) To report a grievance to the authorities was considered bad form—a violation of the code of *omerta*, which dictated that a real man maintains silence and secures his own justice, in his own way. If a life had been taken, the victim's kinsmen would "wash blood with blood."

In America, the Mafia would come to be seen as a vast and many-tentacled organization whose power had reached across the ocean from the Old World to the New. But in Sicily the typical form of organization was the local band, or *cosca*, headed by a *capo*, or chief. (Not a *don*, which was a general term of respect in southern Italy.) The mafiosi of Sicily had much in common with the brigands of other depressed areas—Spain, Ireland, the Balkans, the Ukraine—where the struggle for existence was harsh and the government oppressive and corrupt. Sicily, described by Alexandre Dumas as "a paradise populated by demons," was especially violent, the western half of the island most of all. Eastern Sicily was comparatively peaceful.

---

[2] The Bourbon ruler was popularly known as the king of Naples, but the official designation of his domain was the kingdom of the two Sicilys.

"Palermo is dangerous, Messina is safe," it was said. At the turn of the century, the homicide rate in Palermo was 29 per 100,000, and as high as 44 per 100,000 in some inland districts of the west. In Messina, the murder rate was only 8 per 100,000, not much higher than the contemporary New York City figure, which was about 5.

Buffeted by the sirocco, winds from the deserts of Africa, the climate of this violent western Sicily was hot and dusty. Mountains tended to isolate districts, and many dialects were spoken. Men from one area looked with suspicion on those from another, and even on members of other families living in the same village. The east had more industry and richer soil, and its landlords were more likely to live on their estates, or *latifundas*. In the west, upwards of two-thirds of the estates belonged to absentee owners. It was common practice for them to turn over the management of their land to a *gabellotto*, or overseer, who collected rents, keeping a portion for himself and forwarding the rest to the *signor* in Naples or Palermo. To enforce his orders and guard his estate, the *gabellotto* retained a crew of gunmen, many of them bandits on the side. A particularly ruthless *gabellotto* might even succeed in squeezing out the landlord and taking over an estate himself. Whether to maintain or resist control by the overseers, to avenge an insult or commit a crime, luparas and knives were used with great frequency.

In America, the Mafia would sometimes be portrayed as an ancient organization. This, too, was essentially a myth. In one generally discounted legend it arose out of the Sicilian vespers in 1282 when the natives rose up and massacred French garrisons, supposedly shouting *"Morte alla Francia Italia anela* (Death to the French is Italy's cry)"—a chant whose words form the acronym MAFIA. Sicilians of the time would not have considered themselves Italians or spoken the dialect in which the phrase is couched. Although organized thievery and brigandage had existed for centuries, the Mafia groups of the late 1800s most likely originated in response to Bourbon rule. The term itself was used loosely, to convey an attitude or way of life adopted by many Sicilians who had no ties to any criminal group. To be a *"mafioso,"* one contemporary author wrote, meant to be a brave man.

Neither ancient nor vast, the actual Sicilian Mafia bore little resemblance to the image that Americans were forming. The Neapolitan *camorra* came closer. Tightly organized under a single *"capo in testa,"* or head chief, and twelve district chiefs, the Camorra had functioned since the early 1800s as a guild of thieves, enforcers, and, when the occasion demanded, murderers. Its origins could be traced back to a venerable Spanish secret society mentioned in the sixteenth-century novels of Cervantes. The name was derived from the Spanish word for the cloak in which assassins draped themselves—it also meant a fistfight. In nineteenth-century Italy, it connoted someone looking for trouble. Camorrists, who strutted about wearing a multicolored sash, a red tie carelessly flung over their shoulder, and carrying a cane with brass rings, lived up to that description.

The Neapolitan jails were a traditional Camorra recruiting ground. Incarcerated members would invite a new inmate to perform a series of services for them. If he did well, he could expect to become a *picciotti*, or "young one," in a *brigata* upon his release. The *picciotti* who continued to impress his superiors might, in time, be asked to carry out a murder—the last step to full-fledged membership. A formal initiation ceremony followed, sometimes involving the drawing of blood or the swearing of an oath over a sword, a gun, or a holy picture; the novitiate would promise to obey the rules of the organization, protect its secrets, refrain from sex with another member's wife, and turn over a portion of the proceeds of his crimes. If he broke the code of silence or any other rule, he could expect to receive the kiss of death, and an assassin would be assigned to kill him, perhaps attaining his own membership in the process.

Rites and procedures of the Mafia varied according to time and place. In some parts of Sicily, entrance to a band was difficult, requiring a trial at arms with knives. Elsewhere, Mafia bands dispensed with such rituals. What was true of rural Girgenti on the south coast in the 1870s did not necessarily reflect the practices of urban Palermo on the north coast in 1900. But whether Camorra, Mafia, or the Calabrian Fibbia (Honored Society), all southern secret societies received covert support from a coterie of respectables. These businessmen, government officials, and nobles were known in Sicily as the *alta* (or high) Mafia, and in Naples as "the Camorra in kid gloves." The arrangements between respectables and criminals, and the use of the *gabellotti* as middlemen, provided a business model of crime that later would be emulated by some American gangsters.

In 1860, the Bourbons were finally overthrown, and Sicily and the dynasty's mainland possessions became part of the newly united Italy. Yet the bastions of power remained far off. Many Neapolitans and Sicilians had joined the revolution as members of Garibaldi's legion; nevertheless, the national *Risorgimento* brought no end to the *miseria* of the south. Rural peasants continued to live in one-room shacks with their animals; the lives of slum dwellers in the hovels of Naples and Palermo did not improve much, either. Sicilians—often referred to as "Africans" by the arrogant new officials from the north—continued to regard the government as an occupying force. Rather than establishing order, the replacement of one set of alien rulers by another and the introduction of a new legal code and peacetime military conscription further unsettled conditions in the south, giving rise to even more banditry.

In southern Italy, after 1860, the new government vacillated between ignoring and repressing the *mala vita*, or criminal classes. Under the tenets of Roman law, followed throughout continental Europe, Italy gave its police and courts far more power than England or the United States did. The government routinely used secret service agents to spy on citizens, and a tough militarized police force known as the *carabinieri* dealt with banditry and disorder on a large scale. The legal code strongly favored the prosecution, permitting the introduction of hearsay evidence and the defendant's prior record. Innocence was *not* presumed. As much as the legal process favored the state, even stronger measures were sometimes employed. If conditions got seriously out of hand, the government would declare martial law. In extreme cases, officials would put a price on a wanted man's head—paid on delivery of the severed head. In Sicily, peasants' cottages were occasionally burned with the occupants inside.

Often what set off anticrime drives were attacks on foreigners—the kidnapping of a tourist, for example. In 1877, a young Englishman named John Forester Rose, a member of a wealthy banking family, was seized by a Mafia chieftain named Leone. Holding Rose prisoner in a network of caves, Leone sent a politely phrased ransom note to the victim's family in England. He asked for five thousand pounds. Receiving no reply, Leone dispatched a more threatening follow-up message. The banking Roses understood that if they paid off too quickly, they might get a reputation as easy marks. The next letter from Leone arrived with one of the captive's ears enclosed. That stepped up the tempo of the negotiations, but the family continued to stand firm. It was only after a fourth letter with the other ear (followed, according to some accounts, by a fifth letter with a portion of his nose) that Rose's wife finally prevailed upon her family to pay the ransom.

The case brought disaster to the people of the district as well as the perpetrators of the crime. The embarrassed Italian government sent a large force of troops into the area to hunt down the kidnappers. Their modus operandi was to shoot and hang mafiosi and non-mafiosi alike until one of Leone's men, defying the code of *omerta*, betrayed his capo. Leone and his top lieutenant, Giuseppe Esposito, were captured, but they managed to escape from custody and fled the country. Esposito proceeded to New York and then to New Orleans.

The largest city in the South was a natural destination for Italians. New Orleans had been a terminus for Italian fruit ships since before the Civil War, and descriptions of the city had been carried back to the mother country by sailors and merchants who, by and large, preferred its climate to the colder and less predictable weather of Boston or New York. New Orleans had a Latin Catholic culture derived from the time of Spanish and French rule. With its yearly round of carnivals and feast days, its relaxed attitude toward vice, and its crooked streets and open markets, the city did not seem drastically different from Naples or Palermo. The sugar, cotton, and rice plantations of Louisiana resembled the *latifundas* of the southern Italian gentry. Even the local diseases—yellow fever, cholera, and malaria—were familiar.

Before the Civil War, several thousand Italians lived in New Orleans. By 1890, estimates of the Italian population ran as high as 25,000, or 10 percent of the city, though the official census listed only half that number. Italians "have found here so much that encourages them," an editorial writer for the *New Orleans Picayune* commented, "that we must look for constantly

increasing immigration." For Sicilians, the first stop was "Little Palermo"—
a crowded slum adjacent to the waterfront. But Italians could be found in
the best as well as the worst neighborhoods, owning businesses and real
estate, and serving on boards and in the local government.

For over a decade before Esposito arrived in 1880, New Orleans residents had believed the Mafia operated in the city, but the local culture of
violence and lawlessness went back much further—in fact, to the founding
of New Orleans in 1718. The original French and Spanish inhabitants often
settled their differences with guns or swords, and many of the Americans
who poured in after the War of 1812 adopted similar habits. Anyone with
pretensions to gentility made sure to polish his fencing and shooting skills.
In 1862, the city was captured by Union forces who imposed a harsh rule
that continued through Reconstruction, fomenting more unrest. Italian
immigrants were just one subgroup in a city long renowned for its gangs,
mobs, riots, duels, and assassinations. Only a small minority of Italians
became involved in crime, and of those only a few had actually belonged to
groups like the Mafia—though many more found it advantageous to claim
such associations, the better to instill fear in their victims.

Esposito came from a lower-middle-class family and was fairly well educated. He adopted a new identity, calling himself Vicenzo Rubello, bought a
sailboat, and played at being an oyster fisherman. Beyond these modest gestures, however, Esposito showed little concern for his anonymity. Short,
swarthy, and powerfully built, he had a distinctive knife scar between his
eyebrows which he made no effort to conceal. He walked the streets of
Little Palermo with an attention-getting swagger, and took care that all he
encountered—all the Italians, at any rate—knew they were dealing with a
Sicilian bandit leader. Esposito even flew a pennant with the name of his former chief, Leone, on the prow of his little boat—a gesture that meant nothing to the local authorities but made Sicilians more respectful.

Tony Labuzzo built Esposito's boat and claimed to have been cheated out
of the fee for it. Hesitating to confront Esposito directly, Labuzzo found
another way to settle the score. Esposito had a wife and five children in
Sicily. When he married a New Orleans widow with two children, a relative
of his first wife sent word to her, and the Italian authorities were soon

informed of his whereabouts. They responded by posting a $3,000 reward and retaining two private detectives from New York to capture him. When the detectives arrived in New Orleans, they were pushed aside by the police chief. He assigned two of his own favorites to the case instead—cousins David and Mike Hennessy.

With Labuzzo's covert assistance, the Hennessys managed to bag Esposito on his way to mass at the Cathedral of St. Louis. He was then turned over to the New York detectives, who took him away by boat. Labuzzo was quickly ferreted out and gunned down by Esposito's friends. In New York City, Esposito fought extradition to Italy by insisting that he really was Rubello. He even produced witnesses from both New York and New Orleans to support his story. It took a pair of carabinieri sent over from Italy to settle the identity question once and for all, pointing out the knife scar between his eyes. Returned to his native land under guard, Esposito was tried, convicted, and sentenced in short order. The new kingdom of Italy had no death penalty, but the defendant did not get off easy. He was sentenced to life imprisonment—in chains.

Esposito only pretended to be a fisherman, but many of his countrymen were finding work on the waterfront. Shippers liked to pit the Italians against more established groups of black and Irish dockworkers. When it suited their purposes, they pitted Italians against other Italians. In 1878, the Provenzano family of dockworkers won a contract to unload fruit. But in 1886, the leading shipowners grew dissatisfied with them and cut a new deal with Charlie Matranga, who also ran a combination dance hall and gambling joint catering to a black clientele. Two years later, the Provenzanos were dropped completely and their work was given to the Matrangas, starting a feud, with each family characterizing the other as Mafia. In May 1890, a group of Matrangas were ambushed coming home from unloading a banana boat. Three of them were hit by bullets, including Charlie's brother, Tony, who lost a leg. Real mafiosi weren't supposed to run to the law, but the Matrangas promptly did, identifying the shooters as Provenzano men. Six of the latter were eventually convicted of assault.

Unfortunately for the Matrangas, Dave Hennessy was now the police chief, and he wasn't satisfied with the verdict. Hennessy could well have been in prison himself. He was a popular local figure, tall and handsome with a reputation as a bold, fearless officer—without peer, perhaps, but scarcely beyond reproach. In 1881, after the Esposito arrest, a new administration had taken charge of the police, and both Hennessys had been demoted. The two cousins then got into a shootout with their boss, the chief of detectives, killing him. Pleading self-defense, they were acquitted of murder, but fired from the force. Mike, who had been wounded in the incident, resettled in Houston where he was murdered a few years later, allegedly by a New Orleans assassin. When political tides turned, Dave became the new chief. His record, which might have barred him from the appointment in other places, was no disqualification in New Orleans. Local detectives were known for wearing fancy clothes, smoking expensive cigars, and somehow managing to live well beyond their salaries. Dave's father had come to New Orleans as a Union soldier before joining the Reconstruction-era police, and wound up being murdered in a coffeehouse as a result of a feud among corrupt detectives. Before and after his appointment as chief, Dave Hennessy enjoyed a close relationship with the Provenzanos, especially with Joe Provenzano, their leader. At their trial, at least two dozen of Hennessy's cops testified as alibi witnesses for the defendants, and there were widespread accusations of perjury.

Publicly denouncing the verdict against his friends, Chief Hennessy claimed that it was the Matrangas who had given perjured testimony; he also accused them of murdering an important defense witness before he could take the stand. Hennessy declared that he would launch a new investigation and see the defendants exonerated. He even sent a request to the authorities in Italy for information about fugitives from that country who might be hiding out in New Orleans (there were in fact hundreds of such people). In August, Hennessy received a threatening letter warning him to cease his investigations, and began to hear rumors that he had been targeted for assassination.

When the first group of suspects in Hennessy's murder were swept off the streets—some none too gently—the local Italian consul, Pasquale Corte, went to Mayor Shakespeare to protest their treatment. The mayor waved off Corte's objections. Considering himself a likely next victim and anxious to impress the electorate with his toughness, Shakespeare ordered a second wave of arrests. By now, however, others were beginning to attack the mayor—not for manhandling Italians, but for bungling the investigation. Within a few days of Hennessy's murder a group of leading citizens created a "Committee of Fifty" to assist in combating "oath-bound, hell-born societies." Dissatisfied with the performance of the mayor and his police force, the committee bypassed them altogether, raising what they described as "a substantial amount" of money to bring in the Pinkerton Detective Agency.

The Pinkertons were the largest and most effective investigative body in late-nineteenth-century America. Scottish immigrant Alan Pinkerton opened his agency in 1855 after a brief stint as a police detective in Chicago; his earliest clients included several leading railroad companies. Pinkerton went on to serve as chief of the Secret Service branch of the Union Army under a former railroad president, General George B. McClellan. After Pinkerton's death in 1884, his sons William and Robert took over, and the agency's symbol—a watchful eye—became known far and wide. In addition to the many corporate duties that the Pinkertons performed (spying on labor organizers, for one), they were often retained to investigate robberies, murders, and other major crimes. Not infrequently, they would be approached by private groups like the Committee of Fifty that had lost faith in the integrity or effectiveness of the local authorities.

In the municipal police departments of the day, political patronage governed almost every personnel decision. The Pinkertons, by contrast, hired people on the basis of merit, including women and disfavored minorities. The principal agent assigned to the Hennessy case was a young man of Italian descent, Frank Dimaio, who had worked in the Philadelphia office. Short, muscular, and dark, with jet-black hair and a forceful manner, he would become known as "The Raven." Dimaio had quit a previous job in the insurance industry, craving more exciting work. As a Pinkerton, he got what he was after. Fluent in several languages, he often worked undercover, in guises that ranged from gangster to dance instructor to organ grinder. He had recently been commended by his superiors for his work on an insurance fraud case. The Pinkerton brothers were impressed. With their endorsement, in November Dimaio set out for Louisiana in the guise of a counterfeiter named Tony Ruggerio, a real-life bill passer serving a prison term in Italy. For added credibility Dimaio had $6,000 in high-quality phony money sewn into the lining of his coat when he appeared in a small Louisiana town to establish his bona fides. By prearrangement, he was seized in a boardinghouse by the Louisiana chief of the U.S. Secret Service, who loudly informed a crowd of onlookers what a desperate rascal this Ruggerio was. The lawman was so convincing that some of the boarders ran to get their shotguns to assist in the arrest. When the Secret Service agent delivered Dimaio to the New Orleans jail, he warned the guards that he had fought a gun battle to overcome the prisoner. The Italian inmates were wary just the same. A bribed jail clerk had tipped them to a mysterious prisoner who might be an informer, and when Dimaio was put in a cell block with eight of the suspects they eyed him suspiciously.

Nevertheless he managed to win their confidence. Instead of cozying up to his fellow prisoners he treated them with the scorn of a high-level criminal for small-time punks mixed up in a murder. When one of them approached, Dimaio knocked him down with a single punch. His disdain only increased their interest and respect. A couple of the men began to talk about their personal exploits to gain his approval. Still trying not to arouse suspicion, Dimaio discouraged their overtures.

Like any good detective investigating a crime with multiple suspects, he was looking for the weakest link. His eye soon fell on one of the suspected triggermen, Manuel Polizzi, a simple-minded man who was at the bottom of the jail pecking order. Polizzi worked hard to ingratiate himself with Dimaio. At first the detective held him off, but eventually they became friendly.

Thanks to their many friends on the outside the Italians were sometimes able to order dinner from a local restaurant. On occasion, Dimaio would share a meal with Polizzi. With Dimaio's subtle encouragement Polizzi was beginning to suspect the other Italians of plotting against him. One day as dinner was set down before them, Dimaio knocked the plate out of Polizzi's hand. As an expert counterfeiter he claimed to know all about chemicals; the cheese sauce, he insisted, contained arsenic. Another time he did the same thing with a glass of wine, which supposedly contained cyanide. Polizzi was convinced—and alarmed. But the vile prison conditions had taken their toll on Dimaio, whose weight had dropped from 185 pounds to 140. Alerted to his condition by the lawyer that the agency secretly retained for him, William Pinkerton sent word that it was time to have Dimaio released on bail. Dimaio refused. Although he knew he couldn't hold out much longer, the frightened Polizzi had at last begun to talk about the Hennessy assassination and how the gang had drawn straws to determine who would do the actual shooting (a familiar detail in allegations of murder involving Italian secret societies). Dimaio covertly wrote down everything Polizzi said on scraps of paper, and got him to make his mark on them. Finally satisfied he had enough, Dimaio contacted his lawyer to bail him out.

Although nineteen Matranga men were indicted for murder the district attorney put only nine of them on trial, dissatisfied with the evidence against the other ten. The defendants were a mixed lot: they included Polizzi; Aspara Marchese, the fourteen-year-old whistler; his father, Antonio; crew boss Charlie Matranga; and Joseph Macheca, one of the wealthiest Italians in New Orleans. Macheca lived in a Bourbon Street mansion and owned a considerable amount of local real estate and a small fleet of steamships that hauled bananas up from Central America. A mover and shaker in local politics, Macheca worked both sides of the street. The story went that it was Macheca's influence that got the Hennessys demoted, after Dave refused a $50,000 bribe to back Esposito's claim of mistaken identity. During the Matranga–Provenzano feud, however, Macheca had arranged a meeting between the two factions, bringing in Chief Hennessy as referee. Though both groups agreed to compromise, the bargain did not hold up. According to Polizzi, it was Macheca who had rented the shed near Hennessy's home, installing a man there to track the chief's movements.

Consul Corte kept a close watch on the proceedings, sending regular reports to Baron Fava, the Italian ambassador in Washington. Fava relayed his own strong feelings of concern to the American government. Italian Americans in other cities held meetings to generate support for the prisoners, who were widely believed to be innocent by their countrymen. These far-flung supporters raised a $75,000 defense fund and brought in some high-class legal talent, including a former Louisiana attorney general. "Mafia money" was the way most people in New Orleans described the defense fund, though the average contribution was just two dollars.

Nearly eight hundred prospective jurors were examined before twelve could be seated. Word was out that a juror could make a bundle of money by voting to acquit, and private detectives working for the defense were accused of offering bribes. The trial itself lasted two weeks, with the prosecution presenting sixty-seven witnesses. Polizzi's supposed jailhouse confession was not introduced in evidence—although the information it contained provided useful leads, it was not thought to be legally sound. When the jury finally reached a verdict it was, in the words of a *New York Times* reporter, "like a thunderclap from a clear sky." Six of the defendants were acquitted outright. As for the three others, the jury could not decide. The crowd outside the courthouse was stunned at first. Then came a chorus of loud protests followed by ominous muttering about bribes. Most of the jurors found it prudent to quickly disappear. The *Picayune* described their verdict as one that "astonished every person."

Many people grew angrier when they heard that the city's Italians were openly celebrating the acquittal. The celebrating was real, but mostly unrelated to the case. The verdict had been announced on the birthday of Italy's King Humbert I when local Italians were marking the occasion with flag-waving and outdoor revelry in the manner of their relatives back home. Another rumor had American flags being burned or desecrated; that story evidently stemmed from a drunken Italian sailor hauling down the Stars and Stripes. Nevertheless, the Committee of Fifty called for a mass meeting the next day near the statue of Henry Clay on Canal Street to "remedy the failure of justice in the Hennessy case."

Lynching was not an uncommon practice at the time, and the mobs that carried it out weren't necessarily composed of the communities' worst elements. Just as some people fought duels to avenge insults, others considered lynching to be the normal reaction of an enraged citizenry to acts of blatant and unpunished lawlessness. W. S. Parkerson, an attorney active in the reform movement and close to Mayor Shakespeare, took charge of the rally, delivering a fiery oration. "When courts fail," he declared, "the people must act. . . . Our chief of police is assassinated in our very midst by the Mafia society and its assassins again turned loose on the community. . . . Are you going to let it continue?" His audience roared "No! No! Bring on the dagos!" Parkerson led the way to the parish jail, where the six acquitted defendants were still locked up pending the adjudication of some lesser charges, along with the thirteen others who were still awaiting trial. By the time they arrived the crowd numbered six thousand.

Two detectives had rushed there to warn of the approaching mob. The sheriff had already departed, leaving the warden in charge. "Let them come," he replied. "They won't get in." But his actions indicated less confidence than his words. His first step was to release the Italian prisoners from their cells, telling them to hide in the women's quarters. Meanwhile Consul Corte was pleading for help from Governor Francis Nicholls. His Excellency regretfully explained that he could not act without a request from the mayor, who, like the sheriff, was nowhere to be found. A lynching would not harm any of these men politically—quite the reverse.

Outside the jail the mob began pounding on the doors, which had been locked by the sheriff's deputies. "We want the dagos," people shouted, while others called out mockingly to the prisoners inside, "Who killa da chief, who killa da chief." The crowd included a large black man who hurled a paving block against a side door, splintering it (his presence in the midst of a southern lynch mob attracted little comment from the press). The mob entered the building and they quickly proceeded to the women's quarters after a female inmate pointed them there.

Polizzi was one of the first caught—picked up with one hand by a burly planter, taken outside, hung from a lamppost, and blasted with rifle fire. A second prisoner soon followed. Cornered in a courtyard a half a dozen others, including Joe Machecha, dropped to their knees and begged for mercy. They were all shot down. Two of the prisoners had secreted themselves in a packing crate that normally served as a doghouse for the warden's bull terrier. They too were found and shot to death. Charlie Matranga hid under a mattress with his mouth pressed to a crucifix and was one of eight survivors. Another was the whistling boy, spared because of his age.

When the job was done Parkerson gave a speech of thanks to his helpers. "God bless you," he concluded.

"God bless you, Mr. Parkerson," they shouted back before they dispersed.

In Washington, Ambassador Fava received a short and frightening telegram from his man in New Orleans. "I hold the mayor responsible," Consul Corte wrote. "Fear further murders. I am in great danger." Fava protested to U.S. secretary of state James G. Blaine, and the Italian prime minister, the Marquis Rudini, sent a sharply worded note. Blaine, the 1884 Republican presidential candidate, had won considerable popularity in his long political career by defying Great Britain. He adopted the same stance toward Italy, declaring that the United States "had never taken orders from a foreign government and was not going to start now." In response, Rudini recalled Fava. In Italy, the incident became a source of widespread outrage, with resolutions introduced in parliament calling for a punitive attack by Italy's formidable navy. In response, influential citizens of the wealthy but largely unprotected seaports of the East Coast began calling on the United States to build more warships (helping to ensure that when the Spanish-American War broke out seven years later, the U.S. fleet was, in fact, substantially larger). The Italian threat created a warlike mood and a feeling of national unity. In 1891, many Confederate veterans volunteered to serve in the federal army in order, as one group of ex-rebels put it, to "plant the Stars & Stripes on St. Peter's dome."

Italian-American citizens held mass meetings in a number of cities. In New York, six thousand gathered for an angry rally at Cooper Union. A group in Chicago describing themselves as "Italians by birth, Americans by choice" telegraphed Secretary Blaine to protest against "the cowardly and lawless act of the New Orleans mob, aided by the tacit consent of the local authorities."

Washington ordered an investigation of the trial. After examining the transcripts a government attorney found good legal reason for the acquittal of the key defendants. Jurors asked to explain their failure to convict pointed to the weaknesses of the state's case and vehemently denied being bribed or intimidated. The case essentially rested on the uncorroborated statements of an accomplice—a weak foundation under the best of circumstances. And Polizzi had given signs of mental instability, standing up at intervals during the trial and screaming at the top of his lungs in a Sicilian dialect that no one understood. On one occasion he had attempted to jump out of a window; eventually his outbursts had caused him to be removed from the courtroom.

In the end, the federal government paid $25,000 to the families of three of the lynched men, who were Italian citizens, and President Benjamin Harrison expressed his regrets. Charlie Matranga and the rest of the surviving defendants were not tried again, and the Provenzanos were eventually acquitted of the original assault charges. No member of the lynch mob was ever prosecuted. This was how nasty situations were often resolved: drop the charges against everyone and forget it ever happened. But Americans did not forget what they had heard about the criminality of Italians and the power of the Mafia. The *Baltimore News* spoke of "a dangerous people—cruel, treacherous, vindictive." The *Indianapolis Journal* characterized Italian immigrants as "ignorant, suspicious, and violent." In the decade that followed, Italians would be lynched from West Virginia to Colorado with few non-Italians protesting. Nor, in the aftermath of the Hennessy case, did many in Louisiana seem greatly troubled by the strange career of their murdered chief or by the mayor's inability or unwillingness to halt a lynching. Across the country, many editorial pages all but congratulated the lynch mob. Even a *New York Times* editorial observed that while "this affair is to be deplored, it would be difficult to find any one individual who . . . deplored it very much."

2:

A Place in the Sun:
Italian Gangs of New York

Between 1880 and 1900, the number of Italians in New York City leaped from 20,000 to 250,000. By 1910, immigrants and first-generation Italian Americans accounted for half a million New Yorkers—a tenth of the city's population. Even so, they were only the fourth-largest immigrant group, trailing the Irish, Germans, and Jews in a metropolis where nearly three-quarters of the inhabitants were either immigrants or the children of immigrants.

At the end of the nineteenth century Italians and Jews began to displace Irish and Germans in some of the most depressed areas. Eighty percent of these Italian immigrants came from the southern provinces where the idea of a unified Italy had yet to take hold, so people sorted themselves out by region of birth. The first wave of Sicilians settled uptown between 106th and 116th Streets along the East River. Though distant from lower Manhattan, the neighborhood had the same cheap housing and social problems. Neapolitans congregated on the East Side of lower Manhattan around Mulberry Street, or in Brooklyn near the Navy Yard. Americans called each of these areas "Little Italy." Italians referred to their settlements as "colonies." In 1890, the journalist Jacob Riis brought the New York slums to national attention when he published *How the Other Half Lives*. In it he described Mulberry Street as a "suburb of Naples" and the "foul core of New York's slums." An area known as "The Bend," where Mulberry made a sharp turn, was the most crowded part of a crowded island. One tenement block of 132 rooms contained 1,324 Italian immigrants, sleeping in tiers of bunks, ten people or more to a room.

As tenants, Italians were highly esteemed by the slumlords of the day. According to Riis, the typical Italian "is content to live in a pig-sty and submits to robbery at the hands of the rent-collector without murmur." As employees they were obliged to be equally undemanding. A young man fresh off the boat might earn a dollar for a ten-hour day of ragpicking or "trimming a scow"—leveling off the garbage barges that took the city's refuse out to its deep-water burial grounds. The more fortunate immigrants earned two dollars a day working on construction sites or laying railroad tracks, but the extra money reflected an appallingly high rate of injury and an utter disregard for the few safety regulations that existed. "The slaughter of Italians . . . yesterday was simply awful," one newspaper reported after a group of track workers were hit by a train. "The men were torn and mangled and their blood was scattered all over the tracks, and there can be little doubt [the railroad's] bosses were responsible for the horrible affair."

Few Italians spoke English; most could not even read their own language. As a result, they were easy marks for padrones—unscrupulous labor brokers who recruited southern Italian peasants for what they touted as well-paid work in the golden land across the sea. Those who could raise $30 for steerage passage were required to sign contracts that bound them to a particular employer. In 1885 Congress passed a law making it illegal to recruit immigrants before they landed in the United States. Nothing changed. The padrones simply coached their charges to answer "no" when immigration inspectors asked them if they had signed such contracts. Other padrones lurked at the tip of Manhattan, waiting to waylay the unwary after they came across the river from Ellis Island. And no matter what any padrone promised, the reality for most immigrants was working in a gang of twenty or more as a railroad-track hand or hod carrier and being housed in foul conditions as a virtual prisoner until the job was done. Then, the immigrant would be cut loose with little to show for his work once the padrone had deducted inflated charges for housing and food.

Used to a sunny climate and the lively open-air existence of their home villages, many Italians found New York cold, dreary, and claustrophobic. Yet Italians had a great capacity for taking joy in simple things. In downtown Little Italy and East Harlem good weather was almost a cause for celebration in itself. "When the sun shines," Riis wrote, "the entire population seeks the streets, carrying on its household work, its bargaining, its love-making on street or sidewalk or idling there when it has nothing better to do." In 1930 Mike Fiaschetti, an Italian-born New York policeman describing immigrant life at the turn of the century, noted that when his countrymen managed to save a bit of money they would splurge on a ticket for a minor opera company or standing room at the world famous Metropolitan Opera. Most played the lottery, their lives coming to a halt for the Saturday-night announcement of the results, which were based on the official government-run lottery at home. For a people inclined to distrust authority, Italians had remarkable faith in this particular government service; there were few higher terms of praise than to say that someone was "as honest as the lottery." The winning numbers were cabled to America and distributed by local operators. Someone who came away with one of the small prizes would throw a wine-and-cake party for his friends and neighbors. The losers went back to consulting the *cabala*, a guidebook to the occult that linked certain dreams and experiences to particular numbers. Big prizewinners could return to Italy and retire for life.

New York was the financial colossus of the nation and the world's greatest seaport—the principal route of transit for goods moving between Europe and the United States. It was the most foreign of American cities, and yet also, curiously, the cultural center from which the heartland got its cues. For their knowledge of Italians, Americans looked to New York where two very different pictures were taking shape. On the one hand, many middle-class New Yorkers had a favorite Italian barber, restaurant, or wine-and-cheese shop, and Italian opera was in vogue with the upper classes.

Enrico Caruso's 1903 début at the Metropolitan Opera was the social event of the year. But New Yorkers were also hearing more and more about Italians as the perpetrators and victims of banditry and violence. Italians tended to lack immediate family ties; as many as 40 percent of them were single men planning either to earn some money and return home or to establish an economic beachhead before they sent for their families. Some were fleeing peacetime military conscription or the law. Regardless of their motives, young men far from home were good candidates for trouble.

On Sunday, the workingman's only day of recreation, men played cards up and down Mulberry Street. "The Italian is a born gambler," Riis commented, with dour Scandinavian disapproval. "His soul is in the game from the moment the cards are on the table and very frequently his knife is in it too before the game is ended." Some Italians carried weapons partly to protect themselves from attacks by young men of other nationalities, particularly the Irish. To many Americans, however, knife-play seemed to be rooted in the Italian character. Even the most downtrodden of the older immigrant groups were wary. When Italians began moving into the African-American part of Greenwich Village the established residents moved away in droves, many settling in the tough Irish neighborhoods on the West Side. They could expect a hostile reception there, but they would at least be among people who "talked American."

A more positive view was expressed in the *New York Times* by a former assistant district attorney. He said most Italians were "hard workers, frugal, temperate," who would be assimilated in the course of a generation. A report for the Sanitary Aid Society on the Italian quarters centering around Mulberry Street claimed that "if these tenements were cleared out, many of the temptations to crime would be removed." As in New Orleans the early stories of Italian-American crime in New York depicted a transplanted underworld society in which murder and extortion were widely practiced. Far more than the press or the populace cared to admit, however, the Italians were simply absorbing habits already well entrenched in American urban life. The wellspring of New York City's crime was not in Little Italy but at the Fourteenth Street "wigwam," or headquarters, of an immensely powerful political organization known by the name of an Indian chief, Tammanend or Tammany. Since the mid-1800s Tammany's Election Day victories had been ensured by saloon keepers and gamblers, who provided the money, and local gangs, who furnished the sluggers. In return the organization saw to it that police, prosecutors, and judges did not unduly trouble those gang members who lived by theft, robbery, and vice.

The heavily Irish rank and file of the NYPD treated Italian immigrants brusquely on the whole. Forgetful of the days when their own people had been called "Paddy," Irish cops referred to Italians as "Pasquale." Beyond being patronized or called names, however, Italian criminals and gang members had little to fear from the police as long as they stuck to their own neighborhoods. As Giovanni Branchi, the Italian consul general in New York City from 1895 to 1905, later wrote, "Whole parts of the town . . . inhabited by Italians only [were] virtually without police supervision," except for "the regular Irish policeman at the corner of the street who did not care a rap what Italians did to themselves."

Counterfeiting was a different matter. That was a federal offense, and a serious one for which sentences of as much as twenty years were not uncommon. Most American criminals preferred not to run afoul of the Feds. Those who did "pass the queer" were a small fraternity skilled at handling the plates and inks necessary to print "greengoods." Italian criminals, accustomed to a single system of courts and police controlled by the national government, did not comprehend the greater risk they ran by defying Uncle Sam. Nor did they have the necessary skills at first; the early Italian counterfeiters relied on printers back home who smuggled the phony bills in olive oil cans and other merchandise shipped from the old country.

The United States Secret Service had been formally established in 1865 to combat counterfeiting. In the last decades of the nineteenth century Italian counterfeiters became a high-priority concern at the Service's New York office. From time to time, the NYPD would also rouse itself to deal with such a case when it spilled over into murder. In 1888 Antonio Flaccomio was stabbed to death at the corner of St. Marks Place and Third Avenue by a counterfeiter named Carlo Quarteraro. Carlo and his brother Vincenzo had invited Antonio and his friend Polazzi to dinner in a nearby restaurant, intending to kill Polazzi for informing on them. When the victim got suspicious and excused himself, the brothers started berating Flaccomio. Antonio decided it was time to make an early exit as well, but Quarteraro caught up with him and stabbed him in the heart.

The St. Marks killers were "Sicilians . . . banded together in a secret society known as the Mafia," Chief Inspector Thomas Byrnes told the *New York Times*. "Murder with some of them is simply a pastime." According to Byrnes, "Members of the society that commit a serious crime in this city find refuge among friends in the South and vice versa."

Byrnes, who led the investigation of the case, was known as America's greatest detective. Joining the force after service in the Civil War, by the 1880s this Irish immigrant had created the nation's foremost municipal detective bureau. His sleuths were especially effective against major thefts such as bank robberies. Byrnes and his men also had a good record with crimes of violence involving the city's numerous street gangs. While critics attributed Byrnes's achievements to his cultivation of informants and use of the third degree, his many admirers considered him a master interrogator.

His methods did not seem to work with Italians. Their culture taught them to distrust all arms of government, particularly the police. When an Italian knifed in a Mulberry Street fray was asked by a cop, "Who done it?" the reply was true to the code of *omerta*: "Fix heem myself." Even Italian detectives sometimes shook their heads in wonder at the behavior of their countrymen. One related how when a young Italian was shot and killed on a Manhattan street, an older man who had run out when he heard the firing told investigating officers he had never seen the victim before. When police identified the body it turned out to be the man's son.

The principal suspect in the St. Marks case, Carlo Quarteraro, fled the country disguised as a priest. His brother Vincenzo was captured and charged with murder. When the jury deadlocked, Vincenzo was set free, to Byrnes's considerable embarrassment. Backtracking, he portrayed the killers not as members of a conspiracy but simply as moral reprobates. "The Great Detective," as he was called, made it clear that he would not be responsible for Italian-on-Italian crime in the future. "Let them kill each other," he told the *Times*.

In 1899, twenty-two-year-old Ignazio Saietta arrived in New York fleeing a murder charge in his native town of Corleone. Corleone—the name means "lion heart"—was one of the leading Mafia strongholds on the island. A decade earlier Saietta's brother-in-law, Giuseppe Morello, had made the same trip after killing two men, one of them the chief of a local guard force. By now Morello was an influential figure in East Harlem, along with his brothers Tony and Vincent and their half-brother Ciro, who went by the surname of Terranova. For the next twenty years the extended Morello clan would be the most powerful Sicilian criminal group in New York.

In Sicily Ignazio had acquired the nickname "Lupo," or wolf, suggesting an animal that preys on the weak. In America, he became "Lupo the Wolf." While linguistically redundant, his nickname made sense for a man who was out to inspire fear in two languages at once. Giuseppe Morello was now known as Joe, and didn't need anything fancier—he looked the part of a murderer. Tall, burly, and hairy, he had a droopy mustache, a granite jaw, and thick black hair. Born with a shriveled right arm and no fingers on his right hand, he usually wore a shawl to cover up these defects. On the prowl he sometimes sported the red bandanna favored by Sicilian brigands. In contrast, Lupo was soft-spoken, stocky but smooth-looking, and a bit of a dandy, given to wearing fancy clothes and keeping his hat tilted at a rakish angle.

A law-abiding immigrant tricked into working in their counterfeiting operation described Lupo and Morello as cowards who would never kill anyone personally. Instead, he said, they would assign the job to a "corporal" who would take along a squad of four men to help him do the deed. Both men were experts at intimidation, however. Lupo drove around in a creamy white carriage pulled by a fierce-looking black horse. Spotting a fellow Italian who looked like a promising mark for extortion, he would drive his carriage alongside his target and draw on the reins, causing the horse to rear up snorting. Usually the frightened victim paid off promptly. Those who didn't, regretted it. When a man who rented out workhorses refused to come across, Lupo gave some apples to a small boy with instructions to feed them to the nice horses. The horses fell dead from poison. Another Lupo-Morello specialty was compelling an honest store owner to purchase fire insurance so they could torch his place and share in the proceeds.

Morello was the backroom administrator and Lupo worked the streets. His greater visibility led people to think of Lupo as the boss, with Morello as his number two man; actually it was the reverse. But both men were dreaded. When either of their names was mentioned Italians routinely crossed themselves.

The most sinister property in Lupo and Morello's real estate portfolio was a stable on East 108th Street near First Avenue. Besides being a place to keep stolen horses, it also functioned as a murder factory where victims were reputedly hung on meat hooks or burned in furnaces. Between 1900 and 1920 the East Harlem stable was the scene of anywhere from twenty to sixty homicides, according to official estimates. The Morello crew also set up a command post at 8 Prince Street in Little Italy, with a saloon in front and a spaghetti restaurant in the back. The Prince Street establishment became known among Italians as "Mafia Headquarters."

Lupo and Morello began their counterfeiting career by obtaining product from a printing plant in Salerno. Denominations of 2 and 5 dollars were shipped to New York in cartons containing olive oil, spaghetti, wine, and cheese. Selling these bills to wholesalers at 30 to 40 cents on the dollar for distribution throughout the country was what first brought Lupo and Morello to the federal cops' notice. The head of the Secret Service's New York office was William Flynn, who had acquired his considerable knowledge of crime as warden of New York's Ludlow Street jail. His agents arrested Morello in 1900 for counterfeiting, but the U.S. attorney ruled there was insufficient evidence to prosecute him. In 1902 Flynn's men raided one of his restaurants and found several thousand dollars in phony five-dollar bills, again hidden in cans shipped from Italy. Some of his underlings were convicted but Morello won an acquittal. Within a few years the pair had acquired 200,000 real dollars, which they used to purchase barbershops, groceries, and shoe repair stores.

As the presumed suppliers to Italian counterfeiters in cities such as

Pittsburgh, Buffalo, Chicago, and New Orleans, Morello became known to the Secret Service as the "Boss of the American Mafia" and Lupo as the treasurer. The Mafia, Chief Flynn told the press in 1903, was "the most secret and terrible organization in the world." But though Lupo and Morello adhered to the culture of the Old World Mafia it is not clear that they actually belonged to the society. When Secret Service men raided the home of one of Morello's henchmen they found a notebook, written in Italian, with a list of rules for " Companions of the Society." One of the rules forbade knife fights among members without permission. Another warned against talking about organizational business to nonmembers. But the fact that they had business dealings with Italian suppliers and distributors and imitated Mafia procedures hardly proves that they belonged to or led an American branch of the Sicilian Mafia—or that such a branch even existed. In that era, lawmen frequently described Italian criminals (even many non-Sicilians) as mafiosi and many a local chief was elevated to the post of the "Boss of the American Mafia."

With its emphasis on counterfeiting, it was natural for the Secret Service to regard Lupo and Morello as the most important Italian criminals in New York. The NYPD's detectives, concentrating on the fighting gangs and their frequent acts of mayhem, thought differently. In their opinion the most important Italian criminal was a man with an Irish name, Paul Kelly, né Paolo Vaccarelli. Of Neapolitan descent, Kelly had adopted his Irish handle to improve his image during a youthful career as a middling bantamweight boxer. Short, thin, and soft-spoken, with pretensions to artistic sensitivity, he led the multiethnic Five Points gang that ruled the territory once controlled by the Irish Whyos. By 1900 the twenty-nine-year-old Kelly directed hundreds of thugs distributed across a broad swath of the Lower East Side from his headquarters at the New Brighton Saloon on Great Jones Street. The Bowery north of him was the domain of a Jewish gang led by "Monk" Eastman (who sometimes used the Irish name of Delaney). The Five Pointers and the Eastmans collected protection money from gambling joints and were available as sluggers for hire, particularly at election time, all the while carrying on an almost perpetual state of warfare against each other. The two leaders were arrested many times without serious consequences because both enjoyed the protection of State Senator "Big Tim" Sullivan.

In 1890 Tammany Hall had put Sullivan in charge of the Italian and Jewish newcomers. He was responsible for making sure they voted correctly and that those who were involved in crime paid off regularly. Big Tim was a garrulous, hail-fellow who could dance the tarantella or don a yarmulke when the occasion demanded it. In a nod to the Italians, he sponsored the legislation that made Columbus Day a legal holiday.

Sullivan's position gradually expanded from district leader to overlord of vice and gambling while his territory grew from the Bowery, then Manhattan south of Fourteenth Street, and finally the whole island. His ascent was not without opposition. Patty Divver, an Irish saloon keeper, was the longtime boss of the city's "old Fourth Ward" (officially the state's second assembly district). Nestled along the East River south of Fourteenth Street, it was still an Irish island amid a sea of Italians and Jews. When Sullivan decided to allow brothels in the Fourth Ward, Divver refused. His defiance led Sullivan to put up another Irish saloon keeper, Tom Foley, to oppose Divver in the election of 1901. To improve his chances, Sullivan called on Paul Kelly to organize a voter suppression drive. The night before the election, members of Kelly's gang crossed over from the Five Points and formed a human chain around each polling place. When the polls opened, husky young Hibernians attempted to fight their way through the phalanxes of Kelly's hoodlums, but the Five Pointers wielded blackjacks and were more numerous and better organized. Kelly's boys also managed to cast a few votes of their own. One of them boasted that he did his civic duty fifty-three times that day. The mostly Irish cops patrolling the area remained spectators. Only gunfire would have brought them into action, and Kelly was careful not to make that mistake. Eventually, the Irish boys were, as the newspapers reported, "slugged to the ground," and Tom Foley emerged victorious.

Fluent in French and Spanish as well as Italian, Kelly loved to discuss high culture with the society swells who came slumming at the New Brighton (albeit with an NYPD detective along for protection). Listening to his erudite conversation, the visitors would sometimes mistake him for another uptown slummer, complaining upon their departure that they had never gotten to meet the terrible Paul Kelly. When the escorting detective informed them that they had just spent a half hour in Kelly's presence, they were amazed. For most New Yorkers of the early twentieth century, Italian gangsters meant the Americanized Kelly who operated in the mainstream. Lupo and Morello, who preyed on their countrymen and passed phony bills, were far less well known. When Herbert Asbury published his classic *Gangs of New York* in 1928, he devoted just a portion of two pages to them while giving twenty-five to Kelly.

In 1903 the Secret Service and the NYPD were presented with a golden opportunity to destroy the Morello gang. Early on an April morning an Irish scrubwoman was heading to work when she noticed a coat draped over a barrel in a courtyard near the corner of 11th Street and Avenue D on the Lower East Side. Picking up the coat and peering into the barrel she saw the mutilated body of a murdered man. Her screams attracted passersby and the police. The body, still warm, was that of a husky thirty-five-year-old with his ears pierced, a common practice among Sicilians. He bore several stiletto wounds sufficient to kill him and his body had also been repeatedly slashed with a razor. Some accounts added a grisly final touch that marked him as a squealer, claiming his genitals had been removed and stuffed in his mouth. The *New York Times* called it "An Atrocious Murder," adding: "Police believe that he was a victim . . . [of] the Italian Mafia, because it never secretes a body, leaving it as an example of their work to confirm that they do not fail to carry out their threats."

Once the word *Mafia* had been invoked the choice of a detective to lead the investigation became a foregone conclusion. Like every crime with a Mafia angle the barrel murder was promptly assigned to the NYPD's resident expert in all things Italian, Giuseppe "Joe" Petrosino.

Born in 1860 near Salerno in the province of Naples, Petrosino was thirteen when he arrived in New York with his family. As a boy he shined shoes on Mulberry Street, right outside police headquarters. Later he became a foreman in the street-sweeping department where his two-fisted management style caught the eye of the legendary Captain Alexander "Clubber"

Williams, a police commander temporarily serving as the city's sanitation commissioner. Clubber liked the no-nonsense way Petrosino bossed his group of Italian laborers. The burly Petrosino was a few inches shy of the police department's minimum-required five-foot-seven height, but Clubber Williams's endorsement overcame that problem and Petrosino became a patrolman in 1883; three years later he was appointed a precinct detective.

With Petrosino on hand the NYPD at last began to show some sophistication in its response to Italian crime. Unlike the Irishmen who dominated the detective ranks, Petrosino knew that when searching for a suspect it was important to know his origins. If he was Sicilian he would not be found among Neapolitans on Mulberry Street but perhaps among fellow Sicilians on nearby Elizabeth Street. If he was from the Sicilian village of Cinisi chances were he would be living among two hundred other Cinisian families uptown on East 69th Street. Petrosino understood that threatening an Italian with arrest would only cause him to disappear. Among the handful of Italian-American detectives in that era the rule of thumb was: "Don't talk about locking someone up, do it." Petrosino also knew how dangerous it could be for an Italian to be even seen conversing with a policeman. Petrosino's name resembled the word for "parsley" in dialect, and when he entered a block the street characters would call out, "See the fine parsley!" Anyone who appeared friendly with Officer Parsley was putting his own life at risk, so when he was looking for information Petrosino would often dress as an Italian immigrant—"Luigi off the boat"—to make it easier for people to talk to him. Sometimes he added a false beard.

Though he had a thick Italian accent, Petrosino taught himself to speak slowly and precisely. He was "always striving for accuracy," according to Assistant District Attorney Arthur Train, and determined to solve every case. He was also committed to the cause of his own professional advancement, and Clubber Williams was only the first in a succession of superiors to be won over. In 1895 Police Commissioner Theodore Roosevelt was so impressed that he promoted Petrosino to headquarters detective sergeant, with a roving commission to investigate cases in which Italians were involved.

The Secret Service had its own Italian specialist. Operative Larry Richey (né Ricci) was only eighteen but already a veteran investigator. As a thirteen-year-old boy living in Philadelphia he had served as an aide on a major counterfeiting case, working with the star of the service, William Burns. Where Petrosino was plodding and inarticulate, the American-born Richey was bright, glib, and even more ambitious. In 1901 Richey's mother secured her sixteen-year-old son an appointment as a full-fledged Secret Service man; shortly afterward he Americanized his name. A quarter-century later, he would be a principal secretary (in modern parlance, the chief of staff) to President Herbert Hoover. At the time of the barrel murder he was working undercover, "roping" counterfeiting suspects in the downtown Little Italy.

On two consecutive days before the murder Richey had been with a group of operatives following an unknown counterfeiting suspect whom they dubbed "The Newcomer." At Richey's last sighting the newcomer had just entered Morello's restaurant. Hearing about the body in the barrel, Richey and his coworkers contacted the NYPD. Soon they had identified the corpse as The Newcomer's.

With the Lupo-Morello gang implicated, the investigation got going in earnest and the NYPD and the Secret Service agreed to work together—sort of. Police had found a small crucifix in the barrel, along with some sawdust and cigar stubs and a perfumed handkerchief with a note written in Italian by a female hand. Petrosino translated it as "Come at once," suggesting that a woman had lured the victim to his death. An examination of his stomach revealed evidence of a recently consumed Sicilian meal. Familiar with Morello's restaurant, Petrosino knew it served similar food and had sawdust and cigar butts on the floor. Eventually the police would establish that the victim had been killed there and taken by horse-drawn wagon to his resting place on the Lower East Side. At the moment they had no evidence to back up a murder charge in court and the wisest course might have been to go on shadowing the suspects and looking for a weak link among them. On the other hand, the gang might leave New York or even flee to Italy.

The chief of the NYPD's detectives was a Byrnes protégé, Inspector "Chesty George" McClusky, whose nickname reflected his swaggering air. Chesty George wanted to make sure that the NYPD and not Flynn's Secret

Service controlled the case. Rather than wait, he ordered his men to round up the dozen principal members of the Lupo-Morello gang. As the *New York Times* reported, in some instances their heads "had to be slammed into the pavement to overcome resistance." Among the prisoners were Lupo and Morello themselves. The NYPD detectives then locked up the crew together, which according to Chief Flynn gave them an opportunity to get their stories straight. One of those questioned during the investigation was a mysterious figure known as "Don" Vito Cascio Ferro. He had fled to New York from Sicily two years earlier after running afoul of the law for his involvement in a kidnapping case. Another arrestee gave his name as Tomas Petto, age twenty-four, a.k.a. "Il Bove" (the Ox). A bull-necked man of Herculean frame, according to the *Times* Petto fought "like a wild beast" until a blackjack-wielding policeman felled him with a "stunning blow." Police found a one-dollar pawn ticket for a wristwatch on his person. Assuming that the barrel victim hadn't been murdered for his watch, the detectives did not trace it.

McClusky's next move was to stage what would today be called a perp walk. Using the unlikely excuse that the three patrol wagons assigned to haul the suspects from headquarters to the courthouse did not arrive in time, he ordered them marched there on foot. Given the proximity of police headquarters to Little Italy, the result was to parade them before their countrymen as the Romans had paraded their captives and as the Italian police sometimes did with mafiosi, dramatizing their powerlessness. The *Times* reported that as the procession left headquarters, it was "greeted by an immense crowd . . . many of them Italians suspected of being in sympathy with the prisoners." Suddenly there was "a movement," causing detectives to anticipate a rescue attempt; in response, the police "broke up the crowd . . . knocking down some men and boys."

The papers liked such stories, and so did the police. Portraying the Mafia as an all-powerful organization made their occasional victories seem all the more impressive. At their arraignment Morello was held on $5,000 bail, others on $3,000 or $4,000. Petto, whom the police had yet to focus on, was released on only a $300 bond. Don Vito Cascio Ferro quickly fled the city for New Orleans and then back to Sicily, where he remained a Mafia leader of consequence for another three decades.

The police had a surplus of defendants and a scarcity of evidence. Accounts of those involved in the barrel murder investigation tend to diverge considerably in detail, especially in assigning credit and blame, but all give the impression that the case was investigated first and the arrests made later. Instead, as most cases were handled in those days, the method was to arrest the suspects, then find the evidence to prove their guilt. And as often happened, the police came up short, despite the best efforts of the indomitable Petrosino. He got a convict in Sing Sing, Giuseppe De Priemo, to identify a picture of the murder victim as his brother-in-law Benditto Madonia of Buffalo, New York. De Priemo, he learned, had sent Madonia to collect some money owed him by Joe Morello in connection with a counterfeiting deal. And on the day of the murder Petto "the Ox" had spent a good deal of money around Little Italy, his girlfriend blossoming forth in expensive clothing.

When Petrosino learned in Buffalo that Madonia had carried a cheap watch belonging to his stepson, he wired Inspector McClusky and the police finally linked the watch to the pawn ticket. Petto was indicted for murder. At his trial, however, he claimed he had gotten the ticket from a man named "John," and the pawnshop owner could not identify him. When Madonia's wife and stepson took the stand to testify Morello's followers murmured and shuffled their feet, one even jumping up and putting his finger to his lips as a warning. Not surprisingly the two witnesses were unable to positively identify the watch. Brought down from Sing Sing, the convict De Priemo was equally unhelpful, declaring that his good friend Petto would never have hurt Madonia. Petto was acquitted.[1] The cops had locked up the city's worst gang of Sicilian all-around criminals—and had failed to make a case against any of them.

The police invariably blamed such debacles on the code of *omerta*—an alibi that helped distract attention from a badly botched investigation.

---

[1]Some writers who have studied the case claim that between the first and second arrests another man was substituted for Petto.

Locking up the defendants together made it unlikely that any individual would break ranks. If the police had continued their surveillance longer they might at least have brought counterfeiting charges against a few of the defendants. Instead, the police took a quick-and-dirty approach which suggested that Italian-on-Italian crime was still not important enough to command a serious effort. As a practical matter, Byrnes's dictum, "Let them kill each other," remained in force.

The barrel murder brought forth an outpouring of invective from the American press. The Mafia was "now almost as strongly entrenched in New York, New Orleans, and Chicago as in its Sicilian home," the *New York World* declared. The Italian-language papers, in turn, decried what they considered a wave of ethnic slurs equating respectable citizens with gangsters. Gino Speranza, a New York lawyer of Italian ancestry, wrote a fiery letter to the *Times* protesting against one alarmist article on the Mafia—there was no such organization in Italy, he asserted. A *Times* reporter was then assigned to interview a sample of Italian Americans for a story headlined: DECLARES MAFIA CRYS A POLICE FICTION. The efforts of men like Speranza were futile. Occurring in the media capital of the country, the barrel murder solidified the image of Italians as ferocious criminals.

Tomas Petto left New York after his acquittal and settled in Pittston, Pennsylvania. Fearful of retribution, Petto was careful, particularly after De Priemo's release from Sing Sing in 1905. Not long afterward, though, he heard a low whistle outside his house followed by a knock at the door. Cautiously, Petto opened the door, gun in hand. Before he could make a move he was fatally wounded by five blasts from a lupara. Near his body, the authorities recovered a crucifix identical to one found on the body of Madonia. Whoever fired the shots, rough justice had been done.

While Lupo and Morello continued to prosper, Paul Kelly's fortunes soon took a turn for the worse. A few months after the barrel murder Kelly sent a squad of gunmen into the Bowery to hold up a card game and a gun battle broke out between his gang and a contingent of Eastmans. Not until police reserves arrived on the scene was the shooting stopped, leaving 3 men dead, 11 wounded, and 20 in police custody, including Monk Eastman himself. The blazing guns and headlines did not sit well with Tammany, then in the midst of a tough mayoral election. Any more such incidents, Tim Sullivan warned, and the two gang leaders would lose their protection—and their freedom. Not long afterward, Eastman, prowling through the Tenderloin after midnight, was caught trying to rob a rich young drunk. He spent the next five years in Sing Sing. The following year some rival hoodlums came gunning for Kelly at the New Brighton. His Irish bodyguard spotted them and yelled, "Look out, boss." After diving under a table Kelly came back up shooting, while a quick-thinking employee switched off the lights. By the time the police arrived the bodyguard lay dead on the floor and Kelly was nowhere to be found. The next day's papers prominently displayed the corpse beneath a picture of Big Tim Sullivan. A logical inference was that Tammany was sheltering Kelly. In fact, after being hit three times he had been spirited away to a hideout in East Harlem to convalesce under the protection of Lupo and Morello, who up until then had not been involved in Kelly's operations. Eventually he surrendered and was charged with murder, but the case was dropped for lack of evidence.

It was the beginning of the end of Kelly's downtown career. He closed the New Brighton and opened a café called Little Naples, which failed. Kelly then withdrew from the Five Points, moving into a house on East 116th Street owned by the Morello family. He became partners with them in a local real estate business, using strong-arm tactics to force people to sell their property. In 1910, he tried to open an upscale place in the Broadway theater district that he whimsically called The New England Social and Dramatic Club. His old friends from the Lower East Side were pointedly discouraged from dropping in, but the club failed regardless. Eventually he became a business agent for a union of ragpickers in East Harlem. He preferred this semilegitimacy, and as Italians gradually came to replace the Irish on the East Side docks Kelly moved up in the world, becoming a vice president of the International Longshoremen's Union. In his new position he double-crossed the international by keeping his men working during a waterfront strike. Nevertheless, his image makeover was on the whole successful. He changed his name back to the original and the newspapers gradually took to referring to him respectfully as "Mr. Vaccarelli." Only Tim Sullivan was unimpressed. If it hadn't been for *him,* Sullivan liked to say,

"Mr. Vaccarelli Kelly" would be doing twenty years for the New Brighton affair (a typical bit of Sullivan boasting—after all, in this case Kelly only fired in self-defense, and missed, at that).

Lupo and Morello remained their old vicious selves, but while they may have been immune to the criminal laws they could not escape the economic ones. Continuing to expand their business operations, legitimate and illegitimate, they incurred heavy losses in the panic of 1907. Simple and direct men, they concluded that the answer to their financial woes was to open their own counterfeiting plant in the Catskill Mountains. It was a move that set them up for a rematch with Uncle Sam.

3:   Italian Squads and American Carabinieri: Law Enforcement Wars on the Mafia

No one saw the bomb thrown, but hundreds heard it explode, and within a few minutes the streets around Mott and Mulberry were filled with excited residents. One of those who heard the blast was Detective Joe Petrosino, who quickly arrived on the scene. The entire front of a florist shop on the ground floor of a five-story tenement building had been blown out and its contents strewn all over the street. The shop belonged to the Deodaro brothers who lived with their families on the second floor above it, and this wasn't the first time they'd been bombed. Until a year ago, they had owned another florist shop a few doors down on Mott Street. After the Deodaros failed to respond to letters demanding money, that shop was blown up. They moved to a new location and the letters started coming again. Now another bomb had exploded, shattering the peace of New York City's largest Italian colony, just a week before Christmas of 1906.

Black Hand letters had become endemic in New York. Usually phrased with exquisite Old World courtesy—"Honored Sir, we respectfully request"—the message was always the same: "Pay or die." And die some did, by bullet, knife, or bomb (with many Italians working as laborers on construction sites sticks of dynamite or five-pound metal balls loaded with high explosives were not hard to come by). Some of the letters contained a symbol of a menacing black hand, daggers, or both. An enterprising reporter for the *New York Herald* searching for a fresh angle on a routine story referred to the missives as "Black Hand" letters and the phrase caught on. The new term added to the confusion about criminal societies. Was the Black Hand an organization coincident with or apart from the Mafia, or Camorra, or simply a method of operation? The name had originally been applied to Spanish anarchist groups. Leftist accounts, which have a certain plausibility, claimed that it was popularized in the 1880s by an Andalusian police chief, Don Tomas Perez Monforte. Confronted with a widespread strike of agricultural workers, Monforte hit on a clever ploy to break it. Noting black hands painted on the walls of buildings as directions, he proclaimed that these were warnings placed by an anarchist group. Later, the chief's deputy "accidentally" found the organization's charter hidden under a rock. With this evidence, the police commenced to round up the strike leaders and force the rank-and-file back to work. The story of *"La mano negra"* (*nero* in Italian) was widely publicized in Latin countries, and the symbol was sometimes adopted by Italian criminals as a device to facilitate extortion.[1] It was obvious to detectives that the Black Hand was not an organization like the Mafia but a method employed by individuals or small groups. The use of explosives by Black Handers also popularized another derogatory term for Italians—"bomb throwers."

American law was still reacting sporadically to crimes committed by Italian gangs: arrest a murderer here, a few counterfeiters there. Certain detectives, like Joe Petrosino in New York, Gabriel Longabardi in Chicago, Peter Angelo in Pittsburgh, and John D'Antonio in New Orleans, were assigned to work as Italian crime specialists. The deluge of Black Hand cases prompted the NYPD to establish a five-man Italian squad with Sergeant Petrosino in charge. Since its detectives also "caught" all serious Italian-American crimes it had the unintended effect of ghettoizing the problem.

---

[1]Latin Black Handers had no connection with the Serbian secret society of the same name that organized the assassination of the Austrian archduke at Sarajevo in 1914.

Several hundred thousand Italians in New York City could not be policed by a squad of five men, but its existence meant the rest of the force was off the hook.

In 1907 Commissioner Theodore Bingham expanded the Italian squad to twenty-five men and promoted Petrosino to lieutenant. In his enhanced role Petrosino scored major triumphs over genuine bosses of both major Italian secret societies. In Naples that year a Camorra chieftain, Enrico "Big Henry" Erricino (also known as Alfano), had ordered the murder and torture of a man and his wife, causing the Italian government to proclaim a crackdown on the Camorra and to send 30,000 troops to enforce it. Erricino fled to New York City. Petrosino's squad tracked him down and turned him over to Italian authorities. When Big Henry was returned to Italy he became one of the principal defendants in a three-year state trial of Camorra leaders. The Italian consul general presented Petrosino with a gold watch in gratitude for the capture.

In 1908 Raffaele Palizzollo, a former member of the Italian parliament, came to New York to raise funds to finance a return to political life. A Mafia leader in Sicily, he had emerged a free man after three trials for the murder of a director of the Bank of Sicily. In New York he was greeted by the local consul and a large crowd of Italian notables. Even American officials were respectful and Palizzollo made a big hit on the banquet circuit by attacking the Mafia. Then Petrosino tipped off city officials and Italian colony leaders about Palizzollo's background. The distinguished statesman had to cut his visit short and take the next boat back home. When Petrosino came down to wish him bon voyage, the angry mafioso shook his fist and warned the detective never to come to Sicily. But these were only occasional successes, and criminals styling themselves Black Hand, Mafia, or Camorra continued to flourish in New York City.

The mining areas of Pennsylvania were some of the principal battlegrounds for the industrial strife that was the dark side of the Gilded Age. Waves of immigration from southern and eastern Europe led to the gradual replacement of English, Irish, and Welsh miners by Italians, Slavs, and Hungarians. At first the Italians hired out as strikebreakers. Within a relatively short period they came to identify with the workers. In 1890 two small unions, one of them affiliated with the radical Knights of Labor, merged into the 17,000-member United Mine Workers. In the spring of 1902 they called a general strike to secure recognition for their union and its demands. A private force of 5,000 Coal and Iron Police patrolled the mining districts in addition to the 9,000 National Guardsmen called to duty. By fall the country was facing a fuel shortage and President Theodore Roosevelt intervened, persuading the workers to return to work on the promise that he would appoint an arbitration commission. The arbitration findings compelled the owners to recognize the UMW and abolish their private cops. The common wealth of Pennsylvania responded by creating the state police. Since 228 officers and men were replacing 5,000 Coal and Iron Police, it would have to be a crack outfit. The commanding officer, a Philadelphia aristocrat and National Guard captain named John Groome, was a veteran of both the Spanish-American War and considerable strike duty in Pennsylvania. He opted to recruit ex-servicemen, preferably of American stock, though some Irish and German immigrants were admitted to its ranks. Troopers—a cavalry term denoting their mounted status—were required to enlist for two years, be unmarried, and live in barracks. In effect, they were soldiers of the state invested with police authority. Each of the initial four troops were headquartered in the mining districts. The Pennsylvania State Police became nationally well known and served as a model for the creation of similar forces in other states, thanks in part to their Boswell, Katherine Mayo, who wrote three books about the organization.

Prior to the creation of the state police, the nonchalant policy in Pennsylvania regarding violence by Italians against Italians had been similar to New York City's. Katherine Mayo described its practical application: "At feasts, christenings, balls and the like, these alien people were given to heavy and prolonged drinking bouts, which ended often in wild and murderous disorder. The comfortable practice . . . had been to let them fight out their brawls undisturbed even to the rebeginning of a hearty funeral." She was a prescient observer, though not sympathetic to those whose Americanism failed to meet her standards. According to Mayo, one of the principal tasks of the new state police was to teach the unassimilated foreign element by "small but repeated object lessons that a new gospel was abroad in the land." In anticipation of their duties, the recruits were imbued with the philosophy, "One American can lick a hundred foreigners."

The force commenced operations early in 1906. In the beginning of April Troop B, located in the northeastern part of the state, responded to an Italian settlement called "Boston Patch" where it was reported that striking quarry workers were firing at other workers still in the plant. A dozen troopers arrived and the sergeant in charge ordered the five hundred Italians gathered to disperse. Some of them allegedly aimed revolvers at his head, but the sergeant led his men in a cavalry charge that cleared the area. He then ordered a sweep, sending troopers to search the residents' homes and confiscate all firearms. The United Mine Workers had opposed the formation of the state police, labeling them "American Cossacks," and when they learned of the Boston Patch episode the union secured warrants for the troopers' arrests on grounds of trespassing and disorderly conduct. The charges were eventually dismissed.

A more spectacular incident took place in September at the town of Florence near Punxsutawney. A sergeant and five troopers were fired on when they attempted to enter a house to arrest two Italians charged with murder. One trooper was killed and two were wounded. After reinforcements arrived from Troop D headquarters the officers again rushed the house and another trooper was killed. All through the night they exchanged shots with the occupants of the house. Finally Troop D commander Captain Joseph Robinson ordered the house dynamited, causing it to collapse and burn, killing everyone inside. The *Punxsutawney Weekly Spirit* noted, "There are many differences of opinion regarding the manner of conducting the attack on the house . . . but all who watched agreed that the courage and loyalty of the state policemen was beyond criticism." A sergeant told Katherine Mayo, "Those two [dead troopers] . . . taught us to hold the honor of the force dearer than life." The United States had never seen a police force like this, though some of the immigrants had. One Slavic miner, watching the troopers in their dark blue uniforms and slouch hats riding through his village, muttered, "Ah, hussars, me no like," and quickly walked away.

One of the most violent areas for industrial strife was the Mahoning Valley, particularly in Lawrence County along the Ohio border. Mine owners such as the Bessemer Limestone Corporation claimed that some Italians were shaking down their countrymen on paydays and holding conspiratorial Black Hand meetings. While extortion in the area was widespread, some of the activities the company objected to were likely to have been dues collecting on behalf of a union that had just won a general strike. It was a murder that ultimately galvanized the state authorities. In the fall of 1905 State Fish and Game Warden Seely Houk, patrolling near Hillsville .in Lawrence County, caught an Italian man named Rocco Racco hunting out of season. Houk warned Racco that the next time he would kill Racco's dog. A few weeks later a friend borrowed the dog to go hunting, also out of season, and was caught by Houk, who followed through with his cruel threat and killed the animal. When Racco was told of the killing, he declared, "As my dog died in the woods, so shall this man." The following April, Houk's body was discovered weighted down with stones in the Mahoning River. The Pennsylvania State Police were soldiers, not detectives, so the Bessemer Company and the State Fish and Game Commission, each acting separately, engaged the Pinkertons to investigate the quarry shakedowns and the murder of Warden Houk. The agency assigned Frank Dimaio to the case.

Increasingly the Pinkerton Agency was being called on by wealthy Italians who had received Black Hand letters and Dimaio was still their Italian specialist, assigned to gather information on the Mafia.[2] For several months in 1905 he had wandered through the Italian colonies of cities like Chicago and Pittsburgh dressed in the black pants, checkered shirt, threadbare jacket, and peaked cap of a typical Italian laborer. The report he produced inspired Joe Petrosino to declare that Dimaio was the most knowledgeable man in America about the Mafia. Dimaio then embarked on a career of undercover work investigating Italian gangs in the industrial heartland of

[2]Dimaio did get at least one interesting break from the Italian beat. After New Orleans, he went to South America to search for Butch Cassidy and the Sundance Kid. According to the Pinkertons, he supplied the Bolivian military with the information that led to their discovery and deaths.

America, from Pennsylvania through the upper Midwest. Because there were so few Italian private detectives, his services were in heavy demand. In Columbus, Ohio, he uncovered information leading to the arrest of fourteen Italian extortionists.

When an undercover man is used frequently word begins to get around about him in the underworld. Gangsters whispered about the mysterious man in Columbus who arrived in their circle shortly before a police crackdown and disappeared afterward. As the word was passed confederates in other cities recalled a similar individual whose sudden appearance and equally sudden disappearance seemed to coincide with law enforcement drives. The underworld even gave him a nickname, "The Raven," as in Edgar Allan Poe's poem, which said, "Beware the Raven." In the same year that the NYPD formed its Italian squad, the Pinkertons did likewise and placed Dimaio at the head of it.

The workers in the mill and mining towns of the Ohio-Pennsylvania border were a tough lot. For the Pinkertons to operate undercover was dangerous, especially for Dimaio, who was marked for death by many of the Italian gangs. He and his squad began their assignment by assuming false identities. They went to Ellis Island where they blended in with other immigrants and were eventually hired as a group by contractors from the Pennsylvania limestone quarries and taken to Hillsville. The town was locally known as Hellsville, and according to Katherine Mayo, life there was grim. "Young men who were saving money to send back for their sweetheart soon learned to keep secret their ambitions. Songs in the summer evenings ended, and the homes over which the Black Hand held the menacing stiletto or the smoking revolver never contained a light, for fear of attack by night."

Posing as hard-drinking tough guys, the Pinkerton detectives began to circulate around the county trying to gain the confidence of suspected gang members and to develop informants. One of Dimaio's first contacts in the quarries was a local capo, Sal Candido, who called himself Sam Kennedy. One night while the miners were drinking at Candido's house police burst in and began frisking everyone. One of Dimaio's men spit in a detective's face and was sent flying across the room; he was handcuffed and taken away, presumably to be beaten for his effrontery. The scenario had been pre-arranged with the local police—down at the station, the Pinkerton operative and county detective Creighton Logan had a good laugh and exchanged information.

After this encounter, Dimaio and his crew were hailed as heroes by their drinking buddies. Pretending to open up, Dimaio confided that he was a mafioso and he made his listeners sit up and take notice when he used secret passwords like *monte albano.* It was through Candido that Dimaio managed to meet John Jati, who had been a lieutenant of Giuseppe Musilino, the "Jesse James of Calabria." In 1901, when Musilino was killed by Italian troops, Jati had fled to the United States. Now he was working out of Youngstown, Ohio, running a school for assassins. Jati had a large collection of knives, stilettos, and lead pipes, and he used dressmaker's mannequins with vital parts of the body outlined in red ink to instruct his pupils in the art of striking a fatal blow. Dimaio was even able to sign up for a few lessons.

It became apparent to the detectives that there was no single all-inclusive Black Hand or Mafia in the county. Instead, small bands of Sicilians, Neapolitans, or Calabrians in the various towns had their own rackets. A character named Bagnetto was responsible for some of the payday shakedowns in Hillsville. He made sure to get his money by standing near the pay line where he would stop every Italian after he got his envelope, make him open it up at gunpoint and take out a specific amount. It was claimed that $25,000 a month was collected this way. He and his gang would also kidnap miners and force them to write out checks until their bank accounts were empty.

In July 1907 a plan was laid to arrest twenty-one of Bagnetto's Hillsville extortionists in one fell swoop. On payday a Pinkerton agent assumed the role of paymaster. As a suspect came to the window to get his wages he was told that his envelope was short a dollar and he was asked to step into a back office where it would be made up. As each man entered he found a detective pointing a gun at him while another handcuffed him. After eleven men who had entered the office did not come out, an Italian woman who was part of Bagnetto's crew sounded an alarm and the remaining suspects bolted from the line. Suddenly the engineer of a freight locomotive idling on nearby tracks moved his train forward and frantically blew the whistle. The doors of several boxcars opened and disgorged police who proceeded to complete the roundup. Afterward, John Jati was picked up in Lima, Ohio, and two of his henchmen were apprehended in New Jersey. Thirty-five of the men arrested were eventually convicted and sentenced to terms of three to ten years.

Among those in prison was Rocco Racco, and again the code of *omerta* failed. Sal Candido was the weak link. His wife had recently given birth to their first child. During her pregnancy Dimaio had accompanied the proud young father on trips to buy baby clothes. After her husband went to prison Dimaio visited Mrs. Candido and got her to pose for pictures with the baby and to sign a letter he dictated asking her husband to collaborate. As Dimaio expected, when he showed the letter to Candido in prison the capo cursed the detective and ordered him away. After a passage of time Candido came around and told the story of the murder of Warden Houk. According to Candido, Racco and his brother-in-law had gone into the woods and fired shots to draw Houk's attention. When the warden came over to investigate they killed him and disposed of his body in the river. Candido's statements led to charges against the other prisoners, some of whom had already divined that Dimaio was "The Raven." When he approached them they all cursed and screamed, but eventually they directed the detective to a young quarry worker who had helped to dispose of the body and to the man who had borrowed Racco's dog, seen it shot, and heard Racco swear revenge. Dimaio even got on good terms with Racco's wife, who spent most of her time praying and ended up having to sell her possessions to survive. When a pawnbroker tried to cheat her on some jewelry Dimaio intervened and forced the man to pay her the proper amount. In gratitude she silently delivered the shotgun used to kill Warden Houk to the detective. At Racco's trial Dimaio was called as a witness and the defendant was convicted.

The state and local police had also been busy in the western part of Pennsylvania. Early in 1906 the mayor of Monongahela asked Troop A to help arrest 140 members of the Black Hand Society, whom he claimed were responsible for twenty-one murders. In Pittsburgh Detective Pete Angelo arrested two New York hitmen who had come to town to carry out a murder. They were tried and hanged. Next the police picked up two dynamiters sent from New York, allegedly to blow up the jail. It was rumored that all the law enforcement activity would cause a general uprising of Italians in western Pennsylvania. A whole troop of Pennsylvania State Police under Captain Robinson was assigned to protect the Lawrence County jail. Robinson, an ex–regular army officer, announced his policy was to "shoot first and let the coroner ask the questions." The hanging of Rocco Racco in the fall of 1909 was the final act in the great anti-Mafia drive, which had turned out to be essentially a roundup of ordinary criminals. By Mayo's account, Hillsville's Italian residents now "sat peacefully on their front porches and tipped their hats when state troopers rode by."[3] It would have been appropriate for them to salute the Pinkertons too, but Dimaio's team had moved on. He would eventually become head of the agency's Pittsburgh division.[4]

Back in New York, NYPD commissioner Theodore Bingham was still plagued by the Black Hand rumors. A former general whose spit-and-polish military manner made him unpopular with the cops, his frequent ill-advised comments brought him more criticism from the public. In 1908 he pinned most of the blame for New York's crime problems on Jews and Italians, describing the latter as "a riffraff of desperate scoundrels, ex-convicts, and jailbirds." Taken to task by the more politically sensitive mayor, George B. McClellan Jr., the commissioner issued a formal apology. But his heart wasn't in it and he cast about for a way to save face by shoring up evidence of foreign-born criminality. He proposed to create a Secret Service unit composed of men specially appointed from outside the NYPD to infiltrate foreign criminal groups. The idea was shelved when board of aldermen president "Little Tim" Sullivan (cousin of "Big Tim") voiced disbelief that there was a Black Hand and refused to appropriate the funds. Bingham was not a man to accept defeat lightly, and a recently enacted federal law allowing for deportation within three years of arrival of any alien found to have

---

[3]In 1917, Katherine Mayo was able to persuade the state of New York to create a police force modeled on the Pennsylvania troopers. Later she would arouse a storm of criticism with her book *Mother India,* which voiced strong support for British imperial rule and condemned Gandhi and the Hindu nationalist movement. When she died in 1940, both the New York State Police and the British Navy furnished a guard of honor at her funeral.

[4]At the time of the 1957 Apalachin conference raid, the ninety-year-old Dimaio was still alert enough to provide reporters with background information on the Mafia.

concealed a criminal record provided him with a tool to pursue his theories. A consultant to the federal government proposed that U.S. officials be sent to Italy to investigate the background of Italian criminals now in America with a view toward deporting them.

In February 1909 Bingham announced that he had obtained private funds (from both Italian-American businessmen and leading New York tycoons) to establish a Secret Service branch composed of fifteen civilian investigators—and he revealed that its commander, Lieutenant Petrosino, was already on the way to Italy to implement the consultant's proposal. The federal law would not directly affect men like Lupo and Morello who had been in the country more than three years, but it could mean trouble for more recent arrivals. Petrosino might also be able to arrange the extradition from Italy of fugitives wanted in New York. There were many men in both countries who had reason to fear his trip.

For once the always eager Petrosino did not jump at the assignment. The American press had long heaped praise on his vigilance. "When murder and blackmail are in the air," the *New York Times* declared, "and the men folks are white-faced but searing and the women folk are saying litanies to the Blessed Mother that their dark-haired cherub children may be saved from the Black Hand kidnappers, a telephone call comes to Police Headquarters in Mulberry Street for Petrosino, and all Little Italy looks to the Italian detective for protection." At the same time, the Italian-American press criticized him for what it saw as constant harping on the Black Hand and the Mafia. This complaint was unfair. Despite his propensity for seeking publicity, he did not believe Italian gangs in America were significantly influenced by foreign organizations or that those in New York City were part of a single group. He perceived them as a minority of criminals who preyed on their own people, often escaping punishment because of the weaknesses of the politically influenced criminal justice system. He certainly did not agree with Bingham that Italians were "riffraff."

For much of his career, his dedication to policing the Italian community kept him so busy he had virtually no time for a personal life, maintaining the existence of a lonely bachelor in a two-room apartment away from the Italian colony where his only relaxation was playing the violin. This had changed the previous year. He had married a widow and taken an apartment near the new police headquarters on Centre Street, a few blocks from the old one on Mulberry (but still in the midst of an Italian neighborhood). In his late forties, with twenty-six years of strenuous police duty beginning to wear on him, he was on extended sick leave. His wife had just given birth to a daughter and he wished to be with them. Petrosino's friends counseled him not to go on such a dangerous mission. His deputy, Lieutenant Anthony Vacharis (Vaccarezzi), a Genovese, warned him that "South of Rome, everyone is Mafia." In the end, despite his lack of enthusiasm, Petrosino departed carrying a list of two thousand names. On the ship going over he was listed as Signor Guglielmo DeSimone, drawing suspicious glances from fellow passengers. By the time he arrived, Bingham's indiscreet remarks about Petrosino's mission had been picked up by the Italian press. Petrosino was already known in the country from a series of cheap crime thrillers that portrayed him as the "Italian Sherlock Holmes."

The prime minister at the time was Giovanni Giolitti, who also held the portfolio of minister of interior in charge of police. Though a northerner, he was strongly supported by the Mafia, which controlled most parliamentary seats in western Sicily, and he was widely known as the "Prime Minister of the Underworld." Having left Italy as a child, Petrosino had little understanding of the country's intricate politics and his humble origins presented a social barrier. High-ranking Italian police officers were educated men of aristocratic bearing with *Excellencia* and *Cavaliere* before their names. Even his personal appearance weighed against him. New York prosecutor Arthur Train, who liked Petrosino, described him as "bull-necked with a great round head like a summer squash and a pock-marked face." High police officials were friendly, but privately they were unimpressed with the American detective.

Petrosino was offered bodyguards in both Rome and Palermo, but he refused them—he had always worked alone on undercover assignments. He also knew that some cops were on the Mafia's payroll. Finally, he was a proud man, and like any policeman, he would have felt ashamed to be guarded by another policeman. Still, he was apprehensive. In Palermo, after being recognized by an Italian criminal who had formerly resided in New

York, Petrosino wrote in his notebook, "I am on dangerous ground." He seemed mindful when he registered at his hotel under a false name, but then he opened a local bank account and mail drop under his own, though he must have known that the bank was likely to have Mafia connections. On March 12 he was out and about in the Palermo area meeting with unknown persons. While waiting for a trolley near a statue of Garibaldi in downtown Palermo around 9 P.M., Petrosino was shot to death. According to the American consul four shots were fired by two paid gunman, three of them striking the unarmed detective. The fact that he had left his gun back in his hotel room suggests that he may have been lured to his death by someone he trusted.

Tributes to Petrosino poured into police headquarters. President Roosevelt said, "He was a great and good man. . . . He did not know the meaning of fear." Italian-American leaders expressed outrage that their hero had been sent on such an obviously suicidal mission. Bingham and the NYPD brass struggled to deflect blame, putting out a story that the mission was conceived by Petrosino, who sold it to the department. Another theory advanced was that he had been betrayed by the Italian police. The department then announced that it was dispatching Lieutenant Vacharis to Italy along with an Irish detective to catch Petrosino's killers. Later the NYPD claimed the two detectives were in Sicily working undercover on the case—a questionable notion. Vacharis, a northerner, would have stood out like a Bostonian in Alabama, while the Irish detective—despite the Sicilian he had supposedly learned in the East Side Italian neighborhood where he was raised—would quickly have been spotted by his looks and dialect. The wily Prime Minister Giolitti's government had put out its own cover story that the American cop was killed by anarchists while acting as an advance man for a contemplated visit from outgoing President Roosevelt. Blaming anarchists made sense politically because, unlike the Mafia, they did not support the government. Giolitti barred the two American detectives from traveling anywhere south of Naples, telling U.S. diplomats that their safety could not be guaranteed. No doubt another concern was that they might find out something that would embarrass the Italian authorities. Ultimately, Vacharis and his partner spent most of their time at police headquarters in Rome gathering records on Italian criminals in America.

Petrosino's trip had been paid for out of funds provided by friends like Pioggio Puccio of the Italian Protective Association. They would also pay for his funeral and the Vacharis mission. When Petrosino's body was returned to New York City it was met by a police guard of honor and escorted to St. Patrick's Cathedral where it lay in state. Two hundred and fifty thousand people turned out to line the streets for his funeral procession. Senator Tim Sullivan sponsored a benefit for Petrosino's widow at a Broadway theater and the city's leading impresario, "Yankee Doodle Dandy" George M. Cohan, put together a gala night of stars. The event turned out to be a disappointment, raising only half as much money as expected. American headliners like Victor Moore, Louise Dresser, and Edna Wallace Hopper went on, but at the last moment some of the Italian singers on the bill canceled and many of their countrymen decided not to attend at all. This was an ominous sign. No performer turned down a chance to appear in a George M. Cohan production and no ethnic New Yorker dared to disappoint Sullivan. Some who stayed away claimed that they had received threatening letters or admitted they were afraid of offending the Black Hand. Eventually a fund of $10,000 was collected for Petrosino's widow, though attempts to award her an enhanced police pension were rejected by the board of aldermen. No one was ever officially charged with Petrosino's murder. In Sicily a few low-level mafiosi were rounded up, but they were released in 1911 as part of a general amnesty when Italy went to war with Turkey.

In the immediate aftermath of Petrosino's murder, there were press reports of a plot to kill other Italian detectives like Johnny D'Antonio of New Orleans, Pete Angelo of Pittsburgh, and Chicago's Gabe Longabardi. Over the next few years the papers regularly reported that the Petrosino murder was about to be solved. One time the culprit was identified as a New Orleans gunman. Then it was a Pennsylvania miner sent there by Lupo and Morello. When the Italian government held a massive trial of several hundred Camorrists in 1910, it was reported that "Big Henry" Erricino had ordered Petrosino's murder. The proof offered was that a Camorrist had supposedly sent a coded telegram from Rome to Sicily to warn that the detective was on his way. Why the Camorra man would do such a favor for the Mafia was not made clear.[5] Raffaele Palizzolo, who had warned the detective never to come to Italy when Petrosino ran him out of New York, was frequently cited as the man behind the assassination.

Many accounts of the case claim that Don Vito Cascio Ferro committed the murder personally or at least was present. The noted Italian journalist Luigi Barzini claimed that Cascio Ferro, whom he described as the "greatest head the Mafia ever had," shot Petrosino a few hours after he landed. But Petrosino arrived in Palermo eleven days before he was murdered. While serving a life sentence in one of Mussolini's prisons many years later, the don was supposed to have confessed to the deed. His explanation was that Petrosino was "an honorable man who deserved to die in an honorable way" (rather than be slain by hired gunmen). In the final analysis, whatever his precise role, the murder could not have been carried out in Palermo without Don Vito's assent.

Whoever was behind the assassination, it was a huge triumph for the Mafia or those who claimed to be members, adding to its already fearsome reputation. To counter this sense of growing menace, the NYPD should have launched a vigorous offensive against the local mafiosi; instead it was the Italian squad that suffered. In June 1909 Commissioner Bingham was dismissed after becoming embroiled in yet another controversy because of his unwise remarks. When Vacharis and his partner returned to New York with a list of names, the NYPD was no longer interested. The city had elected a new mayor, the civil liberties–minded William Gaynor, who gave orders to the police department to purge its photo albums and files of suspected criminals. In 1911 Gaynor's socialite police commissioner, Rhinelander Waldo, abolished the Italian squad and transferred Vacharis to City Island—a two-hour commute from the lieutenant's home, causing him to

---

[5]Four years earlier, a duel fought between twelve Camorrists and twelve mafiosi in the yard of an Italian prison left five men dead. If the army had not been called in, it would have gone on until one side was annihilated.

put in for retirement. Byrnes's dictum—"Let them kill each other"—had once again become the semiofficial policy of the NYPD.

In the end, it was the United States Secret Service that struck the hardest blow against the New York Mafia. Late in 1908 Lupo had vanished while owing at least $100,000 to creditors of his East Side wholesale store. When he resurfaced he had the effrontery to claim that his losses were a result of victimization by Black Hand extortionists. Rumor had it that his disappearance was connected to the Petrosino murder, but actually he had been setting up a counterfeiting plant in the Catskills. Soon New York City was flooded with phony bills and the Secret Service went all out to locate the source. Lupo and Morello were obvious suspects, but agents could not trace the bills to them or find the plant. Their ruthless behavior toward their fellow Italians would prove to be their undoing. The gang needed some technical assistance, so they tricked a young Sicilian printer named Antony Comito into working for them.

Before coming to New York, Comito had lived for seven years in Argentina and Brazil, but he was unable to establish himself in his profession and had returned home. Still seeking a better life for himself, his wife, and his young daughter, he decided to join his brother in New York City. Comito took up residence at his brother's place on James Street in downtown Little Italy and eventually found a job in a small Italian-owned printing shop. The shop serviced foreign-language newspapers and Comito's proficiency in Spanish, Portuguese, and French got him hired at $10 a week. He joined the Sons of Italy and the Forresters of America, secret fraternal groups of the type that were then so much a feature of American life. All conferred titles on their members; in the first he was elected orator and in the second, supreme deputy.

But life in New York was proving difficult. Comito's brother was too overbearing and the economy was still feeling the effects of the 1907 financial panic. After six months in his new job Comito was let go because of a lack of work. He was unemployed for several months, then he found a job with a Spanish-language printer. Lonely without his wife and daughter, he met a young Italian immigrant named Katherina and moved in with her. He rationalized his decision by claiming that he did it to avoid becoming a "libertine."

While undertaking his round of meeting new people Comito was introduced to "Don" Antonio Cecala, who claimed to own a Philadelphia printing shop. He offered Comito a job and even said Kathy could come along. The delighted Comito accepted but was puzzled when told they had to take a boat to Philadelphia. He had been in New York long enough to have heard that one traveled there by train. Cecala assured him that he was wrong and not until the Hudson River steamer deposited them in upstate Highland did he tell him the truth.

The next surprise for young Tony was that the printing work he would be doing was in the gang's counterfeiting plant. When he demurred he and Kathy were threatened with death. During the course of his employment he met Lupo, Morello, and other members of the ring. Comito was a good printer, but he was not up to mixing the proper shade of green ink for a new batch of bills. Morello, who planned to use him again, allowed him to go back to New York with the warning that "if you so much as whisper our secret to the trees, you will die! If you are arrested, you must not tell about me or you will die. But if you are in trouble we will help you with everything we have."

In New York the Secret Service was already maintaining a tight watch on some of the gang. A baby-faced young Irish kid who shined shoes down the street from Morello's house was actually operative Tom Callaghan. Another operative, Sam "Pete" Rubano, was roping in Little Italy when one of his informers tapped Comito and Cecala as part of the Lupo-Morello gang. Late one night the Feds swooped down on Comito and took him to Secret Service headquarters. There he quickly broke down in tears and told the whole story. As a result of his confession the two principals and six other members of the gang were rounded up.

In February 1910 the defendants were tried in a federal courtroom packed with their supporters. When Comito was called to testify one of them on a front bench clenched his fist, crooked the index finger, and gripped the bent finger between his teeth, then pulled the finger away and ran the fingertip around his collar. It was the Mafia sign of death. Comito was terrified but decided "it is better to die than to live so miserably." He gave a detailed explanation of his work for the gang, estimating that he had personally printed about $46,000 in phony bills. As far as it is known nothing untoward happened to him after the trial.[6]

During the course of the trial the judge had received many threatening letters, but he ignored them and all of the defendants were found guilty. When Morello stood up to be sentenced he made a bid for sympathy by displaying his withered arm and missing fingers, and with tears in his eyes declared, "You see how I am crippled. This arm I have had from the day I was born. I have family—a big family. They need me. If the judge will suspend my sentence, I promise to take my wife and children and go back to Italy." When the judge gave him twenty-five years Morello fainted dead away. When Lupo had his turn to address the court he protested that he had done nothing wrong and had been "hounded by police of two countries." The judge thought even less of his performance and gave him thirty years. Both defendants spent some time on the floor writhing and wailing. Another one, when he heard his sentence, let out a scream that was described as the most chilling sound that had been heard in the courthouse since a visitor had gotten mangled in the elevator.

Chief Flynn and his agents had done what the NYPD had failed to do— jailed the leaders of the preeminent New York Italian gang. Flynn was appointed deputy commissioner in charge of New York City detectives, but he didn't last long in the chaotic Gaynor administration. In 1912 he was made chief of the entire United States Secret Service. Lupo was paroled in 1920. He ran a minor Italian lottery in Brooklyn and shook down Italian bakers but never regained his former standing. The governor of New York asked President Roosevelt to revoke Lupo's parole in 1936 and he was sent back to prison. Morello was released in 1928 and two years later was assassinated.

---

[6]Following the Morello gang trial, a full account of Comito's confession appeared in *Everybody's Magazine,* though how it was obtained was not revealed. Perhaps not so coincidentally, Larry Richey, who had left the Secret Service in 1909, was then employed as a reporter for the magazine.

4:

Diamond Jim:
Overlord of the Underworld

Today it is difficult to understand how in the early years of the twentieth century many people believed that thousands of their fellow Americans were being held as slaves in cities and towns across the country. These were not blacks in the South, Chinese on the West Coast, or Italians in the clutches of an eastern seaboard padrone but white women, like their own sisters or daughters. "White slavery" was a term that aroused primal fears. In its most lurid version, gangs of swarthy foreigners—Italians, Frenchmen, and Jews—supposedly kidnapped, imprisoned, and raped thousands of girls and women annually. The women were then placed in houses of prostitution and kept there against their wills. Like any legend it had an element of truth. But a 1911 Chicago commission investigating vice found that though some women were forced into prostitution, it was not the usual route. Some had been persuaded by boyfriends to sell sex rather than give it away or seduced by apprentice pimps, known as "cadets," who acted as recruiters for prostitution rings. Others, like the eponymous *Sister Carrie* in Theodore Dreiser's novel, preferred being a prostitute to working for a few dollars a week as a salesgirl or waitress.

Crusades against white slavery were usually aimed at closing the officially tolerated red-light districts found in most cities of any size. One of the most famous and rip-roaring was the Chicago Levee. Its name connoted the tough and racy waterfront districts of southern river towns whose waters were held back by banks or levees. Reformers constantly attacked the Levee. Revivalists like former baseball star Billy Sunday would assemble a crowd of a thousand or more and parade through the streets, occasionally stopping in front of bordellos to recite the Lord's Prayer and the Twenty-third Psalm or sing "Where Is My Wandering Boy Tonight." In 1910 a Republican congressman from Chicago, James Mann, struck a blow at the Levee and its kind by obtaining passage of a federal law outlawing the interstate transportation of women for immoral purposes.

At the same time Congressman Mann was securing passage of his act his constituent, vice lord "Diamond Jim" Colosimo, was polishing his. Everybody in Chicago knew of Colosimo, who rode around in the contemporary version of a pimpmobile—a huge, shiny Pierce Arrow with a uniformed chauffeur at the wheel. A broad-shouldered giant, Colosimo had dark skin, jet-black hair, a bushy mustache, and a room-filling personality. He spoke in a booming southern Italian accent, his arms flailing whenever he was excited, which he frequently was. Even in Colosimo's quieter moments he was hard to miss, owing to his fondness for white linen suits with garish checks—made of material so fine that his underwear showed through. He wore diamonds all over—diamond rings on every finger, diamond shirt studs, diamond cuff links, and diamond belt and suspender buckles topped by a huge diamond horseshoe pin on his vest. If one of his trouser legs rode up, another diamond could be glimpsed on a garter clasp. He carried a bag of jewels with him and frequently took out a couple of stones to play with.

In 1910 he opened a cabaret restaurant in the heart of the Levee. Colosimo's, as he proudly named it, was as much of an eye-catcher as its owner. The two-story white-brick building stood out in a row of run-down wooden and red-brick structures. The dining room was paneled in silver and gold, the walls adorned with red velvet drapes, the chandeliers made of solid gold. Crude and flamboyant as he was, Colosimo was a sharp student of public relations. He encouraged newsmen to stop by, making sure to pick up their tabs. This practice resulted in a raft of favorable stories and, before long, in the patronage of important members of the cultural and business establishment. The regulars eventually came to include America's most famous trial lawyer, Clarence Darrow; the tenor Enrico Caruso; and all three of the acting Barrymores, Lionel, Ethel, and John. These worldly-wise clients did not feel embarrassed to be greeted by the owner and have him join them at their table. Many regarded Colosimo as a friend, and society ladies were thrilled to meet such a handsome rogue (those who dropped by in the afternoons without their husbands were sometimes invited to join him in a private room upstairs). New York's Paul Kelly had entertained—even charmed—the elite, but his place was a dive; the society folks who went there were slumming and none of them considered Kelly a personal friend. Jim Colosimo was the first Italian-American gangster to cross over from the underworld to the fringes of respectability, building a network of valuable connections as he did so. Reformers might denounce him, evangelists pray for his destruction, lawmen seek to imprison him—no matter, Jim was close to untouchable.

He had arrived in Chicago as a boy in the 1880s, brought from Calabria by his family. At the time Chicago had only 4,000 Italians out of a total population of half a million, but their numbers were growing fast. Like many immigrants the Colosimos disembarked at the Dearborn Street Railroad Station in the heart of the "Old Levee" and took up residence in the shadow of the terminal. There young Jim became a newsboy, a bootblack, and, finally, a "gandy dancer" or railroad section hand—a breed known for their rough-and-ready ways.

As he entered young manhood, Chicago played host to the 1893–94 Exposition, which celebrated the four hundredth anniversary of Columbus's discovery of America (albeit a year behind schedule). Many of the visitors traveled from downtown hotels to the fairgrounds by way of the Clark Street trolley, which took them right through the heart of the red-light district, revealing prostitutes hustling in the streets or leaning, half-naked, out of windows. One visitor, the English celebrity journalist William T. Stead, wrote a book with the catchy title *If Christ Came to Chicago,* in which he described every Levee dive. After the fair closed a group of business leaders mobilized behind a plan to move the district to a less conspicuous "New Levee" a mile southward, stifling criticism and conveniently opening up a large swath of choice real estate for development.

Because he came from the southern Italian mainland and was often referred to as a Neapolitan, Colosimo was sometimes called a Camorrist. But it was the local politics of the Levee that made his career. The red-light district fell within the boundary of the First Ward, the city's most powerful neighborhood political organization. In 1898, under the ward's sponsorship, Colosimo donned the white uniform of a city street cleaner. The pay— $1.50 a day—wasn't exalted, nor were the duties, which basically consisted of shoveling horse manure. But for an Italian (whose countrymen constituted just 5 percent of the ward's 28,000 residents) it wasn't bad. Only an Irishman could hope for a clerk's position, which paid $4 a day. Colosimo did well as a street sweeper. His fistic prowess was an asset in bossing Italian laborers and he soon rose to foreman. He even found time to organize a group of fellow workers into a social and athletic club. Impressed by his skills, particularly at getting out the vote, the two aldermen of the ward, "Bathhouse John" Coughlin and Michael "Hinky Dink" Kenna, made him a precinct captain—the Chicago equivalent of what other cities called a ward heeler.

Coughlin, a former bathhouse rubber (masseur being too effete a term for the Levee), was a burly six-footer who strutted like a peacock in a red vest, lavender trousers, green tailcoat, silk hat, and pink gloves. Kenna, called "Hinky Dink" because of his five-foot-one stature, owned a saloon with the longest bar in town. Although he habitually dressed in black mourning clothes, said little, and shunned the spotlight, the Dink was the brains of the operation. The Bath, who put his name to such ghostwritten poems as "Dear Midnight of Love" and "Ode to a Bathtub," was the front man.

The ward's considerable graft-generating capacity depended not only on its gamblers, madams, and saloon keepers, but on businessmen seeking electrical and trolley franchises in the core downtown area known (because of its encircling elevated lines) as the Loop. The Levee's numerous flophouses also provided voting addresses for the thousands of "floaters" the organization turned out on Election Day. The gregarious Bathhouse John made it a practice to be up and out early every day touring his fiefdom, and one of his favorite guides was jovial Jim Colosimo, who taught him to greet the Italian-speaking populace with a well-pronounced "*Salute!*" or "*Buon giorno!*" Over the years, a close friendship developed between the two men.

Colosimo's career got a big boost around the turn of the century when he met a Levee madam named Victoria Moresco. According to romantic legend, Victoria looked out of the window of her brothel on Armour Avenue one day and saw the handsome, bare-chested Colosimo swinging a pick. She liked what she saw and called down for him to come up and see her—not some time, à la Mae West, but right away—and they fell in love. Or so the story went. In the pecking order of Chicago ward politics, it is doubtful that a foreman would have been swinging a pick. As for Vickie's attractions, she was tall with dark hair and eyes and a full figure, but she was six years older than he and beginning to run to fat. Her bordello may well have been a significant factor in Jim's thinking. They were soon married and as a wedding present the bride installed the groom as manager of her establishment, which he named The Victoria (some wives might have objected to having their name on a whorehouse; Vickie was evidently delighted). Within three years they had opened a second place, the Saratoga, on the New Levee's main drag, 22nd Street.

The gold standard in big-city bordellos at the time was the Everleigh Club, a couple of blocks away from the Victoria, on Dearborn Street. It was run by two ostensibly genteel southern sisters, Ada and Minna Lester, who had both married and divorced young before running off to the 1898 Omaha World's Fair where they first cut their teeth in the whorehouse business. From Omaha they went on to New York, Philadelphia, and Washington before finally settling in Chicago, where it seemed that as total strangers unconnected to the world of Levee vice, they catapulted to the top of their profession.

The place had actually been opened by one Christopher Columbus Crabb. When the Lesters came into his life, Crabb was a wizened gentleman nearing fifty, well-known and powerfully connected. He was generally acknowledged to be the lover of Carrie Watson, longtime madam of the old Levee's finest house, and like her he catered to an upscale crowd. That meant meeting certain basic criteria: a place had to be safe for the customers and the girls had to be inspected frequently for disease. The patrons, too, were screened for proper dress and manners.

Crabb wanted his place to be the best in town. Toward that end, he recruited Ada and Minna. They would run the place with their refined lady act while he operated behind the scenes. The sisters could start afresh, free of undesirable connections with either lower-class girls or lower-class johns. If the Lesters ever had to be fired, they wouldn't have any powerful friends to appeal to. As for the name, Everleigh had a usefully aristocratic ring.[1]

The Everleigh was an instant success. To enter one had to be known or recommended to the sisters, who greeted each customer personally. The furnishings, haute cuisine, and liveried servants were the equal of any downtown gentlemen's club. The girls didn't line up for inspection as they did at other brothels; they were properly introduced, as if at a dance class. Fees were never discussed, though the least it would cost for a night of sex with Champagne and supper was one hundred dollars—about one-sixth the average annual wage in 1900. After expenses, including heavy bribes to cops and politicians, the place averaged about ten thousand dollars a month in profit.

Like Colosimo, the Lester sisters understood the power of the press. Their policy was to let reporters eat and relax—though not go upstairs— without charge. At night, the Everleigh functioned as an alternate city room: if an editor needed to contact a wayward scribe, he dialed Calumet 412, the club's well-known phone number. The press responded by buying the sisters' life story without question and, on more than one occasion, saving them from disaster.

Despite the great success of the Everleigh, Jim Colosimo did even better. He parlayed his leadership position among the Italians of the First Ward

---

[1]According to the sisters, it came from the way their aunt or grandmother—they could never get it straight— signed her letters, "Everly yours."

and his friendship with Coughlin into a role as collector and overseer for a portion of the Levee's vice operations. Money poured in, and he became recognized as one of the most important figures in the "vice trust," a combine of two hundred or so houses. With success "Big Jim" became "Diamond Jim." As a boss, Colosimo enforced the Levee's many business rules. Houses had to patronize taxi services, grocers, and clothing stores recommended by the First Ward. They had to buy their liquor from Hinky Dink and their insurance from Bathhouse John. To square a pimping rap cost a thousand dollars; for harboring a prostitute, it was double. By now Colosimo was beginning to develop national connections. He and a fellow bordello operator, a dandified Frenchman named Maurice Van Bever, worked with bookers who furnished them with a steady stream of fresh talent, much as the Keith-Orpheum Circuit supplied the nation's vaudeville houses.

Success carried its burdens, however. Black Hand extortions had become a headache for prominent Chicago Italians on both sides of the law and Colosimo made an obvious target. His first response was to pay some of the Black Handers off while having others killed. Eventually he grew impatient with this ad hoc approach, and in 1909 he sent to New York for Vickie's twenty-six-year-old cousin, Johnny Torrio. Johnny—born Osario Depuglia—had arrived in New York at age two from Naples. As a young man he belonged to Paul Kelly's Five Points gang. In Chicago his first assignment was to throw some fear into the Black Handers. He organized a team of some of Chicago's top hired guns, the star of whom was Mack Fitzpatrick, formerly W. E. Frazier of San Francisco's tough Barbary Coast. After a few murders, the letters subsided and Johnny was elevated to the post of manager of the Saratoga.

Uncle Sam, too, was threatening Colosimo. Before passage of the Mann Act the United States subscribed to a 1902 Paris Agreement suppressing the international "white slavery" traffic. The Colosimo–Van Bever syndicate received a few of its girls from overseas courtesy of French pimps, and in 1909 the Feds arrested Van Bever and Torrio. The government had even begun to prepare a case against Colosimo himself. Van Bever and his wife were convicted and sentenced to a year in prison, but the investigation ground to a halt, allegedly because a prostitute who was scheduled to be a key witness was found murdered in Connecticut. As a result Colosimo was never charged and the government dropped its cases against Torrio.

After his narrow escape and the passage of the Mann Act, Jim began to distance himself from interstate prostitution and opened his café. As a restaurateur he fashioned a new persona for himself. The pimp image receded, to be replaced by that of a beaming host to the elite. Even civic reform types like John Lyle of the Municipal Voters League remembered Colosimo fondly, as "a smiler and glad-hander" with a boisterous and infectious charm. Colosimo had men on his payroll who carried "Betsys" (from "Old Betsy," the frontiersman's affectionate name for his hunting rifle), and one of his favorite expressions was "Remember the Maine"—meaning, be careful, you're sailing into dangerous waters. But he was also an attentive and sympathetic listener, providing a broad shoulder for troubled patrons and friends to lean on. A problem was as good as solved if Jim gave someone a pat on the back and told him not to worry. Soon, a few of his boys with Betsys would visit whoever was causing the difficulty and remind them to remember the Maine.

Colosimo was not the most important organized crime figure in Chicago. That honor fell to Jacob "Mont" Tennes, who had started out as a small-time gambler on the North Side. Tennes lived a quiet life, always claiming to be a simple real estate dealer. When the heat was on, he would hold a party and publicly announce his retirement. For years, the press dutifully wrote farewell stories. In 1907 his rivals decided to speed his departure by bombing his home and gambling establishments. Tennes returned the compliment. Around the same time, the Payne Racing News Service in Cincinnati transmitted the wrong odds on a race, costing bookies a fortune. Tennes moved quickly to set up his own service, making many gamblers around the country dependent on him for the timely results they could not do without.

Gamblers had long been the heavyweights of the Chicago underworld. Mike McDonald, boss gambler in the days when faro and roulette games flourished, helped mold the shape of Chicago politics from the 1870s to the mid-1890s. It was McDonald who orchestrated the mayoral election of Carter Harrison, an aristocrat of southern lineage. In the last of his five terms, which coincided with the Columbian Exposition, Harrison incurred the enmity of a man he had refused to appoint as head of the city's law department. Since the fellow had no legal training and appeared deranged, Harrison's refusal was understandable, though not by the applicant, who assassinated him. A few years later the dead mayor's son, Carter Harrison the Younger, was elected to the first of *his* five terms. In 1911, after a four-year absence, he was returned to power with the usual strong support from the First Ward.

Harrison the Younger was a distinguished-looking gentleman whose southern origins, Yale education, and ability to work well with northern political machines led influential Democrats to think of him as a logical candidate for president in 1912. But the party would never nominate a man seen as a protector of vice.

Other American cities were already wrestling with the problem of their red-light districts. In New York, the pendulum swung wildly back and forth between periods of reform and machine rule. The reform mayors would crack down on areas like the Tenderloin and the Bowery; within a few years, though, the tide would turn, and Tammany Hall would let things rip. New Orleans's Storyville and San Francisco's Barbary Coast were invariably open and notorious, while Boston's Scollay Square and Washington, D.C.'s "Division" were relatively discreet year in and year out. This was the approach that Chicago's leaders decided to follow. The Levee could not be eradicated, but it might be toned down. Just as Harrison began to contemplate the idea of a less flamboyant Levee, however, his attention was called to a booklet distributed to tourists in which the Everleigh Club described its attractions. The embarrassed mayor responded by ordering the place closed.

Caught between City Hall and the First Ward, the police brass hesitated. To achieve his aim, Mayor Harrison had to transfer the divisional inspector and threaten to fire the police chief. According to their reporter friends, the Lester sisters went out like ladies, with Minna declaring, "I'll close up the shop and walk out with a smile on my face." In reality, Minna screamed her head off and prepared a sworn affidavit cataloging the whole system of pay-offs, threatening to spill the beans to the newspapers. At this point Diamond Jim dispatched his boys with the Betsys to remind the sisters to remember the Maine. After six months out of town they took up residence in an exclusive neighborhood on the far West Side, waiting for the climate to change. Over time they became convinced it never would and they fled Chicago permanently—not for the South they claimed to dearly love, but for New York City. As a farewell present they sent their affidavit to the chief justice of the Municipal Court. It caused a brief sensation, but since they were not about to come back and testify in court, it did little more than confirm what everybody already knew.

Short-lived cleanups were a regular feature of Chicago politics, and after the initial attacks on the Levee and the 1912 nomination of Woodrow Wilson as Democratic standard bearer, Harrison might have been expected to back off. Instead the attack on the Levee continued to gather momentum, and Mayor Harrison became increasingly dissatisfied with his police commanders. The captain of the 22nd Street station was Michael "White Alley" Ryan. Despite his nickname—the evangelists' term for the sinner's road to salvation—Ryan was an enthusiastic graft-taker who had been put there by Kenna and Coughlin to ensure that things ran smoothly. The 22nd Street cops received regular monthly payoffs from Colosimo, who sometimes put a diamond or two in the envelope as a bonus.

Elsewhere in the ranks were officers capable of cleaning up the Levee. One was Captain Max Nootbar: a 280-pound giant who had been born in Hamburg, Germany, attended Heidelberg University, and had done a hitch in the imperial army before emigrating to America and joining the U.S. Cavalry. In 1896, Nootbar joined the Chicago police department. "Big Max" was famously incorruptible. During one of the earlier cleanup moves in 1912, he had been assigned to command the Levee district with orders to check the worst excesses but not to kick over the traces. Chafing under the restrictions, he repeatedly asked for a transfer. Each time, it was refused—his presence was a sop to public opinion. Finally, on a cold February day, Nootbar went down the line raiding bordellos and throwing the inmates out into the snow. When he got back to the station there was a telephone order from headquarters transferring him immediately.

His attitude never changed. Once a black dive owner known as "The Emperor" hired a gunman to protect him and declared that if Nootbar even came near him he would be shot. Max promptly flattened the bodyguard.

The Emperor retained Clarence Darrow to sue Nootbar for $50,000. Captain Max acted as his own lawyer, winning the case. Afterward, Darrow shook his hand and told him that he should have been an attorney. Nootbar held no hard feelings. Not long after that, he took a gun away from a man who was holding it to the Emperor's head. In doing so Nootbar made a friend. In 1919, when Chicago was rocked by a race riot, the two men worked together to halt the violence.

Mayor Harrison might have simply named Nootbar to replace Ryan. But that would have meant an open break with the First Ward. Instead, he established a centralized morals division and recruited a core group of fifteen detectives from outside the regular force to set the tone. Heading the squad with the rank of inspector was W. C. Dannenberg, who had already acquired considerable knowledge of Colosimo and the vice trust from his days as a federal agent working on white slave cases. The fiery redhead Dannenberg was a man who liked action. His hobby was racing down country roads in the newfangled and dangerous automobiles.

The leaders of the vice trust recognized the crackdown for what it was: a mortal threat to their existence. By now, Johnny Torrio had risen to be Colosimo's first lieutenant handling the day-to-day business and power had shifted within the district. Kenna and Coughlin were embarrassed by their inability to persuade Mayor Harrison to back off. What use were payoffs, the dive owners asked, if they did not secure protection? With their political influence waning the aldermen had to cede strategic direction to others, much as politicians give way to generals in wartime. The obvious commander in chief was Colosimo. He had the necessary money and prestige along with an impressive record of immunity from law enforcement. With Torrio as his deputy commander and Van Bever, dive owner Roy Jones, and two 22nd Street station detectives as his general staff he formulated a battle plan.

The first move was to send a former cop to buy off Inspector Dannenberg. The offer was twenty-two hundred dollars a month (about forty thousand in today's money); all Dannenberg had to do in return was confine himself to a few staged raids for show purposes. Instead Dannenberg chose to arrest the briber and go after the dive owners full blast, employing a crew of paid informers. Within six months his squad made three hundred and fifty arrests, closed a number of joints, and brought grafting charges against some members of the Chicago Police Department.

The contest became a game of thrust and counterthrust, the vice trust utilizing its own force of cadets and toughs to warn people about raids and ferret out informers. When Dannenberg swept in, the grapevine would sound the alarm. If his men crashed into a bordello, secret panels allowed the inmates to escape into an adjoining building. After the detectives got wind of this ploy, they resorted to faking a raid in one place as they broke into another. The vice trust, with equal ingenuity, sent prostitutes dressed in their tartiest outfits into respectable neighborhoods to inquire about apartments for rent. Squads of whores began ringing doorbells from millionaires' mansions on Rush Street and Prairie Avenue to middle-class apartment buildings in Hyde Park and Woodlawn, on down to modest workingmen's cottages nestled alongside the South Side tracks of the Pennsylvania and Illinois Central railroads. The most shocking feature of their appearance, according to contemporary accounts, were the cigarettes that dangled from their painted lips. The idea was to scare good citizens into pressuring the mayor to call off the raids. But the ploy failed, as did the follow-up tactic of having girls go out in demure dresses, confess to being prostitutes, and beg for lodging far from their sadistic masters in the Levee. The reform societies offered to accommodate the ladies in the existing shelters for wayward girls. The whores told the societies what they could do with their shelters.

As the vice trust escalated its tactics so did Dannenberg & Co. In the past their arrests had been confined to the girls and their madams and pimps. Johns were generally told to "put on your trousers and get out of here." Now they too were hauled in, making them fodder for photographers' cameras and reporters' pencils. The old phony-name dodge became harder to pull off. Newspapermen would recognize that John Jones, laborer, was actually the Loop businessman they knew from Colosimo's or the Everleigh's parlor.

Some members of the trust—Roy Jones, for one—began to call for sterner measures. He was married to a prominent madam, Vic Shaw, and her trade was being affected. But others doubted that Dannenberg, a police inspector backed by the mayor, could be gunned down like any little Black Hander. The plotters compromised behind the idea of a warning shot—an attack on the morals squad rather than on Dannenberg himself. Roy Jones was delegated to arrange things and given the promise of political support if the plan went awry. It did. One night in January 1914, a Dannenberg informer named Ike Henagow was in Jones's dive on Wabash Avenue. Suddenly Henagow was confronted by a mysterious Levee tough with a slew of names: Jim Franche, "Frenchy," or Duffay—a French-Canadian on the run from Montreal, where he had been mixed up in a murder. Frenchy had a reputation as a savage brawler, his favorite tactic being to lower his head and charge headfirst, earning him another nickname, "Duffy the Goat." In normal times the Goat would have settled for giving the stoolie a beating, but this was war and he shot Henagow in the heart.

Jones tried to pass the incident off as a mere barroom brawl, but the authorities weren't buying. They indicted the Goat for murder. Jones's place was shut down and Dannenberg redoubled his efforts. In April, one of his detectives was stabbed in another joint. Jones began drinking heavily and complaining that he had not been given proper political protection. He even admitted to morals detectives that Colosimo's gunmen had planned to assassinate Dannenberg. When word of this leaked out it should have meant a death sentence for Jones. But Levee protocol dictated that Colosimo could not kill Vic Shaw's husband without giving him a chance. So Jones was offered a bribe to go to South America with the understanding that if he stuck around, he would be eliminated. He fled as far as Detroit.

At last Torrio sent to New York for help. It came in the form of his cousin Roxy Vanille, or "Vanilla." As an outsider, Vanilla presumably could get close to Dannenberg without being recognized and slip out of town without being missed. One night in July, Dannenberg's detectives raided a dive on 22nd Street, accompanied by one of their informers. Following the usual procedure they left the prisoners out front to await a patrol wagon under the guard of two detectives; the rest of the squad rushed on to other raids, eager to strike before the Levee grapevine could warn anyone. The wagon was slow in coming, perhaps because the regular cops from "White Alley" Ryan's station had little love for the downtown morals detectives. A crowd of street toughs gathered and began harassing the two cops. After the wagon took the prisoners away the detectives sought to catch up to their partners and the emboldened crowd followed, hurling abuse and finally surrounding the officers. Just then, Johnny Torrio pulled up in a red car. With him were Roxy Vanilla and Mack Fitzpatrick.

Although accounts differ, Torrio and his friends were probably there only to eyeball the Dannenberg squad and give Roxy a good look at his target. On the sidewalk the two detectives pulled out guns to defend themselves from the mob just as two headquarters detectives happened to pass by. Seeing the altercation they drew their guns, neither group of law enforcers recognizing the other. According to some witnesses Roxy Vanilla jumped out of the car and fired a shot. Others attributed all the shooting to the detectives. In any case, when the smoke cleared one of the headquarters men was dead and two morals cops had been shot, as were their informant, several bystanders, and Roxy Vanilla. Torrio and Mack Fitzpatrick helped Vanilla back into the vehicle and fled the scene. The next day, the *Chicago Tribune* ran a story based on information from an anonymous Chicago detective. The man he described as the shooter, though unnamed, was obviously Fitzpatrick.

The massacre pushed the murder of the Austrian archduke and his wife off the front pages of the Chicago papers. Torrio and Van Bever both left town in haste. Colosimo stayed put, confident he was above the law. Now that he was getting more press coverage than the German kaiser, however, the state's attorney ordered him arrested and for the first time in his life Jim was lodged in the 22nd Street station—for half a day. Mayor Harrison personally ordered "White Alley" Ryan relieved of his command and installed Nootbar as his replacement. The Levee was hard hit. For nearly a year Dannenberg and Nootbar's troops made so many raids that, according to a contemporary chronicler, it was not uncommon for one group to be breaking in through the front door, unaware another group was smashing in through the back.

But the reformers had gotten seriously out of synch with the public mood. Chicago in the ragtime era was a fun town. Forty years later, aging inhabitants would recall the excitement of going to the giant South Side amusement park called White City or of rooting for the Cubs and Sox in an era when they actually won pennants. Carl Sandburg celebrated Chicago as the "stormy, husky, brawling City of the Big Shoulders." It winked at vice— the town, as its signature song boasted, that the evangelist could not shut down.

In the 1915 Democratic primary the vice trust backed Harrison's opponent, who was duly nominated. Then in the general election Colosimo mysteriously threw his support behind a wealthy Republican, William Hale "Big Bill" Thompson, who triumphed in a close race. Thompson was in tune with the Chicago spirit. As a young man he had played football and water polo by day while making himself at home in the Levee by night. His administration was to be one of the most corrupt in the city's history. Inspector Dannenberg was soon fired and Captain Nootbar transferred—and that was just the beginning.

In less than two years the police chief and three of his key officers had been indicted for taking bribes (Clarence Darrow ultimately got all of them acquitted). This time Colosimo and Torrio were not involved. They had begun to thin out their operations in the Levee. Wide-open red-light districts were becoming passé, and the advent of World War I created a draftee army whose parents demanded that the morals of their boys be protected. The United States government was cracking down on vice from coast to coast. Recognizing the changing times, Colosimo and his allies began offering new services and expanding geographically.

It was in the Thompson era that Johnny Torrio earned his nickname "The Fox." He had married a respectable woman he had met on a visit to Kentucky and spent most of his nights at home with his eyes closed, dreamily listening to opera records. His pride and joy was his fire engine–red Cadillac runabout. Automobiles had opened up the suburbs to easy access, and Torrio was quick to appreciate the implications for people in his line of work. Just south of the city limits in the little town of Burnham he opened up a large café and stocked it with prostitutes. The village president was a twenty-five-year-old layabout, Johnny Patton, who had taken the post when no one else wanted it and under his dubious leadership the city fathers did not object. In fact, Patton eagerly signed on as manager of the joint while the town board of trustees waited tables and the police chief tended bar. Located along the Indiana state line, the place drew much of its clientele from the nearby steel mills. In case of a raid Torrio and his crew could easily slip into another jurisdiction. Suburbs also had the advantage of being easier to control than Chicago, with its multiplicity of interest groups. The boy mayor cum brothel keeper showed so much aptitude for the job that Torrio and Colosimo put him in charge of all their suburban operations.

Now effectively Colosimo's full-fledged partner, Torrio had learned a lot from the Levee wars. Like the reformers he concluded that a single, concentrated red-light district was a bad idea. It gave the authorities too good a target. Profitable as sex had been over the years, it was not the best racket to be in because of the moral stigma it carried. Gambling and liquor were much more broadly acceptable, Torrio concluded. Violence should be avoided whenever possible because bullets brought headlines and crackdowns.

With direct access to a Republican city hall, Colosimo was in a position to bypass his old friends Coughlin and Kenna and the other leading Democrats in the First Ward. For the first time an Italian mob boss was more powerful than the political machine. But he remained respectful, partly out of loyalty and partly in the knowledge that Irish politicians would continue to play a critical role in the city's affairs. There were too few Italians in Chicago— 125,000 out of an overall population of three million in 1920—to serve as an adequate political base. Colosimo continued his payoffs to Kenna and Coughlin, even allowing them to make a red-faced little man, Dennis "The Duke" Cooney, overlord of what was left of Levee vice.

Colosimo's approach contrasted with the career of the city's other major Italian crime boss, Anthony D'Andrea, a defrocked priest who had emigrated from Sicily to the United States in the 1890s. A man of driving energy and high intelligence, D'Andrea became heavily involved in counterfeiting and prostitution, and ultimately staked out a position as leader of the Sicilians in the Nineteenth Ward on the Near West Side. Allied with Lupo and Morello in New York, he was the closest thing Chicago had to a Mafia boss. Eventually, he became president of the Unione Siciliana, a national fraternal organization founded in Chicago in 1895. Both his personality and career were polar opposites of Jim Colosimo. Where Jim was sunny by nature, a fellow Mafia leader described D'Andrea as "savage and fierce." Jim managed to avoid prison; D'Andrea had been sent up for counterfeiting in 1902, though President Theodore Roosevelt had commuted his sentence the following year. Colosimo abandoned the union movement after a brief attempt to organize a group of Italian street workers. D'Andrea, by contrast, became business agent for the sewer and tunnel workers' and the hod carriers' unions—occupations in which many Italians were found. And while Jim played ball with the Irish politicians, D'Andrea fought them relentlessly. In 1921, with his countrymen now constituting over 70 percent of the Nineteenth Ward, D'Andrea stood for alderman against the local Irish boss, Johnny Powers, known to his Italian constituents as "Johnny De Pow." Even many Sicilians considered D'Andrea's move foolhardy. As the election approached, the ward exploded in an all-out shooting and bombing war between rival factions. The mayhem ended when D'Andrea was killed by a shotgun blast while entering his home.

Colosimo had no political ambitions. He enjoyed the life he had created for himself, gradually turning over his day-to-day operations to Torrio. His greatest pleasures were his restaurant and a young singer who turned up there one day in 1917. Twenty-five-year-old Dale Winter—a wholesome American beauty with raven hair, gray eyes, fair complexion, and an hour-glass figure—had been stranded in Chicago when a musical she had been scheduled to appear in closed unexpectedly. When she took the stage at Colosimo's in a white low-cut evening gown with a red rose pinned to her bosom, Dale was an immediate hit. Her boss was especially impressed. If Colosimo had lived up to white-slaver legend, he would have sold her into a bordello; instead, he treated her like a princess.

Jim encouraged Dale to move to a nice apartment far from the Levee and he personally escorted her home in his limo every night. According to his chauffeur he acted like a schoolboy, not even attempting to steal a kiss at the door, and on the way back he would whistle or hum, happy as a lark. Although Dale was already a star at Colosimo's, Jim wanted more for her. One night Florenz Ziegfeld dropped into Colosimo's and offered Dale a contract. She declined, in part because Jim had plans to make her an opera star. Like most cabaret singers of the day Dale sang such staples as "I Dreamt I Dwelt in Marble Halls" and "Every Little Movement Has a Meaning All Its Own." Contemporaries who heard her forays into semiclassical music and opera remembered her voice as pleasant and energetic, if limited in range. But that was not the judgment of Enrico Caruso and several of Jim's other opera-star friends who came to hear her at his request. Perhaps they were only being diplomatic, but they pronounced her voice trainable and Colosimo accordingly enrolled her in the Chicago Musical College.

Colosimo was in love. He was also, in his imagination, a new man, the husband of a concert singer, sitting with the elite and listening to her perform at the Chicago Auditorium, then proceeding across the street to the elegant Pompeian Room of the Congress Hotel, where the diners would applaud them as they walked to their table. To all appearances, Dale was also captivated by her almost-fifty boss. One group, though, was growing very upset by Jim's aspirations—his family. Victoria had played an important role in his career and southern Italian men generally made a point of not embarrassing their wives, to say nothing of divorcing them. When he separated from Vickie in 1919, her brothers, all employed in various capacities at the family's vice operations, began to ponder their own fates if they ceased to be his in-laws. One night Dale was entering the cabaret when Vickie suddenly emerged from the shadows and pushed her up against a wall, accusing her of having sex with her husband and demanding that she get out of Jim's life or she would kill both of them. When the frightened singer told Colosimo about this encounter he burst in on Vickie and harsh words were exchanged. She accused him of marrying her for her whorehouse and said that at the time of their first meeting he had been "shoveling horseshit." Jim demanded a divorce.

Although Johnny Torrio apparently warned Colosimo against the idea— "It's your funeral," he was said to have advised him—Vickie obliged in return for a payment of fifty thousand dollars. In early 1920 the decree was granted and Jim and Dale promptly eloped to an Indiana spa. Colosimo rented the ballroom of their hotel and hired a passing circus to perform on the lawn, inviting the other tourists to come as his guests. Apart from a woman who got nipped by a bear cub, the affair was a smashing success. When the happy couple returned from their honeymoon they set up house in a nine-room, two-story brownstone in a middle-class neighborhood a couple of miles south of the Levee, inviting Dale's mother to move in with them. By now, Jim's friends had begun to notice that he no longer wore such loud clothes.

The Prohibition era had commenced. A few months earlier Torrio had convinced Jim to invest twenty-five thousand dollars in a bootlegging operation, promising to keep its operations distant from the boss. Now Torrio wanted them to get into bootlegging in a big way—not just because of the money to be made but to keep rivals from outbidding them for police and political protection. A pair of Irish gangsters had already teamed up with a wealthy Chicago brewer in a million-dollar deal and Near West Side Sicilians were manufacturing booze in their basements. The manager of Colosimo's café was also telling him to take the plunge: customers were beginning to bring their own drinks and forcing the house to serve setups.

Colosimo had reached that stage in a successful man's career when he had to change with the times or step down. He did neither. Like most of his political friends Jim subscribed to the maxim, "Never get between the people and their beer." He didn't expect Prohibition to last long and he was deeply afraid of federal law enforcement. How could they hide a brewery or the open sale of liquor? He assumed that Prohibition enforcers would be as incorruptible as the other federal agents he had known. While younger associates longed to expand their turf and increase their take, Colosimo was basically content with his lot. The last thing he wanted to do was endanger his new life with Dale.

A year earlier a scar-faced, twenty-year-old Italian had left New York after falling afoul of both the law and some Irish gangsters. His flight had been arranged by a Brooklyn friend of Torrio's, Frankie Yale, who convinced Johnny to give him a chance in Chicago. Torrio liked the young man, whose name was Al Capone, and made him a brothel manager. Torrio and Capone would be hurt if Jim fell from power. They came to the reluctant conclusion that their boss, lovable as he was, was no longer up to his responsibilities.

Shortly after his honeymoon Colosimo got a call that required him to make a quick trip to the restaurant. It was late afternoon. The place was empty of customers. While peering out through the glass windows of one of the entrance doors, apparently looking for the person he expected to meet there, Jim was shot twice in the back of the head. He died instantly. Many theories have been advanced about the killing: robbery, revenge by Vickie's family, politics, etc., but almost certainly Torrio arranged for another New York hitman to do the job. Immediately after the shooting police grabbed Frankie Yale at a local railroad station trying to board a train back to New York. And while some have claimed the murderer was Capone himself, at the time he was too young and inexperienced to have been entrusted with the task. The fact that Torrio used Yale to carry out an important murder four years later virtually clinches the case.

Jim did not leave a fortune, at least not in his will. He had supposedly withdrawn two hundred and fifty thousand dollars in cash from the bank and hidden it away from possible seizure by Vickie's lawyers. Those who were close to him estimated he had double that amount. Though no money turned up, not long afterward Torrio made some substantial investments in a brewery operation. Jim's legal estate—including cash, bonds, and a house—totaled only about eighty-one thousand dollars and neither Vickie nor Dale received a bequest. Under Illinois law ex-wives were not eligible, and his marriage to Dale was not recognized because it took place before expiration of the required waiting period. Thus the estate went to Jim's father, who gave Vickie twelve thousand and Dale six thousand dollars. Dale remained steadfast throughout her ordeal and spoke out in defense of "the dearest husband a girl ever had." Chicago's press corps could be rough on people, but everybody who knew Dale always liked her and the papers played her quotes straight and with sympathy.

Colosimo's funeral was as contradictory as the rest of his life. After the archbishop of Chicago forbid a Catholic burial, Jim's friends convinced a Presbyterian clergyman to perform the rites and Bathhouse John Coughlin knelt beside the coffin loudly leading the mourners in Hail Marys. Despite the church's disapproval, five thousand people followed the hearse to the cemetery. Judges, politicians, and notables of the Chicago opera marched along with the likes of Johnny Torrio, drawing a great deal of criticism. The *Chicago Tribune* asked how so many leading citizens apparently unconnected to the vice trade could "pay homage to the memory of the man who for more than a decade has been recognized as the overlord of Chicago's underworld." Some of the more respectable guests had been warned to stay away for the sake of their reputations. A reporter from the *American* described their reaction: "No matter what he may have been in the past, no matter what his faults," they replied, "Jim was my friend and I'm going to his funeral."

5:   In the Footsteps of Petrosino: Big Mike

At about the time the Chicago Levee was under attack, the whole structure of organized crime in New York was reeling. In the summer of 1912 Lieutenant Charles Becker, who headed a police squad operating out of the commissioner's office, was accused of ordering the murder of a gambler who was squealing to the district attorney's office about the system of police payoffs. The affair was long on drama and would dominate the headlines for the next couple of years: Lieutenant Becker was sentenced to the electric chair; Mayor Gaynor dropped dead; the police commissioner was fired; and the Tammany organized-crime czar Tim Sullivan went insane, escaped from his keepers, and was run over by a train. At least, that was the story put out—the body lay unidentified in Bellevue for ten days, until a patrolman checking the slabs let out a scream and went running through the halls shouting, "It's Big Tim! Lord God, it's Big Tim." Even worse, from Tammany's standpoint, was the installation of reform administrations in New York City Hall and the state capitol in Albany.

One of the results of the upheaval was the semi-restoration of the NYPD Italian squad under the leadership of a young detective named Mike Fiaschetti. In 1914 reform mayor John Purroy Mitchel had appointed Arthur Woods as police commissioner, a man who knew a lot about gangs in

New York. When he was deputy commissioner in charge of detectives Woods had been a strong supporter of Lieutenant Petrosino and the Italian squad; however, he did not formally revive it. He may have wanted to avoid a repeat of what had happened to Petrosino. The commissioner was a rare combination: a white-gloved socialite—a product of Groton and Harvard allied through marriage to the family of financial tycoon J. P. Morgan—who was not afraid to get his hands dirty working alongside street cops. As a practical man he realized that if the commander of a high-profile Italian squad were assassinated again it might have dire consequences for his commissionership. Instead he employed the familiar NYPD practice of having sensitive functions carried out by units with bland names. He created a small "special service" squad of Italian detectives under the command of Fiaschetti, a bandmaster's son born in Rome and raised in North Adams, Massachusetts. He had been mentored by Petrosino, who had immediately picked the tall, rugged twenty-two-year-old for the Italian squad when Fiaschetti was appointed to the NYPD in 1908. Fiaschetti was another man who hated hoodlums and was not reluctant to meet them with force. The title of his autobiography, *You Gotta Be Rough,* summed up his philosophy. At the trial of a Black Hand extortionist he had arrested, the defense lawyer was able to obtain a hung jury by asking the panel who they would be more afraid of encountering on a dark street—his meek-looking client or the big brute of a detective. Unlike the old Italian squad, Fiaschetti and his crew spent most of their time on regular precinct duty and were called together as a team only when there was a major crime involving their countrymen. Since Black Hand bombers and extortionists were still active, the squad had plenty to do.

Tammany also regrouped under new leaders and organizational arrangements. Tom Foley inherited Sullivan's position as overlord of organized crime. But he and Tammany boss George Murphy knew something had to change if they were going to avoid another debacle like the Becker case. They concluded that instead of a Tammany functionary being directly involved in the supervision of organized crime, they would filter their control through a mob chieftain: a system analogous to Jim Colosimo's role as head of the Levee vice trust on behalf of the First Ward. But who would be

New York's Colosimo? Clearly, whoever was selected would have to bridge the two worlds of organized crime. The first and most lucrative was the milieu of gambling joints and deluxe nightspots that stretched along Broadway from the 30s to the 60s. This was the playground of New York's sports, who dined at Delmonico's and played roulette in the nearby private gambling clubs and high-stakes card games in hotel rooms. The other was the gamblers and gunmen from the mostly Irish West Side and the mostly Jewish and Italian Lower East Side. These were the areas that produced the muscles and guns necessary to collect debts, settle quarrels, keep gamblers and madams in line, and, if necessary, eliminate troublesome individuals. When Becker had put out the contract on the squealing gambler Rosenthal, it had gone to one Italian and three Jewish gunmen from downtown. The new overlord would also have to know how to work hand in glove with politicians and cops.

Paul Kelly might have been a possibility, but his stock had gone down after he had been driven from his Lower East Side base amid a blaze of guns that created equally inflammatory headlines. His departure and Lupo and Morello's trip to the Atlanta penitentiary did not rid the city of Italian gangsters. Plenty of others were around, but because they still confined their activities to the Italian colonies, they did not draw much attention. The story of Italian organized crime in New York City during the second decade of the twentieth century was the rapid rise and equally rapid fall of various leaders. Up until 1911, one of the most fearsome was Giuseppe Costabile. He had come to New York from Calabria at the turn of the century, when he was about nineteen. After a couple of years criminal charges sent him home again. In 1907 he returned to New York City and plunged into Black Hand extortion activity. In one month in 1911, police credited thirteen Manhattan bombings to him. Finally, a team of detectives grabbed him walking down the street with a bomb under his coat and Costabile was sent to Sing Sing.

Uptown, in East Harlem, Caspare Gallucci (or Carlucci) moved in to fill the vacuum left by Lupo and Morello. Gallucci forged a relationship with Tom Foley and by 1915 was probably the most politically influential figure among New York Italian criminals. In that year an Italian challenged Foley for district leader. Given their numbers in the district, if his fellow Italians had stood behind him he probably would have won. But blood took a backseat to business and both Gallucci and Paul Kelly gave strong support to Foley, who survived the challenge.

According to Mike Fiaschetti, for a while Gallucci was the uptown "King of Little Italy." Pretender to the throne would have been a more precise description, since many rivals did not concede his right to the crown. Among them were the Morellos, the family now led by Nick, Vince, and their half brother, Ciro Terranova. For several years they blazed away at Gallucci, and they were not alone on the firing line. Despite the fact that he and his henchmen wore bulletproof vests, rivals managed to kill ten of them and wound the boss.

The internecine warfare was carried on in an exceptionally brutal fashion. Fiaschetti related how in one instance Morello gunmen went to the sweetheart of a Gallucci lieutenant and played to her superstitions, telling her that if she did not help them get rid of her boyfriend they would put a fatal curse on her. They even named the day that she would die. The woman became so worried that one night after some lovemaking at her house, she shot and killed her boyfriend as he lay resting on a couch.

Gallucci's most lucrative holding was the Italian lottery, and he broke with tradition by not maintaining its integrity. Not content with the abundant earnings he was already receiving, Gallucci substituted false numbers on the big hits to prevent having to pay off any large sums. Since Italian-American newspapers were forbidden by law to print lottery information, local people had no immediate way of checking up. Papers from Italy arrived days after the event and most Italian Americans never saw them. Occasionally a cheated customer would note that the number listed in the Naples *Mattino* was different from the one announced by the lottery, grab a gun, and go after Gallucci.

Gallucci not only rigged the lottery, but he failed to follow the code of conduct for a Sicilian assassin. When one of his gunmen scored a fatal hit, he would wait on a street corner until the victim's body was borne past and then spit at the coffin, shouting, "Another dog gone to hell." A gentleman murderer was expected to doff his hat, weep over the death of his dear friend, and offer his condolences to the victim's family—while preparing to repel their revenge.

One night when Gallucci and his twenty-year-old son were sitting in a 113th Street restaurant, a Morello gunmen entered and shot the King in the head. When Gallucci's son tried to shield his dad from the bullets, they killed him, too. Despite the fireworks, Italian colony crime was still not big news in New York. The gun battles between the Galluccis and the Morellos were reported on the inside pages of the newspapers, and when Gallucci was killed the *Times* devoted only fourteen lines on page 7 to his passing, even though they identified him as "The King of Little Italy." In his day, Paul Kelly had been front-page material.

Having asserted their preeminence, the East Harlem Morellos sought to regain their hold on downtown Little Italy's high-stakes card games and to take over the lucrative artichoke trade. The flowery artichoke cones, which were a staple of Italian housewives' kitchens, provided a source of substantial income for the suppliers. The invasion provoked resistance and led to shooting wars between the Morellos and some downtown gamblers. Then Neapolitans from Brooklyn began moving in on the Morellos, leading to what has been described as the "Mafia-Camorra War." The label is a convenient way to describe the struggle between Manhattan Sicilians and Brooklyn Neapolitans, but it can be misleading.

The Brooklyn Neapolitans comprised two groups. Those from the neighborhood around the Navy Yard were led by Allesandro Vollero and Leopoldo Lauritano, who operated a coffeehouse on Navy Street. "Don" Pelligrino Morano directed the other group from his restaurant, the Santa Lucia, near the Coney Island amusement park. The Brooklynites' principal rackets were gambling, cocaine trafficking, and extortion from legitimate Italian businessmen. Testimony at a later trial disclosed that a council of war held at the Santa Lucia was attended by the "Camorra boss" of Philadelphia and other supposed members of the organization. The testimony also described a symbolic rite of passage into the society involving the drawing of blood and a warning to the initiate: "Whatever is done between us, not a word should be breathed on the outside. When you're ordered to do a job or kill anybody, whatever it is, even if you are arrested, never say a word and do not talk at all." Like the Manhattan Morellos, the Brooklynites could be seen as an American imitation of an Italian criminal group, but no evidence was offered to prove that they were an extension of one in the old country.

Assistant district attorney Arthur Train prosecuted Black Hand cases in New York and observed the Camorra trials in Naples. In his 1912 book about his experiences, Train said that both the Mafia and the Camorra influenced Italian-American criminals, the former more than the latter because Sicilians outnumbered Neapolitans in New York. But he also argued that in America the differences between the two groups had largely disappeared and they were "essentially of a piece." Certainly ethnic lines were not clearly drawn in New York. Neapolitan Paul Kelly was an ally of the Sicilian Morellos. The Sicilian Frank Uale (or Ioele), who Americanized his name to Yale (completing the process in 1917 by naming his Coney Island dive the Harvard Club), was a friend of Neapolitan Johnny Torrio and employed another Neapolitan, Al Capone, as a bouncer.

During the Mafia-Camorra War the Brooklyn and Manhattan gangs had the advantage of being able to move freely across the river, while Fiaschetti and his detectives were prevented from doing so by administrative protocol. Brooklyn was still treated as if it were a separate city; cops who worked on the Manhattan side confined themselves to Manhattan cases while their opposite numbers in Brooklyn concentrated on problems in their borough. Unfortunately, the Vollero-Morano crowd had made certain "arrangements" with Brooklyn detectives that afforded them protection, leaving half of the problem basically unpoliced. After some skirmishes, the Brooklynites decided to make their opponents an offer and they invited the Morellos to discuss a deal at the Navy Street coffeehouse. On the agenda was the possibility of a share in the Brooklynites' narcotics trade in return for a piece of Manhattan's gambling business. The restaurant was an ideal site for negotiations. Upon entering patrons were required to deposit their guns in a secret wall compartment covered by a sliding panel. This made it easier for hot-tempered hoodlums to eat their meals in safety, both from each other and from the police, who had a habit of entering mob watering holes, lining up the customers, frisking them for guns, and blackjacking anyone who showed signs of resistance. The cops had heard about the Navy Street gun cache and would frequently appear unannounced at the restaurant to tap the walls with their blackjacks. The panel, however, was thick enough to mask the hollow area behind it, and the police always went away muttering.

New York had a tough gun law, put on the books by none other than Big Tim Sullivan. During Mayor Gaynor's "be nice to hoodlums" administration—a by-product of which was the abolition of Petrosino's old squad—Italian and Jewish gangs of the Lower East Side took advantage of the newly popular automobiles to move around the city and invade places like the Broadway nightlife area. Even Tim Sullivan disapproved of his boys' boldness, and he rushed a law through the Legislature forbidding the carrying of firearms without a permit. Under the Sullivan Act a gangster found guilty of possessing an unlicensed pistol could receive up to seven years in prison.

Because of the Sullivan law, a hoodlum found with a gun could be in serious trouble. At the time, New York State rules of evidence were not restrictive. The U.S. and New York constitutions required that searches be reasonable, but even if a state court ruled that one was not, the gun could still be admitted into evidence. The legal remedy was for the aggrieved party to sue the arresting officers, an unwise and futile recourse for gangsters. Of course, gun arrest cases could be fixed. At the time, however, most Italians did not yet have armies of slick lawyers on call or judges on their payroll. Irish bosses ran the criminal justice system, and, despite protection payments, a double-cross was always possible.

Not about to walk blindly into enemy headquarters, the Morellos sent their scouts out to Brooklyn to pick up information. The word came back that the restaurant was a safe harbor. After some negotiations they agreed to send just two representatives, Nick Morello and his bodyguard. The information that the Sicilians had received about the safety of the restaurant turned out to be right, as far as it went: they were ambushed and shot dead by five gunmen a few feet outside its door. The Brooklynites followed up by invading East Harlem, forcing the Morello clan to hide in their house on 116th Street. The local Sicilian neighborhood remained loyal and the Neapolitans were rebuffed in their attempts to rent nearby flats to use as snipers' nests.

In the spring of 1917 a Navy Street gunman who had fled to Nevada was brought back to Brooklyn, where the district attorney threatened him with the electric chair. The code of *omerta* dissolved before the prospect of several thousand volts of electricity and he talked. The erstwhile Camorrists were indicted by a Brooklyn grand jury for the murders outside the coffeehouse. During the trial, evidence was admitted identifying Morano as a Camorra leader (and although challenged, on appeal the verdict was upheld by New York State's highest court). The United States had recently entered the Great War, and in his summation to the jury, the Brooklyn prosecutor did a bit of flag waving, declaring, "Every gunman and every gunman's boss in the City of New York is interested in this trial. There isn't one who is not following this trial in which you are to decide whether American law is to rule or Italian customs and Italian traditions to continue." Both Morano and Vollero were sentenced to life imprisonment. In Manhattan some of the Morello gang shooters were sentenced for their work downtown, but Ciro Terranova went free because under New York law the uncorroborated word of an accomplice was not sufficient for conviction.

In 1917 Tammany backed a Brooklyn judge named John Hylan for mayor, and Mitchel's reform regime was swept out, including Commissioner Woods. The trials had brought attention to Italian crime and the new police commissioner, Richard Enright, the first career cop to hold the job, decided to re-create an official Italian squad with Fiaschetti in command. Later Enright expanded it to 150 men and named Fiaschetti an acting captain. Big Mike took up where Petrosino left off and did not confine himself to New York. No sooner was the squad back in operation than the police in Akron, Ohio, sought its help in locating a group of New York gunmen who had killed four of their officers. Fiaschetti quickly picked up two of the suspects, transported them to Ohio, and obtained a confession: a local Italian brothel keeper had paid them $150 each for the murders. Fiaschetti received permission to remain in Ohio and to continue his investigations, and because of his work a number of men received life sentences and four were sent to the electric chair. Big Mike was now the new King of Little Italy, entitled to the best seat in any Italian restaurant and a complimentary box at the Metropolitan Opera. That a cop and not a gangster was so exalted provided a positive image for young Italian men.

The World War I era was a time of advancement for Italian Americans. Italy was an ally of the United States. When it entered the war in 1915, its consuls in the United States urged Italians to go home and fight for king and country. Few did. In 1917, when America declared war, Italians flocked to the colors. U.S. propaganda chief George Creel later claimed that although they made up only 4 percent of the population, Italians sustained 10 percent of the total American casualties.

Some Italians were also becoming prominent in public life. One was Fiorello La Guardia. In the 1880s his Italian father and Austrian-Jewish mother had emigrated to New York City, where Fiorello was born. Like Fiaschetti's, La Guardia's father was a bandmaster—Italians with artistic skills found it easier to win acceptance in America. La Guardia senior joined the United States Army and was placed in charge of the regimental band of the Eleventh Infantry. Young La Guardia spent most of his boyhood on western army posts and would always consider Prescott, Arizona, then a frontier settlement, as his hometown. Returning to New York he became a lawyer and joined the Republican Party; he had no use for the corrupt Tammany system. In 1916 he was elected to Congress from the Lower East Side, and then went off to serve as a bomber pilot on the Austrian front. In 1919, La Guardia was elected president of the New York City board of aldermen— the job just below the mayor—ensuring that he would be seen as a strong candidate for the top job in 1921.

While Fiaschetti's squad was cracking down on Italian gangs, Tammany found the man to be its liaison to the gambling world—Arnold Rothstein, or A.R., as he was generally known. Born in 1882, Rothstein started out as a salesman in his father's small cotton goods business, with a gambling hobby that soon became his profession. Around the turn of the century he ran a small operation on the Lower East Side with Monk Eastman as his protector. He became a bail bondsman on the side and forged a close alliance with Tom Foley. Soon the gunmen and gamblers of the East Side began to look to A.R. for direction. He worked up to the ownership of a Broadway gambling house that drew an upscale crowd and became an intimate of people like suave gambler Nicky Arnstein, husband of Ziegfeld Follies star Fanny Brice. Another close pal was *New York World* reporter and future top editor, Herbert Bayard Swope, the man who broke the Becker police corruption story.

Rothstein's reign began at 11 P.M. on July 30, 1915, when Lieutenant Becker was executed at Sing Sing. Broadway wise guys believed up to the last moment that Becker might reveal Tammany and organized crime secrets in return for a commutation, touching off a new scandal and disrupting all previous arrangements. Becker remained close-mouthed to the end. Rothstein was sitting with Nicky Arnstein at Jack's restaurant in the heart of Times Square when he got the news of Becker's death. He immediately got up and went out into the Broadway night to begin running organized crime.

Within a few years he was so powerful nobody could touch him. When detectives tried to break into one of his gambling joints in January of 1919, Rothstein mistook them for holdup men, opening fire and wounding two of them. Though charged with assault to murder, he managed to get the case dropped. The only one who went to prison was a police inspector charged with perjury.

In 1920 he became one of the best-known and most reviled men in America when he was accused of fixing the 1919 World Series. At the time everybody believed he had paid off eight Chicago White Sox players to throw games. Modern research suggests that while he loaned money to the fixers, he did not participate directly. It was a classic Rothstein deal: put up the money and take the profits, but allow others to do the dirty work. Both players and fixers were indicted but Rothstein was not charged. As Jay Gatsby explains to a friend in F. Scott Fitzgerald's classic novel of the era, where Rothstein appears as Meyer Wolfsheim, "They can't get him, old sport. He's a smart man." During Prohibition, Rothstein's brains, and especially his financial skills, would make him the top figure in organized crime in New York.

Also in 1920, an Italian gunman named Papaccio (or Pataccio) shot at another man on a Lower East Side street, killing two innocent women instead. Mike Fiaschetti found out who the killer was and that he had fled back to Naples. Fiaschetti was ordered to go there and apprehend the fugitive, and to take along the records of some other American gangsters who had fled to Italy and pick them up, too. Perhaps remembering what happened to Petrosino, the NYPD brass assigned Fiaschetti a companion, Detective Sergeant Irving O'Hara, Mayor Hylan's brother-in-law. For a mere sergeant, O'Hara exercised considerable influence in the police department. Hylan's previous police commissioner had been dismissed after just twenty-three days in office for ignoring Sergeant O'Hara's unwanted advice.

The Italian police picked up Papaccio before the detectives landed but refused to extradite him because he was not a U.S. citizen. Fiaschetti then presented them with a list of thirty-four other fugitives he wanted picked up. While O'Hara returned to New York, Fiaschetti remained in Italy to press the issue.

For a time, he accompanied the Italian police on a series of raids. Then Fiaschetti decided to go undercover in Naples, headquarters of the Camorra. Realizing that being Roman-born he would stand out there, he returned to the capital, adopted the guise of a criminal fugitive, and was accepted at a rooming house run by a Camorra confederate. After a time he won the man's confidence and persuaded him to arrange his passage to America, which would mean having to go to Naples to board a ship. The man handed him a torn five-lire note and mailed the other half to a Camorra leader in Naples as a means of identification.

When Fiaschetti arrived at the Naples railroad station a pair of detectives moved quickly to either side of him and one tapped him on the shoulder saying, "Come, we have a word to say to you." "But I do not know you," the suspect protested. "Come along, your curiosity will soon be satisfied," he was told and was led into an anteroom of the station where he was confronted by a ranking police official. The prisoner made bold to address him, "Commissioner Cernelli, accept my compliments." "I can do without them," the commissioner snorted, and the startled detectives quickly frisked the suspect, finding two automatic pistols, cartridges, and a big stiletto. As they roughly slapped the handcuffs on him he cried, "It's me, Fiaschetti." The cops were stunned. They knew the story of Lieutenant Petrosino's ill-fated trip to Sicily twelve years earlier. Now, another New York detective was about to create a political furor by getting himself killed. Fiaschetti was allowed to proceed on his way, but when he left the station he noticed he had a shadow. Cernelli had assigned one of his detectives to follow him.

The street-smart Fiaschetti quickly shook off his police tail and went to a house run by the "Oyster Woman," a name she had acquired selling fish when she was a young beauty. She was a gray-haired but still good-looking matron, and when Fiaschetti gave her the five-lire note she immediately welcomed him. For the next few weeks he was an honored guest in Naples. According to Fiaschetti, during this time he came across the identity of the triggerman in Petrosino's murder—it was not Don Vito Cascio Ferro, he reported. Interestingly, in the account of his trip, Fiaschetti does not mention any organizational ties between the Naples Camorra and their alleged New York counterparts. Fiaschetti was having such a good time hoodwinking his hosts that he seemed to lose track of his mission. His behavior may explain what happened to Petrosino earlier. The two men thrived on danger. In Fiaschetti's case he was finally brought to his senses at a gathering of Camorra leaders, when it was announced that the head of the New York Italian squad was traveling around Italy in disguise, attempting to penetrate the society. The startled Camorrists rose in fury, vowing to "hunt this policeman by the blood of the Madonna." Fiaschetti departed posthaste for New York, though he later returned to testify against Papaccio, who received eleven years in prison (counting time served while awaiting trial).

Italy was to change considerably the year after Fiaschetti left. In October 1922 Mussolini staged a so-called march on Rome and the king named him premier. He instituted a drive on the criminal societies, and in Naples the Black Shirts began clubbing Camorrists. At first the society fought back, but when the Fascists began breaking up Camorrists' meetings with hand grenades the opposition ceased.

During the war, the Mafia in Sicily had thrived. It expanded into large-scale black-market activities and ran a racket selling horses to the army—many of them stolen or too old to be of any use. By now Don Vito Cascio Ferro, Mafia chief in Palermo and the man most often tagged with responsibility for Lieutenant Petrosino's murder, was at the height of his career. According to Luigi Barzini, Don Vito's power was based on "his natural ascendancy and his awe-inspiring appearance." Barzini described him as "tall, spare, elegantly but somberly dressed (with) a long white beard (that) made him resemble a New England preacher of the last century, or respected Judge." Wherever he went, mayors dressed in their best clothes would await him at the entrance of their village, kiss his hand, and pay him homage much as if he were the king. Barzini also claims that in the territory Don Vito controlled, peace and order were preserved, and according to a report prepared by an Italian high-government official, "The Mafia dominated and controlled the whole social life. Its orders had the force of laws and its protection was . . . more effective and secure than that which the state offers to its citizens."

Sicily had always managed to overcome foreign occupiers, and the first Fascist officials appointed were murdered. Mussolini himself was embarrassed when he came on a visit. A local Mafia mayor made a laughingstock out of him when, riding in an open car with the dictator, he stood up and announced Mussolini was under his personal protection. The mayor also made sure that the only people who came to the town square to hear Il Duce speak were a handful of local layabouts and village idiots he had selected himself. Furious, Mussolini named Cesare Mori prefect of the island. The dictator ordered Mori, a former army officer who had begun his career as a police officer in Sicily, to crack down with *"ferro e fucci"* (steel and fire). Togged out in black Fascist uniform with a silver dagger, Mori personally led roundups of mafiosi and posed for pictures standing over handcuffed prisoners on their knees. Among the first arrestees was the mayor who had proclaimed himself Mussolini's protector.

Mori knew the mafiosi well. Wary men, they would often enter or leave their homes by the windows and surrounded themselves with watchdogs to raise the alarm when strangers approached. If a suspected Mafia member were summoned to police headquarters for questioning he would immediately disappear or send a substitute to represent him and ascertain the nature of the police inquiry. Mori decided to employ some of the same tactics. Sometimes he would appear in public dressed in a tailcoat and bowler hat, looking every inch the dignified prefect. After he returned home he would change into a black shirt, slip out a side window, and personally lead a force of carabinieri, local police, and Fascist militia in a surprise raid.

Cattle sales always brought Mafia members out in force, so Mori made it a practice to swoop down on them and round up suspects. Torture was applied freely to the prisoners and Mussolini swore to put them in cages and exhibit them like wild animals.

On a more systematic basis, Mori developed a tactic of moving investigators into particular districts to determine the situation with the local Mafia and make a few arrests. Then his forces would withdraw. After the mafiosi were lulled into resuming their activity, suddenly Mori would launch a massive invasion and arrest every suspect. In 1926, Don Vito Cascio Ferro himself was sent to prison where he would remain until his death in 1943. By the late '20s, Mori's campaign had effectively crushed the Mafia. According to official governmental figures, the number of murders in the Palermo district fell from the 200 range early in the '20s to an average of about 30 annually from 1926 on. Mussolini's tactics won wide praise outside of Italy. Winston Churchill declared that if he were an Italian, he would "don the Fascist black shirt."

The thoroughness of Mori's crackdown caused many mafiosi to leave the island, and some who reached New York eventually became major figures in organized crime. Among them was Joe Bonanno. In his memoirs, Bonanno reports the reason for his departure in heroic terms. He claims that, as a nineteen-year-old student at an academy for maritime cadets, he refused an order to wear a black shirt and was dismissed. In 1924 he arrived in Cuba and subsequently entered the United States illegally.

In America, terms like Mafia, Camorra, and Black Hand were beginning to disappear from news stories about Italian gangsters when in 1921 Fiaschetti found himself at the center of an alleged massive Mafia murder plot. An eighty-seven-year-old mafioso named Bartolemeo Fontana reported that his former associates were threatening to kill him because of his knowledge of a series of murders. Fiaschetti assigned a squad of detectives to accompany Fontana to Grand Central Station to trap a Mafia emissary. A detective named Reppetto (no relation), posing as a suitcase-carrying traveler, stayed close to Fontana and took into custody Stefano Magaddino, another fugitive from Sicily who would later become head of an organized crime family in Buffalo, New York. At headquarters, the thirty-year-old

Magaddino knocked the octogenarian Fontana down, attacking him until Fiaschetti came to the rescue. "Big Mike" was now in his element, providing reporters with colorful, though highly speculative, accounts of Mafia plots. For a time New York papers blazed with headlines about Mafia and Camorra murder squads, and detectives from Detroit, Chicago, and elsewhere rushed in to clear up unsolved murders in their own jurisdictions. At one time, the press inflated the body count to 125. In the end, the case turned out to be grossly exaggerated. In his memoirs written nine years afterward, Fiaschetti makes no mention of the affair.

Commissioner Enright became uneasy with publicity about organized crime, particularly because he was taking a good deal of heat from critics over his failure to enforce the Prohibition laws. In February 1922 he merged the Italian and bomb squads. "Greater efficiency and broader activity" was the reason the commissioner cited for the change. Observers were quick to note, however, that Acting Captain Fiaschetti had been dropped to his substantive rank of detective sergeant and subordinated to an Irish lieutenant. Headquarters spokesman also explained to reporters that "conditions which seemed to require the formation of the nationality organization of detectives some years ago have to a large extent disappeared." In a sense this was correct. Even the original formation of the Italian squad might have been ill conceived, since in Petrosino's day it had been too small to deal with crimes affecting 10 percent of the city's population. In the 1920s, though, Italian criminals taking advantage of Prohibition began moving out of their ethnic enclaves into the mainstream of crime, ultimately leading to the ascension of men like Lucky Luciano and Frank Costello to the top of New York's underworld. Thus, while it may no longer have been necessary to have a distinct Italian squad, it was even more essential to retain a group of specialists on Italian crime and to have a man like Fiaschetti as a headquarters captain of detectives (an appointment that was discretionary with the commissioner). Instead, the abolition of the squad dispersed the detectives and removed the larger-than-life Fiaschetti completely. Big Mike, who had survived so many dangerous situations, would be eliminated by politics after an Italian-American lawyer connected with Tammany tried to force his way into Fiaschetti's office while the detective was conducting an interrogation.

Fiaschetti threw him out, and as a result was himself thrown out of police headquarters and assigned to the district attorney's office. In 1924 he was pressured into early retirement.

Another Italian leader who was sidelined in the early 1920s was the equally flamboyant Fiorello La Guardia. The year 1921 was supposed to be the one in which he ran for mayor, but before his campaign could get started his young wife and baby daughter both died. Grief-stricken, he abandoned his ambitions. Eventually he was elected to a seat in Congress from Italian East Harlem. He continued to serve in Congress through the 1920s, but in the Coolidge-Hoover era there was no chance of a liberal Republican like La Guardia attaining any influence in Washington. Back in New York, the Democrats controlled City Hall and the Statehouse, so he was marginalized locally as well.

All through the Prohibition era, men like La Guardia and Fiaschetti, who might have been able to check the worst excesses of the gangsters, could do nothing but watch. Not until 1934 would La Guardia become mayor. As part of his war on hoodlums, he would make Fiaschetti deputy commissioner of the Department of Markets, with a mandate to clean up produce rackets, especially the artichoke business. By that time the mobs, led by Rothstein's apt pupils, were so entrenched in New York life that it would take more than a mayor to smash them.

6:   Prohibition: The Mobs Strike a Bonanza

On January 16, 1920, the First Congregational Church in Washington, D.C., held an unusual evening service. An overflow crowd of conservatively dressed and decidedly sober citizens had gathered for the equivalent of a New Year's Eve party. At the stroke of twelve, they would celebrate something more than a new year—a whole new era, and the triumph of a cause for which many of those present had labored long and hard. The manufacture and sale of alcohol was about to become illegal throughout the United States.

Methodist bishop James Cannon sat in the front row, representing the Protestant churches who had been in the vanguard of the Prohibition movement for years. Nearby was Minnesota congressman Andrew Volstead, who had sponsored the law spelling out penalties. The honored guests also included the man who had actually written that law, Wayne Wheeler, general counsel of the dry movement's main lobbying organ, the Anti-Saloon League. The most prominent figure was the nation's best-known temperance advocate and most stirring orator, William Jennings Bryan. On the eve of this great political victory, he delivered a thunderous speech ending with a quote from Matthew: "They are dead which sought the young child's life." The applause was deafening. As the celebrants streamed out of church, many felt they had witnessed a historical moment comparable to the reading of the Declaration of Independence or the storming of the Bastille.

Their opponents also saw the coming of Prohibition in cataclysmic terms. The fervor of that Washington gathering was matched by the gloom of many New Yorkers. Prohibition was aimed at their city—"Satan's seat," Bishop Cannon had called it. The owners of the famed restaurants on the "Great White Way"—Broadway from roughly 39th to 50th Streets—took it for granted that their days were numbered. At Maxim's, the waiters dressed as pallbearers right down to white gloves. The Cafe de Paris (formerly Rector's) gave a "Cinderella Ball" where, at midnight, the guests' liquor glasses turned into water glasses. At the Golden Glades a coffin containing a bottle of Champagne was wheeled around the room as the clock struck midnight.

A decade earlier, the idea of a flat-out ban on the sale of alcohol was far-fetched even to most of the temperance ladies and hellfire preachers crusading against liquor. Kansas went dry in 1880 and by 1914 eight more states had done the same; still, few Americans expected to see the whole country embrace such a drastic step. Nationally, the campaign didn't really gain steam until a group of shrewd politicians and well-funded lobbyists focused on the task of securing enough congressional votes to send a constitutional amendment to the states. Even then, their cause might never have carried the day if not for the world war, which led to grain-saving limits on alcohol production and heightened concern for the moral well-being of young men in uniform. The fact that most of the nation's beer brewers were German gave saloons and taverns an added aura of menace.

In 1917 the Senate passed the Eighteenth Amendment with just thirteen hours of debate. The House vote took even less time. By January 1919 the amendment had been ratified by the required thirty-six states, eventually passing the legislatures of all but Connecticut and Rhode Island. The victory of the drys was so sudden and so complete that the movement's leaders dismissed the possibility of serious resistance. Even some wets expected Prohibition to be on the level. "Christy, are they really going to enforce it?" a bartender asked Christy Sullivan, a Manhattan congressman (and a blood member of Big Tim Sullivan's tribe). "Yes, I think so," Christy replied. "There won't be any more liquor."

Sullivan's opinion was not shared by his fellow congressman and political foe Fiorello La Guardia. He recognized that Prohibition's opponents were concentrated in the big cities of the Northeast and Midwest. Drink was not the first urban sin that rural-dominated legislatures had attempted to stamp out over the years: there were laws against prostitution and gambling, too. Instead of halting or even greatly reducing those activities, their main effect had been to provide organized crime with a business opportunity and law enforcement with a constant source of temptation. La Guardia estimated it would take 250,000 cops to enforce the law in New York City and another 250,000 to police the police.

In contrast, de facto leader of the Prohibitionists Wayne Wheeler expected the liquor interests to fold their tent. Under his sway, Congress entrusted the job of enforcement to a new bureau housed within the Treasury Department, with just 1,500 agents to cover the entire country. In its hiring practices the Prohibition Bureau wasn't even a match for the typical big-city police department. Agents were exempted from the civil service laws, and political connections mattered more than experience or ability. Training was all but nonexistent; with the right sponsorship an agent could be hired and on the street, armed with a .45-caliber revolver, in a matter of days. The top salary was only $2,300 a year (later raised to $2,836); but even at twice that amount the pay would have been dwarfed by the potential for graft. In New York, a dry agent could make $50,000 a year on the side. Even in less lucrative jurisdictions, agents tended to see the position as a temporary one—an opportunity to get rich quick and move on. Bribe-taking became the rule, not the exception, and it was not the only blemish on the bureau's record. Between 1920 and 1931, 1,600 agents were fired and 257 were prosecuted as criminals. Bureau agents also managed to shoot and kill at least 137 citizens. State authorities sometimes brought charges when low-level violators or innocent bystanders were hit; but the local U.S. attorneys would invariably transfer such cases to federal court and have them dismissed.

In the final stages of their long legislative crusade, the Prohibitionists had seemed all-powerful. A good deal of their power, however, consisted of the lip-service support of officials who, regardless of their votes or public statements, had no intention of giving up drink themselves or forcing their fellow citizens to do so. In the corridors of the Capitol building, whiskey was peddled from suitcases to senators and congressmen, who sometimes appeared visibly intoxicated on the floor of their chambers. At the White House, the liquor flowed freely after the inauguration of President Warren G. Harding in March of 1921.

Prohibition is often portrayed as a bizarre and comical idea foisted on an unwilling nation. Yet the liquor and saloon industries had been a target of feminist groups for decades, and for good reason. There was much to be said, in principle, for a national effort to help the countless women, and their children, whose lives had been blighted by the excessive drinking of their husbands. For any such campaign to have made an impact, however, its focus would have to have been on manufacturers and distributors. Instead, the authorities went after the places where ordinary people drank—corner saloons, or "speakeasies" (the English word for an unlicensed liquor establishment).

Because the temperance and women's rights movements were closely entwined, even the hard drinkers of President Harding's Ohio Gang considered it appropriate to appoint a woman, thirty-two-year-old Mabel Walker Willebrandt, as assistant attorney general in charge of prosecuting Prohibition violations. Small and spare, she was often ignored by her male colleagues in Washington, and, in turn, was not impressed by them. She was quick to assess her boss, Attorney General Daugherty, as "incompetent." Some Prohibition agents, she later wrote, were "no more fit to wear a badge and carry a gun than Jesse James."

Of all the nation's big cities, the most hostile to Prohibition and most openly defiant of the law was Chicago. Less than an hour into the "Noble Experiment" six armed men entered a railroad switching yard, bound and gagged a watchman, and emptied two freight cars of medicinal whiskey worth $100,000. At about the same time, another gang stole four barrels of grain alcohol from a government warehouse and a third hijacked a truck transporting liquor.

Because of his strong ties to the city administration of Mayor Thompson, Johnny Torrio had become the most powerful organized crime figure in

Chicago. The Thompson administration essentially made him their middleman, or controller, of bootlegging, the way Rothstein handled gambling for Tammany in Manhattan. He set out to organize the new industry much as J. P. Morgan and John D. Rockefeller had consolidated railroads and oil. His aim was to establish combines in which the various players recognized one another's territories and agreed to keep prices and business practices in line.

One of Torrio's first steps was to form a partnership with Joseph Stenson, the youngest of four brothers who owned a number of breweries.[1] Stenson had kept some of his in operation for the presumed purpose of making "near beer," a legal beverage containing no more than half a percent alcohol. Since he needed a market as much as Torrio needed a supply, they came to a swift agreement: Stenson would provide 4 percent alcohol beer; in addition, he would act as a conduit to influentials in the upper world. With Torrio running things at street level and Stenson supplying the goods, they each cleared about $12 million a year in the early 1920s.

From his headquarters at the Four Deuces cabaret (2222 South Wabash) Torrio functioned as a corporate manager and political fixer. Although he was prepared to use violence when necessary, he did so regretfully. He had learned from the Levee wars that gun battles and assassinations foretold trouble: bad publicity followed by heightened pressure from the law. Temperamentally, Torrio was too reserved to play the Colosimo role of the lovable hoodlum with a heart of gold. He preferred to remain an obscure figure, often using the name Frank Langley.

Torrio relied on diplomacy as well as muscle. He sought to win people over by spelling out the services he could offer in financing, supply, and political protection and by emphasizing the disadvantages of wasteful competition—something he abhorred no less than any corporate tycoon. Not everyone found him convincing. Several Irish gang leaders balked at doing business with what some of them called a "dago pimp." Torrio got a similar response from Frank McErlane and his partner Joe Saltis. McErlane

---

[1]Stenson is proof that bootleggers could come from all walks of life. He lived on the ritzy Near North Side Gold Coast and the *Chicago Tribune* once referred to him as "The Silk Hat of Organized Crime." Typically, though, when the papers were talking about crime, Stenson's name went unmentioned.

was a stocky, red-faced, repulsive sort, by young manhood a leading contender for the title of Chicago's most vicious killer. Saltis was a big cheerful type who looked as if he ought to be lugging beef in the union stockyards adjacent to the district he and McErlane controlled. Neither man saw any reason to pay for liquor when they could hijack somebody else's truck or distillery. Torrio did not care for these men or their methods, but McErlane and Saltis were too important to alienate. Instead of calling on his gun squads or Mayor Thompson's equally obliging police, he smiled, took his leave, and waited for the next opportunity to press his case.

In his negotiations with certain key groups, Torrio was willing to offer unusually generous terms. After his failed meeting with McErlane, he proceeded to the headquarters of another group of stockyards gentlemen, the Irish Ragen Colts. Chicago's toughest gang, the Colts were a small army—"Hit one and you hit 2,000" was their motto. They were especially noted as Election Day sluggers, which is perhaps why their neighborhood produced more successful politicians than any other. The only way to beat them down was to call out the National Guard, as Governor Frank Lowden had done the previous year during a bloody race riot. Torrio offered to sell them beer at ten dollars off the established price, leaving him and Stenson with a mere thirty dollars profit per barrel. As a political club, the Colts knew a good deal when they saw one. Torrio got a new customer and ally.

Dion "Deanie" O'Bannion's North Side gang was the most powerful group in Chicago, apart from Torrio's own. Johnny had considerable (and justified) doubts about O'Bannion's judgment. Nevertheless, he agreed to recognize O'Bannion's autonomy, even giving him a strip of his own section of the Loop to administer along with a partnership in the Sieben brewery. Deanie, then just twenty-eight, could be an endearing man—when he wasn't engaged in shooting, slugging, and other mayhem. An altar boy and choir singer, he had become known for the sentimental ballads he sang at various saloons in the North Clark Street vice district. With his sweet voice and crippled leg, young O'Bannion attracted generous tips and the paternal interest of several prominent local thugs and killers. By his late teens, he was cracking safes and killing people. He loved flowers and opened a shop across from the Holy Name Cathedral, where he fussed over every floral arrangement until it was just so. At mob funerals, O'Bannion sometimes supplied not only the posies but the corpse.

His subordinates and allies were a cross section of ethnic Chicago—Poles, Italians, and Jews—though it was not always easy to tell who was which. His top lieutenant, Hymie Weiss, was a Polish Catholic, born Earl Wajciechowski. George "Bugs" Moran was also Polish, and, like Weiss, a proficient killer. So were Vincent "Schemer" Drucci, an Italian, and Sam "Nails" Morton, né Markowitz. For these young men bootlegging was a quick and equal-opportunity pathway to the American dream. It could also lead to an early grave. Between 1919 and 1934 Chicago recorded 765 gangland murders.

O'Bannion and his followers would contribute more than their share to the tally, both as killers and victims. And on more than one occasion, their wild ways made Torrio cringe. Despite their wealth and power, the O'Bannion crew were, at heart, still corner punks. In May 1923, Nails Morton died after being thrown from a horse during one of his morning canters through Lincoln Park. The gang responded by kidnapping and killing the horse. Torrio could not abide this sort of juvenile conduct. The differences between his leadership and O'Bannion's illustrated why the former's group emerged from the '20s wealthy and powerful and the latter ended up dead or in jail.

Another group of troublesome allies were the Genna brothers, who ran the toughest outfit in the Near West Side Sicilian district. In their neighborhood, the Gennas had forged an army of "alky cookers"—neighborhood men who were paid fifteen dollars a day to brew rotgut whiskey in their homes. Johnny agreed to buy their cottage-industry product at $1.60 a gallon over cost and peddle it in cheap dives at a 200 percent markup. But O'Bannion had a habit of encroaching on the Gennas' territory, and vice versa. When this happened, Torrio would call on Mike Merlo, the leader of the Chicago branch of the Unione Siciliana, a social worker type who was constantly striving to improve the lot of his people. Mike eschewed violence, and many Sicilians regarded him as a living saint.[2] A word from Mike was all that Torrio needed to keep the Gennas in check.

[2]When he died of cancer at forty-four, a life-size wax replica of Merlo was placed in the backseat of an open touring car and driven through the streets of Little Italy as the crowds knelt down and prayed.

Things ran fairly smoothly until the beginning of 1923, when Mayor Thompson announced he wasn't going to run for a third term. Many Chicagoans had laughed at Big Bill's cowboy posturing and his isolationist fulminations against England's King George V. Thompson's retirement reflected growing public disenchantment with his histrionics and brazen corruption. But during his tenure, Torrio had been able to keep the bootlegging gangs under control.

The new mayor, Judge William Dever, was a man of probity, but he owed his election to Democratic Party bosses. Dever's chosen police chief, Morgan Collins, had previously commanded two of the city's most vice-ridden police districts; in the 1916 scandal, he had been identified as a member of Thompson's Sportsman's Club, the organization that funneled payoffs to the police. His fellow members included Colosimo, Torrio, and Mont Tennes, the gambling magnate. Under Dever, control over bootlegging and other vice was decentralized to the city's fifty Democratic ward committeemen—a formula for anarchy.

Torrio's troubles began immediately after Dever took office, though the first blow was struck, unexpectedly, by the Feds. Through the efforts of the Anti-Saloon League a straight-arrow Oklahoman, Brice Armstrong, had been appointed a Prohibition agent in Chicago. Strapping on two guns, Armstrong began to make raids, always ensuring the press would be notified. (Despite his zeal for Prohibition, he would let the reporters take away a few bottles for "medicinal purposes.") His enthusiasm did not sit well with his superiors and he was soon shipped out to the suburban boondocks. There Armstrong became curious about the operations of a near-beer brewery on the Indiana state line owned by Torrio and a front man for Stenson. Determining that its beer exceeded the .5 percent limit, he obtained warrants and raided the place. Officially a first offender, Torrio got off with a fine, but his conviction set him up for a jail sentence in the event of another arrest.

With Torrio's influence waning, interlopers began to challenge his combine. Newly released convict Spike O'Donnell and his brothers, small-time criminals from the stockyards district, went into the beer business, invading territories previously controlled by Torrio and the McErlane-Saltis faction.

As usual, Johnny tried to negotiate. He enlisted a local police captain to suggest some boundaries for Spike's operation. O'Donnell refused to listen. Johnny's next step was to lower the price of his beer in an effort to force the newcomer out of business. The O'Donnells retaliated by slugging saloon keepers who switched to Torrio's brand.

Torrio could not allow his customers to be molested. He formed an alliance with the McErlanes and sent his own gun squad to assist them in a war of extermination. The automobile age had made it relatively easy to transport victims to out-of-the-way places for execution and burial. Within a short time, several of the O'Donnell gang had been "taken for a ride." Spike himself was hit a couple of times and temporarily retired from the business world to reassess his marketing strategy.

Torrio resorted to violence reluctantly, but the young protégé who had come to him from Brooklyn had no such qualms. Lacking Torrio's business skills or smooth ways, Al Capone was essentially a thug. But Torrio was oddly fond of him—or perhaps not so oddly, now that conditions had begun to render his own, more polite methods obsolete. Johnny decided it was time for a vacation. In the fall of 1923 he took his wife and mother off to Italy for six months, purchasing a mansion for his mom in the Neapolitan village of her birth. In his absence, Capone ran things and shooting became the order of the day.

Before his departure, Torrio had decided to add another suburban enclave to his empire as a hedge against further trouble with the new Chicago administration. The real estate he had in mind was the town of Cicero, just west of Chicago—a blue-collar enclave of 50,000 Slavic immigrants already under the control of an Irish gang led by "Klondike" O'Donnell and his brothers (no relation to the South Side O'Donnells). Johnny persuaded Cook County sheriff Peter Hoffman (immortalized by Charles MacArthur and Ben Hecht as the bumbling sheriff in *The Front Page*) to seize the community's chief recreational device—slot machines. When Torrio sent word that the next raids would be on the saloons, Klondike agreed to share Cicero, and Capone was given the task of equipping the town with an adequate supply of prostitutes and gamblers to serve the trade coming in from Chicago.

While Torrio was in Italy, Cicero held an election. Outraged citizens joined with bootleggers fearful of a Torrio/Capone takeover to put up an opposition slate. On Election Day, the leaders of the opposition were kidnapped and held captive while Capone's gunmen began patrolling the streets and polling places. Their adversaries retaliated with guns of their own, and three men were killed. After a few hours of warfare, a county judge swore in a force of Chicago detectives as special investigators and fifteen squads of them raced to the area. A group of officers promptly got into a gun battle with Al Capone's brother Frank, killing him. At the polls, however, the Capone forces emerged triumphant, and they didn't leave much doubt about who was running things. Soon after his election, the new mayor got into a dispute with Capone over a facet of municipal administration. Al, not being schooled in the fine points of parliamentary procedure, whipped out a blackjack and knocked the mayor down the steps of City Hall as a town cop looked on.

In the city proper the booze business was also becoming increasingly unruly. When Torrio returned from Italy, he received a surprising but welcome message from O'Bannion. Deanie was going to leave Chicago and the whole dirty business to live on a ranch in Colorado—or so he said, offering to sell his share of the Sieben brewery to Torrio. The deal was consummated for $250,000 and Johnny's promise to personally go to the brewery to assure O'Bannion's associates that they would continue to receive their regular supply of booze. Shortly before dawn on a May morning in 1924, Torrio arrived at the plant for his meeting with the O'Bannions. Before it got under way, Chief Morgan Collins arrived and arrested everybody at the scene, announcing that he was taking his state prisoners to a federal courthouse for arraignment. O'Bannion did not have a Volstead Act conviction on his record, so he would only get a fine. As a second offender, Torrio faced a jail sentence. Though the brewery had been padlocked, O'Bannion kept his quarter of a million dollars. Johnny had been flimflammed.

A few months later, the death of Mike Merlo provided Torrio with an opportunity to settle the score. Johnny hatched a scheme with the Genna brothers to order flowers from O'Bannion's shop and send some gunmen to pick them up as a means of getting close enough to Deanie to kill him. The

Gennas nominated two recent immigrants from Sicily, John Scalisi and Anthony Anselmi, for the job. Since the young men were a bit green, Torrio suggested that they be accompanied by Frankie Yale—the same Frankie Yale who most people believed had been brought in four years earlier by Torrio to hit Colosimo, and who had sent his young bouncer, Al Capone, to Chicago. By now Frankie was a prominent bootlegger in Brooklyn, and the source of the high-quality imported liquor sold by Torrio at his Chicago outlets. In addition, Yale owned a number of legitimate businesses, including a cigar company that sold five-cent Frankie Yale stogies with his picture on the box. Yale and the young Sicilian gunmen went to O'Bannion's shop together and when O'Bannion extended his hand in greeting, one of the trio grasped it and held on so firmly that Deanie was unable to reach for his own piece when the other two shot him.

After putting in the ritual appearance at the victim's wake, Torrio went about his daily business unarmed and without bodyguards. But no one was fooled. Two months after O'Bannion's death, Weiss, Moran, and Drucci caught up with him. He was returning home from a shopping trip with Mrs. Torrio in their chauffeured limo. The car pulled up outside the elegant South Side apartment building where they lived and Mrs. Torrio got out. While Johnny fumbled with some packages in the backseat and the unarmed chauffeur remained behind the wheel, a man opened fire from the front with a .45-caliber pistol, while another began pumping shotgun slugs through the rear window. The chauffeur was hit almost immediately. Johnny managed to get out of the car, but he had gone only a short distance before fire from both directions struck him in the jaw, liver, and abdomen. The man with the .45 ran up, put the weapon to Johnny's temple, and squeezed the trigger. The chamber proved to be empty. As the shooter prepared to slip in another magazine, the third accomplice shouted a warning, and all three jumped into their vehicle and fled. Although Torrio recovered, the experience understandably soured him on the idea of settling back into the life of a Chicago gang lord. After a brief jail sentence on the Sieben brewery charges, he turned the mob over to Capone and sailed to Italy once again, where he continued to receive a 25 percent share of the profits.

Chicago might have been wilder than some cities, but drinkers had little difficulty quenching their thirst no matter where they were. Detroit, just across the river from Windsor, Ontario, was ideally located to tap into Canada's liquor supply. A gang originally made up of toughs from the Jewish ghetto dominated bootlegging. When some of their co-religionists described them as being purple, that is, tainted, the group got a name. In addition to taking care of local needs, vessels chartered by the gang hauled Canadian liquor across the Great Lakes to cities like Cleveland. The Purples' role caused the booze-hauling fleet to become known as the "Jewish Navy."

Egan's Rats, founded in St. Louis early in the century by "Jelly Roll" Egan, specialized in strikebreaking. In the 1920s, they emerged as the city's top bootleggers. By the end of the decade both the Purples and the Egans would be decimated by the law and rival gangsters; Italian groups would gradually replace them.

The Pacific Coast was as wet as the Great Lakes region. San Francisco's Pete McDonough, a saloon keeper sent up for bootlegging, emerged from jail to become the coordinator of organized crime. Enforcement was so casual that a well-known speakeasy, the Blue Fox, operated directly across from police headquarters.

In Seattle, an ex-police lieutenant named Roy Olmstead was the top bootlegger and booze runner. He employed fifty people, operated several vessels, and maintained a suburban ranch for storage. His initial $10,000 investment for half ownership of the business soon blossomed to an annual gross of $2 million. Olmstead also owned a radio station, and one of KFOX's most popular programs featured Mrs. Olmstead reading children's stories at bedtime. Local lawmen believed that the broadcast adventures of Peter Rabbit, Flopsy, Mopsy, and Cottontail were actually messages to her husband's liquor fleet, warning them where Coast Guard vessels were patrolling. When the Feds brought a case against Roy Olmstead based on wiretap evidence, the ex-cop was certain the tactic would not stand legal muster. Even Assistant Attorney General Mabel Walker Willebrandt thought the authorities had gone too far, declaring the practice "dangerous and unwarranted." The case eventually went to the U.S. Supreme Court and Justice Holmes sided with the defense, declaring, "I think it a lesser evil that some criminals should escape than that the government should play an ignoble part." Five of the nine justices, led by Chief Justice William Howard Taft, did not agree, and Olmstead went to prison.

In Los Angeles's Little Italy section where Tony "The Hat" Cornero held sway, shootings were so frequent that one block of Darwin Street was known as "Shotgun Alley." When a new mayor was elected in 1925, a war broke out for control of the bootlegging business and Cornero's liquor ships and trucks hauling booze were hijacked. Distribution of $100,000 hadn't secured his protection, so Tony organized his own force. With a hundred guns on the payroll, the hot-tempered Cornero counterattacked, killing two men. The local cops were a rough bunch, applying the same methods to gangsters that they used to keep union organizers out of the "open shop" town. The lieutenant in charge of the "Crime Crusher Squad" called the technique "pinning their ears back." They ran Cornero out of town and he was replaced by Jack Dragna (Anthony Rizzotti).

As the nation's trendsetter, New York City was the place that taught the rest of the country that defying the law was acceptable, even chic. The number one man in bootlegging—and in almost every other illegal enterprise—was the remarkable Arnold Rothstein, christened "The Brain" by Damon Runyon. From his table at Lindy's, the Broadway in-spot noted for its cheesecake, Rothstein presided over bookmaking operations, Wall Street bucket shops, and international drug rings. Like the smart banker he was, Rothstein did not personally engage in such enterprises—he backed those who did. Women responded to his dark hair, flashing blue eyes, pale skin, and good manners, but when Rothstein was business, he was all business. A drug dealer applying to him for a loan would have to take out a life insurance policy for the designated amount with Rothstein as beneficiary; that way, a deadbeat couldn't argue that killing him wouldn't get the money back. Gangsters and politicians alike sought his guidance.

Unlike Chicago, New York was too big to be run by a single political machine. Rothstein and Tammanyite Tom Foley had to maintain an alliance with Brooklyn, particularly when that borough's own John "Red Mike" Hylan was in the mayor's office. Rothstein could not control bootlegging citywide the way Torrio did in Chicago. At first he didn't even want to get into it—a non-drinker himself, he thought that the banning of liquor might give people more inclination to gamble. One of his lieutenants, a former East Side pickpocket and labor slugger named Irving Wexler, a.k.a. "Waxey" (because his fingers were so smooth) Gordon, talked him into it.

Gordon got $175,000 from Rothstein to establish a system for smuggling liquor in from Britain. Tramp steamers carried the goods across the ocean, and then the cargo was transferred to speedboats just outside the three-mile limit of U.S. territorial waters, to be delivered to any of a number of carefully chosen beaches on Long Island and the northern New Jersey coast. Soon this stretch of the East Coast became known as the heart of "Rum Row," and officials of the U.S. Coast Guard—an arm of the Treasury Department—were being pressed to do something about the problem. To make their task easier, they called for the territorial limit to be expanded to the distance a speedboat could travel in an hour. And in order to get as much mileage as possible out of that rule, the nautical cops requisitioned a souped-up powerboat. Unfortunately it broke down during testing, raising derisive howls from a group of rumrunners who had gathered to watch. The United States then unilaterally declared the limit to be twelve miles.

Rothstein and Gordon did not waste time arguing the niceties of international law, preferring to employ the bribes that had proven so effective on dry land. When their rumrunners were plying one part of the ocean, Coast Guard skippers would arrange to be in another part. When the cargo was landed, police were there to protect the goods, often providing a motorcycle-cop escort to the nearest warehouse. Smugglers without such connections had to battle lawmen and hijackers alike on the water, the beaches, and the highways.

In 1923, thirty-one-year-old Owen "Owney" Madden was released from state prison after serving nine years on a murder charge. A product of the Liverpool docks and Hell's Kitchen—two of the world's toughest neighborhoods—Madden had emigrated with his parents at the age of eleven. He was only a teenager when he picked up his nickname, "The Killer."[3] While still on parole, he started hijacking booze trucks belonging

---

[3] Some of Jimmy Cagney and George Raft's gangster roles were based on Madden's character and career.

to a West Side Irish longshoreman named Bill Dwyer, another New Yorker skilled at bribing the Coast Guard. Then they became partners. Soon Owney and "Big Bill" (the name came from his importance, not his size) became a potent force in New York organized crime.

New York's Italians were not as quick off the mark as the city's Jews and Irish, and several years would pass before they felt emboldened to expand beyond the Italian colonies. But when Prohibition began they started a curb exchange in the Mulberry Street area, where Italian bootleggers gathered daily to deal for a dozen cases of whiskey or a truckload of beer (the New York Stock Exchange had begun in similar curbside fashion a century earlier). The problem with the Mulberry Street liquor market was that its products were illegal, and its location practically next door to police headquarters. When business disputes erupted into gunfire, cops would come running out, and after a couple of years the exchange had to be shut down.

The most prominent figure in the area was Giuseppe "Joe" Masseria, a Sicilian who had fled the homeland at the turn of the century to avoid murder charges. In New York, he worked as a burglar and small-time associate of the Morellos until they were sent to Atlanta. Branching out on his own, he had to contend with rivals like Umberto Valenti and his sometime ally, Ciro Terranova. In May 1922, Masseria managed to ambush some Valenti gunmen sent to assassinate him. Both sides opened up, and two Masseria bodyguards and four innocent bystanders were hit. The chief of detectives himself led the cops out of headquarters and the short, stocky Masseria was not fast enough to outrun two detectives. But no witnesses were able to identify him, and he produced a pistol permit signed by a state supreme court justice for the gun he had tossed away while being pursued.

Two months later, another pair of gunmen tried to kill Masseria near his Second Avenue home. One assailant chased him into a nearby store and fired a shot at his head from point-blank range, but Joe managed to jerk out of the way. Twice more, the assailant fired, and twice more Masseria dodged the bullets. Unnerved, the gunmen jumped into their car and fled. Nearby, a group of garment workers coming out of a union meeting blocked their escape. The gunmen shot five of them and ran down two more. The affair produced headlines, but little outrage. Gun battles had been a regular feature of life on the Lower East Side for generations.

Masseria proposed a peace conference with Valenti to settle their differences. In contrast to the 1916 Navy Street ambush, Valenti and his bodyguard were not murdered on the way in—they were killed going out. Masseria's skill at dodging bullets and putting them into his opponents brought him great acclaim from his fellow Italians. The more superstitious ones believed he would never die, and even the bosses fell in line. Ciro Terranova accepted the role of overseer for uptown and the Bronx. In Brooklyn, Masseria formed an alliance with Frankie Yale, who was busy slaughtering Irish gangsters in a war over control of the Brooklyn docks. Despite the many services he had rendered to the Chicago mob, Yale was murdered in 1928 by a squad of Capone's gunmen who chased his car through the streets of Brooklyn with guns blazing. Frankie had evidently shorted Al on some liquor deliveries.[4]

The Prohibitionists wound up doing more damage to the restaurant business than the liquor business. In the past, New York's nightlife had revolved around elegant establishments known primarily for their food. Now Delmonico's, Louis Sherry's, and a score of others were gone, along with their gentlemanly proprietors. In their place, Midtown abounded with joints where the cuisine was minimal, the liquor outrageously expensive, and the management made up of Sing Sing alums. Opening one of these establishments required the permission of a top mobster or politician, and anyone who proceeded without it could expect to have his place smashed (and his head with it) by hoodlums or police raiding parties. Instead of shunning such dives, Wall Street brokers, Park Avenue socialites, and their ladies flocked to them. Larry Fay was typical of the proprietors spawned by Prohibition. A couple of years earlier, he had been a cab driver; now, as the owner of El Fey on 45th Street, he was a millionaire. His girlfriend, Mary Louise

---

[4]The news coverage of Yale's death concentrated on his lavish funeral and the battle that broke out between his two widows, each claiming to be the legitimate Mrs. Yale. Since Jim Colosimo's demise, gangster funerals had become one of the great spectacles of the day.

Cecilia Guinan, a former rodeo rider and B-movie actress better known as "Texas," proved to be an expert at fleecing the chumps with heavily padded checks and inferior booze poured into bottles that bore fancy labels. "Hello, suckers!" she would shout, standing on the stage at El Fey, and the suckers loved it.

West 52nd Street between Fifth and Sixth Avenues was an almost unbroken row of speakeasies. The owners of the one or two brownstones resisting the tide were forced to put signs in front proclaiming "Private residence—do not ring the bell." Owney Madden had a couple dozen spots, including the luxurious Club Napoleon in an old three-story mansion on 56th Street; it featured velvet carpets, revolving bars, and a tennis court in the rear. Up in Harlem, Madden and Rothstein were co-owners of the popular Cotton Club, where an all-white audience was entertained by an all-black cast. Copycats opened a similar place named the Plantation Club nearby, which also enjoyed considerable success until strong-arm guys from the West Side wrecked it. Madden did not care for competition.

With girls and gangsters mingling with the elite night after night, the boozy nightclubs became great social levelers, erasing class barriers as no socialist agitator could have done. Even a cold-blooded killer like Owney Madden, who now brewed the city's premium beer, Madden's No. 1, could do the Jim Colosimo number, coming on as a philosopher, guide, and friend to the swells. Madison Square Garden was another lively meeting ground for New Yorkers who might not have previously crossed paths. In the first ten rows of the Garden on the night of a major prizefight, show business luminaries and Park Avenue aristocrats would sit elbow to elbow with "more murderers than there were in the death house at Sing Sing." Detectives loved the Garden, because it was a convenient place to find a hoodlum who had slipped his police tail.

A platoon of writers relayed the city's raucous doings to the country at large, generally neglecting to mention the grubby tourist traps that now stretched up and down Broadway. Instead Americans read Damon Runyon's *Guys and Dolls* fairy tale, in which Armand Rosenthal (Arnold Rothstein) was rendered as a lovable teddy bear. One of Rothstein's best gambling patrons was Herbert Bayard Swope, executive editor of the *New York World* and confidant of statesmen and tycoons. When Swope lost heavily, the normally implacable A.R. was always willing to carry him for long periods. As Swope's biographer noted, he frequently had disputes with bookmakers "over the precise term of bets he had made with them"—a polite way of saying he welched. Bookmakers frowned on such behavior, but it was good business to be lenient with Swope. One notice Swope posted in the city room of the *World* read: "Members of the staff are doubly cautioned not to take the oftentimes irresponsible utterances of the police as final or authoritative."[5]

After a few years of seeing its will flouted, Congress increased the size of the Prohibition Bureau to 2,500. For the most part, that simply meant an expanded collection of crooks and Keystone Cops. In New York, $2,800-a-year Feds acquired diamonds and flashy cars within a short time of being sworn in. Again and again, Washington sent in new supervisors with orders to clean house. They never got very far. Some were veteran revenue officers who had spent years tracking moonshiners in the southern backwoods. "Reven nooers," like "Cap'n Dan" Chapin, were a tough lot, used to dodging rifle balls aimed their way. When Chapin took over the New York office, his first act was to assemble his troops and order them to put both hands on the table. He promptly fired all those wearing expensive jewelry. But the replacements were no different and Chapin went back to the hills.

Why would an honest man accept a penny-ante salary to enforce an unpopular law? It was a question that might have been put to Izzy and Moe—the country's best-known Prohibition agents. In 1920, Isadore Einstein was a forty-four-year-old New York City postal clerk. An agent's salary was slightly more than he was making already, so it looked good to a man with a wife and four kids. Einstein went to a local Republican politician and wangled an appointment. Later he persuaded his friend Moses Smith to join him. They didn't look much like cops: at five-foot-five and five-foot-seven inches, respectively, each tipped the scale at around 230 pounds. Their

---

[5]In the 1930s Swope was named chairman of the New York State Racing Commission. According to historian Stephen Fox, he eventually became indebted to Frank Costello's gambling lieutenant Frank Erickson for $700,000, which was one of the reasons that Swope was forced to resign from the commission.

unlikely bearing made it easy for them to gain entrance to speakeasies. As they became better known they had to resort to disguises, decking themselves out in shamrocks on St. Patrick's Day or pretending to be violinists or society swells in evening dress. Izzy was the comedian of the pair. He would stand up in a crowded speakeasy and announce, "Oh there is bad news, the joint is pinched." The press loved them. Over five years of service, they averaged one thousand arrests a year—and 20 percent of the convictions for the whole New York district. But eventually they were called down to Washington and fired, essentially for violating a cardinal rule of bureaucracy: never upstage your bosses. Their fame eventually translated into successful careers selling insurance.

New York officialdom was openly hostile to Prohibition. At the executive mansion in Albany, Governor Al Smith—a product of the Lower East Side—served liquor at public receptions. In 1923, under Smith, New York was one of the few states to repeal its own Prohibition statute. While the governor decried the law, Mayor Jimmy Walker trampled on it. "Beau James," as he was dubbed by an admiring biographer, was a Tammany stalwart who had been Rothstein's choice in the primary contest against his predecessor Hylan. Walker was the ideal mayor for Prohibition-era New York. He spent most of his nights carousing with his mistresses, rarely arriving at City Hall before noon. He had started out as a Tin Pan Alley song writer, and bandleaders would invariably strike up his only hit, "Will You Love Me in December as You Do in May?" whenever he entered a nightclub. Show business remained his true love, and his mistresses were chorus girls and leading ladies whose professional fortunes sometimes improved as a result of his attentions. Theatrical producers who didn't make room for Jimmy's favorites might be confronted by an army of municipal inspectors citing serious violations and threatening the theater's immediate closure. Sometimes a city work crew would set up in a nearby alley and begin tearing up the pavement with such a roar of jackhammers that you had to be in the first row to hear the music onstage.

Prohibition generated vast sums for bootleggers, greatly strengthening the power of organized crime. But Arnold Rothstein and Johnny Torrio, the men who provided the organizational models that made the gangs successful, both paid a heavy personal price. In November 1928, Rothstein got up from his regular table at Lindy's, handed his pistol to a friend, and said he was "going to meet McManus" at the nearby Park Central Hotel. George McManus was a well-respected and well-connected gambler around Broadway. A few months earlier he had introduced some friends into one of Rothstein's high-stakes card games; they came out over $300,000 ahead. At the time A.R. had cash problems and did not pay up promptly. Under the gambler's code it was McManus's responsibility to see that he did. Time passed and Rothstein's cash was always tied up somewhere. When he took the phone call at Lindy's, he had half a million dollars on the presidential race between Herbert Hoover and New York governor Al Smith. Treating McManus as though he were an insignificant chump was a risky move. Shortly after leaving the restaurant Rothstein was fatally shot in room 349 of the Park Central Hotel. Police found McManus's Chesterfield overcoat in the closet. Two days after Rothstein's death Al Smith lost the presidential race. Though Smith was a Tammany favorite, the unsentimental Rothstein had bet against him. Had he lived he would have won enough money to pay off his debts.

Johnny Torrio remained exiled in Italy recovering from the wounds he received in Chicago until 1928, when Mussolini's threats to put gangsters in cages propelled him to New York. His return coincided with Rothstein's death, and in the vacuum Johnny's managerial talents proved useful. The business of manufacturing, importing, and distributing liquor required elaborate organizational structures, so Torrio became coordinator of a combine of East Coast bootleggers known as the "Big Seven." It included gangs from New England, New York, New Jersey, and Philadelphia. Torrio would not become as prominent as Rothstein; he wanted no part of that notoriety. Instead, he settled into the role of elder statesman, leaving the management tasks to younger men he and Rothstein had tutored. In the 1930s it was these Chicago and New York gangsters who would create a national organized crime syndicate.

7:

The "Get Capone" Drive: Print the Legend

Shortly before his fatal heart attack in April of 1957, Eliot Ness was reviewing the galleys of a book about his youthful exploits as the head of a Prohibition Bureau raiding squad in Chicago. The squad had played a part in the effort to put Al Capone behind bars, but the book gave him a starring role and its title—*The Untouchables*—would pass into the language as a synonym for an honest law enforcement officer. The author, Oscar Fraley, had been inspired to add a few action scenes and hair's-breadth escapes to the story of an investigation that had been heavier on paperwork than derring-do. "Don't get scared if we stray from the facts once in a while," Fraley reassured Ness when he questioned some of these liberties. "We've got to make a real gangbuster out of this thing."

And a gangbuster it was, though Ness wasn't around to enjoy it. The book inspired a popular TV series and later a blockbuster movie. Today Ness, a relatively minor figure, is one of the best-known opponents of twentieth-century organized crime. When truth and legend collide, the saying goes, print the legend.

The more serious piece of hype was committed by all the participants in the "Get Capone" drive and that was to inflate not their own importance but their target's. Ness's glory is rooted in the idea that his nemesis Capone

was one of the towering figures of modern crime—the century's most important gangster. In truth, Capone's effective rule over Chicago's leading gang
lasted just three years, during which he was almost constantly at war with
rivals or the law. After a series of massive blunders culminating in the Valentine's Day Massacre, he was forced to flee Chicago and hide out first in a
Philadelphia jail cell and then at his Florida estate. When he finally returned
to Chicago an avalanche of federal law enforcement descended on him
resulting in an eleven-year prison sentence. Mobsters have since avoided his
kind of brazenness, and the few exceptions—John Gotti comes to mind—
have brought disaster on themselves. The organized crime world was quicker
to absorb the lessons of Capone's downfall than the criminal justice world
was. For fifty years after his conviction and imprisonment American law
enforcement went right on launching drives against big shots while ignoring
their organizations. And one drive after another ended with a chief going off
to prison, a successor stepping in, and business continuing much as before.

The groundwork for what became the "Get Capone" drive was laid long
before Eliot Ness arrived in Chicago. In a sense the effort began even before
Capone himself got there. In August 1917 a journeyman crook named
"Ammunition Eddie" Wheed and three followers killed a pair of Brink's
guards in a payroll robbery at the Winslow Iron Manufacturing plant on the
West Side. For want of a better hideout they repaired to Eddie's mother's
house, where they quickly found themselves besieged by a force of 250
police officers. After three detectives were wounded the police threatened
to dynamite the house, whereupon the suspects promptly surrendered.

Spectacular crimes were not uncommon in Chicago, and Allied soldiers
were dying by the thousands in a world war that the United States had
recently entered, so normally the deaths of two Brink's men would have
been quickly forgotten. The fact that they weren't was due largely to the
efforts of one man, who decided that Chicago had had enough.

Educated as a lawyer, Colonel Henry Barrett Chamberlain had once been
the director of the Municipal Voters League, one of Chicago's many civic
reform groups. He had begun his career in the 1890s as a reporter for
William Jennings Bryan on the *Omaha World Herald*. Around the turn of
the century he came back to Chicago to work as a reporter and editor for the

Hearst papers, acquiring his military title in the Illinois National Guard. A combination investigative journalist and reformer, Chamberlain called on Chicago's business community to fund a permanent group to reduce crime and improve the workings of the criminal justice system. After two years of effort the Chicago Crime Commission was established, with Chamberlain as operating director. He brought to his role a gift for the colorful turn of phrase—he coined the term "public enemy"—and an equally rare ability to fuse hardheaded businessmen and unworldly civic reformers into an effective lobby.

Reform societies did not have a good record in Chicago. Preachy types from the ritzy Near North Side Gold Coast had little rapport with the blue-collar people hauling beef in the stockyards, making steel in South Chicago, switching freight cars in a West Side rail yard, or pounding a typewriter in a Loop office. "Goo-goos," they were called—derisive shorthand for good-government types. Anti-vice societies had been known to produce 400-page reports describing in convoluted language what the whole town already knew. One such study exposed the existence of a luxurious brothel at "X-523, 24 and 24A Dearborn Street." Why the code, when everyone over twelve knew they meant the Everleigh Club? James T. Farrell, author of best-selling novels about life in his South Side Chicago neighborhood between the two world wars, snorted that a sociologist was "a man who spent $50,000 to find a whorehouse." Chamberlain didn't have $50,000 to throw away. Instead he kept the commission visible by a combination of pithy quotes (Capone was "the gorilla of gangland") and the use of crime statistics and court records to highlight the failings of the justice system. With his patient work Chamberlain carved out a place for the commission apart from the ineffectual white-gloved do-gooders.

Until the late 1920s, however, Chamberlain and his commission were no more than a minor annoyance to Chicago's gangsters. Prohibition was supposed to keep the urban masses sober. Instead, it spawned escalating levels of violence as Colosimo was replaced by Torrio who was succeeded by Al Capone, who made his predecessors look benign.

Capone flaunted his power, riding around in a $30,000, five-ton, armor-plated limousine. When he went to the opera or a ball game he would make a grand entrance flanked by a squad of bodyguards. Onlookers craned their necks to see him. A few even cheered, although some Chicagoans were known to complain about being seated too close to him—not because they feared moral contagion but because they didn't want to be in the line of fire. Whether in evening dress or casting a fishing line, he always obliged reporters by posing for pictures.

Capone was not physically attractive: he was burly, often ballooning to 250 pounds, with a bullet-shaped head, a flabby face, thick lips, a flat nose, and—his most noticeable feature by far—long ugly scars on his left cheek, jaw, and neck. "Scarface," his enemies called him, though when they did they were wise to keep their voices down. His followers generally referred to him as the "Big Fella" while intimates were allowed to call him "Snorky," a slang term for a sharp dresser. Where Colosimo would euphemistically advise someone to "Remember the Maine," Capone would bluntly snarl, "Ya keep ya nose clean, ya unnerstan?" He had married his Irish sweetheart in Brooklyn after she gave birth to their child, but also liked to sample the merchandise in his whorehouses. The only hint of taste in Capone's personality was his fondness for jazz, the hotter the better. His favorites were King Oliver, Louis Armstrong, and the bandleader Paul Whiteman's young crooner, Harry Crosby, whom everyone called "Bing." On one occasion, he even sent his limousine to pick up Crosby after his regular show and whisk him out to Cicero to perform at a private mob party.

In the late '20s federal tax agents estimated Capone's annual income at fifty million dollars. As befit a businessman of such wealth and prominence, Capone moved his headquarters from the Four Deuces cabaret to the Metropole Hotel, a block away on Michigan Avenue. Later he moved again, to the nearby Lexington, where he occupied a ten-room suite and his followers took rooms on several floors. Fifty million dollars bought a lot of political clout. It also allowed Capone to keep a small army of hired guns on his payroll. When a man needed protection from some racketeers who were trying to muscle in on his business, the authorities couldn't—or wouldn't—help. He turned to Capone instead, voluntarily making him a partner. "Now," the man told the press, "I have the best protection in town." The galling fact was that he was right.

The new Thompson submachine gun added menace to Capone's reputation. This hand-held weapon capable of firing at a rate of a thousand .45-caliber rounds a minute had been developed for the army by General John Thompson but came too late for the world war. In 1925 it was introduced into the Chicago beer wars. Soon local hoodlums became virtuoso performers on what was known as the "Chopper" or the "Chicago Piano." The "Betsy" of Jim Colosimo's heyday would be replaced by "Tommy" in the era of Capone.

Most of the violence was directed at gangsters. Small armies were mobilized to carry out commando-style raids. Hymie Weiss, now head of the O'Bannion gang, sent a dozen carloads of gunmen into Cicero to rake Capone's local command post with bullets. A couple of people were wounded but Al emerged unscathed. Three weeks later his own shooters returned the compliment, killing Weiss and another man and wounding three of their companions at 4 P.M. outside Holy Name Cathedral. Bugs Moran succeeded Weiss as boss of O'Bannion's old outfit.

Alliances were formed and broken, and periodic summit conferences were held at downtown hotels, usually with police there to keep the peace. When the conferences ended the shooting resumed, and if any of the peacekeepers got in the way, too bad for them. When Capone's favorite killers Scalisi and Anselmi mistook a squad of detectives for some rival gangsters, a gun battle broke out in which two detectives and Mike Genna were killed. Scalisi and Anselmi beat the murder rap by their insistence that they didn't mean to do it and because the Illinois supreme court ruled that to kill a policeman making an unlawful arrest did not constitute murder. Naturally the police found such incidents upsetting and responded in kind. Chief of Detectives William O'Connor organized a special anti-gangster squad equipped with tommy guns. He told them, "Shoot first and shoot to kill. . . . If you meet a car containing bandits, pursue them and fire. When I arrive on the scene, my hopes will be fulfilled if you have shot off the top of their car and killed every criminal inside it."

Capone's gunmen did things that Torrio would never have sanctioned. In 1927 a rival hoodlum named Joey Aiello set up a machine-gun nest in a hotel room overlooking "Hinky Dink" Kenna's Clark Street saloon, where

Capone was known to drop in from time to time. A stoolie told Al, who told the cops, who raided the place and hauled Joey in. Capone wasn't satisfied. In his rage he dispatched half a dozen cabloads of gunmen to surround police headquarters and kill Aiello when he came out. This Chicago police force was the second-largest in America, but for a time all the cops did was gaze out the window while reporters in the pressroom phoned their editors to send photographers. Finally, after an exasperated captain saw three Capone men standing at the front door, one of them openly readying a pistol for action, he shouted to some detectives to follow him and they went outside and arrested the gunmen. Simultaneously, an emergency call was sent out to patrolling squad cars to respond to headquarters and chase the rest of the gang away.

In the spring of 1927 Big Bill Thompson returned as the mayor of Chicago. Reformers despaired, although the more astute ones, including Chamberlain, realized that the worse things got the greater the pressure would be to do something about Capone and his minions. But what could be done? To Chamberlain's group the answer was clear: get the federal government to send in a force of smart, honest lawmen to smash Capone's empire. This would require pressure on Washington from business community leaders, not just a professional reformer like Chamberlain. In 1928 the man who could spearhead such a drive arrived on the scene.

Frank Loesch was a seventy-six-year-old lawyer and church elder given to spouting biblical phrases. Since the 1880s he had maintained a flourishing law practice while also serving as general counsel for the western division of the powerful Pennsylvania Railroad. Railroads still swung a lot of weight, especially in Chicago, America's rail hub. Loesch's connections and his long and distinguished career at the bar gave him credibility in influential circles. In 1928 he was named president of both the city bar association and the crime commission. In the latter position he was Henry Chamberlain's boss, providing the inspirational force and political clout for the organization while Chamberlain kept track of where the bodies were buried.

Their first break came in the Republican primary of that year. Robert Crowe, the Thompson candidate for state's attorney, was opposed by John Swanson, the choice of a faction led by United States senator Charles

Deneen. Al Capone rode to Big Bill's rescue. One of Deneen's strongest supporters was "Diamond Joe" Esposito, the political leader of West Side Sicilians like the Gennas. Al's gunmen shot Esposito dead in front of his own
home. Next, bombs went off at the homes of the senator himself and the
insurgent candidate Swanson. So many exploded that the campaign became
known as "the pineapple primary." On Election Day Deneen workers were
slugged and kidnapped and a black Republican ward leader was pursued
through the streets and filled with lead. Despite the fireworks the Deneen-
ites emerged victorious. News of the carnage was prominently featured in
papers all over the country and a U.S. senator called for President Hoover to
dispatch marines to Chicago. At last the state of Illinois felt impelled to act.
The attorney general appointed a special prosecutor to investigate the mini-
war, and the job fell to Frank Loesch.

He began by asking the county board to pay for lawyers and the police
department to assign detectives. The elected county commissioners were
not interested in probing voting irregularities, so Loesch wound up raising
his funds from private sources. Thompson's police commissioner "Iron
Mike" Hughes assigned, then withdrew, detectives from the investigation.
Loesch responded by hauling the commissioner in front of a grand jury and
threatening to indict him for obstructing justice. The iron flowed out of
Mike's veins and he quickly rescinded the order. Still not trusting him,
Loesch retained as special investigator John Stege, a former chief of detectives who was fired by the Thompson administration at the behest of
mobster Joe Saltis. The lawyer and the cop managed to secure a series of
indictments against powerful West Side political figures, including a judge
and ward boss who were bulwarks of the Thompson machine.

The next step was to keep the November election from being a repeat of
the pineapple primary. Loesch decided to go right to the source, arranging a
meeting with Capone at the Lexington Hotel. The tall, elderly, white-haired
Bible scholar came alone and unarmed; the dark-haired, swarthy young
bruiser was surrounded by gunmen. Loesch held the typical nativist views of
reformers in his time, attributing the crime problem to immigrants from the
wrong part of Europe. He was immediately offended that the bodyguards
spoke to each other in Italian and that Capone's office was decorated with

portraits of American icons George Washington and Abraham Lincoln (as well as Mayor Thompson). After some preliminary small talk during which Capone informed Loesch that he had no fear of the law because he expected to be murdered before the justice system caught up with him, Capone inquired as to what Loesch wanted. The lawyer replied in language not usually heard in church: "Keep your damn cutthroats and hoodlums from interfering with the voting." To Loesch's surprise Capone agreed to help. His conciliatory attitude might have been prompted by the senator's call for marines, or the announcement that hundreds of federal marshals were being assigned to the polls. Or it might simply have been that after the defeat of the Thompsonite slate in the primary Capone had no preference in the general election. Whatever his reasoning, Capone promised to keep his hoodlums leashed on Election Day. He even vowed to use his influence with the police to keep other gangs in check. As a result, the general election was the quietest in memory, and the reform candidate, John Swanson, was victorious in the state attorney's race.

A few weeks later the cases Loesch had brought against the West Side politicians were thrown out. Undeterred, he got Swanson to appoint him as a special prosecutor while a new Thompson administration police commissioner, William Russell, promised to join the drive against Capone. Russell had been a lieutenant in the Levee, a regular at Jim Colosimo's, and a captain in Johnny Torrio's Loop fiefdom. Reporters who remembered him from the old days took his pledge with a grain of salt. Loesch and Chamberlain also realized that promises of cooperation from local officials were likely to have short shelf lives. Loesch decided the time had come to appeal to the highest possible level, incoming president of the United States Herbert Hoover. As it turned out Capone himself provided the issue for the reformers to seize upon just before the president's inauguration.

After Mike Merlo's death, Neapolitan Capone had installed a harmless Sicilian, Tony Lombardo, as president of the Unione Siciliana. Moran's gunmen killed him one afternoon in September 1928, at the busiest intersection in the Loop. Capone responded by replacing him with the equally inoffensive Pasquale "Patsy" Lolordo. In January 1929 Joey Aiello turned up with two of Moran's hitmen, the brothers Pete and Frank Gusenberg, and killed

Lolordo, too. Capone realized that Moran and his allies were never going to give him any peace short of the cemetery. He had been concentrating on killing rival gang leaders, but the Morans contained enough swashbucklers to fill any leadership vacancies. Capone's answer was to take out the whole gang at once. He gave the assignment to Vince Gebardi (DeAmore), who retained the name he had used as a professional boxer, Jack McGurn, and was known to the press as "Machine Gun Jack." A few months earlier Jack had been talking in a phone booth when one of the Gusenbergs opened up on him with a tommy gun. Badly wounded, McGurn was burning for revenge.

He learned from his informants that the Morans frequently assembled at a garage on North Clark Street. McGurn arranged for a stooge to contact Moran with an offer to sell a hijacked truckload of whiskey. As expected, the seller was ordered to deliver it to the Clark Street garage for inspection. When the gang gathered to accept the shipment, McGurn planned to dispatch a crew of gunmen posing as police officers to execute them on the spot. No one has definitively identified all the members of McGurn's crew, though by common consent they included Scalisi, Anselmi, and Fred Burke, formerly a member of the notorious St. Louis gang, Egan's Rats.

The delivery was scheduled for the cold snowy morning of February 14, 1929, a date that would become emblazoned in local memory. For years afterward Chicagoans could recall where they had been when they heard about the Valentine's Day Massacre. Watchers posted in windows overlooking the garage were instructed to make sure the entire gang had assembled before they called for the gunmen. They observed six men enter the place, including the two Gusenbergs and three petty criminals who worked as mechanics, managers, or bookkeepers. One non-gangster showed up as well—a respectable optometrist who enjoyed hanging around with hoodlums and had just dropped by for a cup of coffee. When a seventh man entered, the watchers identified him as Bugs Moran and set their plan in motion. That last arrival was actually another low-level gang member. Moran came along a few minutes later accompanied by Ted Newberry and Willie Marks. As they approached they saw a squad car pull up and two men in police uniform alight. Puzzled, they did an about-face. The phony cops entered the garage and "arrested" the seven men present. Though there were grumbles—and threats to have the cops transferred—all seven submitted. Only the mechanic's German shepherd watchdog, Highball, growled and struggled to break free from his leash. Then two or three men in "plain-clothes" entered, removed machine guns from under their coats, and mowed down the prisoners.

After the killers departed the dog's frantic cries prompted neighbors to peer into the garage, where they saw the seven bodies. By the time the real police arrived, only Frank Gusenberg was still alive. Questioned by a detective who had gone to grammar school with him, Gusenberg refused to identify the shooters and died shortly after arriving at the hospital. Highball was so crazed that the officers debated whether to shoot him. They took him outside and got him to calm down, but the dog had to be put to sleep within a year.

Witnesses who had observed the phony squad car arrive picked McGurn and Scalisi as two of the men who had gone into the garage. But Jack had a perfect alibi—a girl described as the "blond witness" swore he had spent all of Valentine's Day with her doing what lovers are supposed to do on such a romantic occasion. No charges followed—the identifications were weak and McGurn took the precaution of marrying his blonde. As his wife, she could not be made to testify. Capone was wintering in Florida, where he had arranged to be visiting the office of the Miami prosecutor at the time of the massacre in Chicago. Not long afterward Fred Burke went on a robbery spree in Michigan, killing a local police officer. Lab tests determined that two machine guns taken from a house he occupied there had been used to kill the Clark Street victims, and one had been fired in the Yale murder. The Michigan authorities distrusted their Chicago counterparts and refused to extradite Burke, but got him sentenced to life in prison for the killing of the policeman. Scalisi and Anselmi began to put on airs, strutting around and implying that they might be planning a more ambitious move. Capone thereupon threw a banquet at which he beat them both to death with a base-ball bat. Machine Gun Jack McGurn became increasingly unstable and drifted downward in mob ranks. When the badly shaken Moran was asked the usual "Who did it?" he replied, "Only Capone kills like that." The remark is often cited to illustrate how uniquely vicious the Capone mob was, but Moran and the late Hymie Weiss had attempted a similar massacre of Capone's gang in Cicero three years earlier—an attack that, unlike the garage shooting, jeopardized many innocent bystanders.

Uniquely vicious or not, the Valentine's Day Massacre set off a public outcry that posed a problem for all mob bosses. The year before, after Capone's crew had chased Frankie Yale's car across Brooklyn, machine guns blazing, Frank Costello had expressed the consensus view of the eastern bosses: "If effin' Capone wanted to kill Yale, why didn't he just do it instead of making such a big effin' deal about it." Johnny Torrio persuaded the eastern leaders to summon Capone to a conference that the Big Seven bootlegging combine was about to hold in Atlantic City. When the meeting ended Capone departed for nearby Philadelphia. Within two hours of his arrival a pair of sharp-eyed local detectives spotted him and his bodyguard carrying guns and arrested them. It seemed Al had forgotten that the big boss is not supposed to pack a gun. Philadelphia was just as corrupt as any other mob-infested city, but on this occasion its law enforcement machinery moved surprisingly swiftly. Capone was immediately arraigned in court. Normally, a platoon of lawyers would have appeared, gotten their client released on bond, and dragged out the proceedings for a couple of years until the case could be fixed. Capone and his bodyguard pleaded guilty and were quickly sentenced to a year in jail. They began serving their time a mere sixteen hours after setting foot in the City of Brotherly Love. The only sour note in the story was the subsequent disclosure that the two Philadelphia detectives had previously been Capone's guests at his Florida estate. It was all a setup. The Atlantic City conclave had ordered Al to drop out of sight for a while, implying that if he did not they would arrange a more long-term departure. A friendly Philadelphia jail cell out of the reach of Chicago investigators was the perfect answer.

The New York bosses had been right to be fearful. The massacre had given Loesch the opening he needed. In March 1929 he assembled a group of prominent Chicagoans, including the publisher of the *Daily News,* to join him at a meeting with President Hoover where they made a collective appeal for an all-out drive against Capone. Hoover promised his support. Doubtless Hoover consulted with the man he always turned to in such matters, former Secret Service agent Larry Richey, who had been his principal aide since the world war. The crackdown was shrewd politics. The reputation of the whole country, not just Chicago, was at stake: Capone and his gunmen had become worldwide symbols of American lawlessness.

In the course of the ensuing investigation, Loesch would enlist half a dozen of Chicago's most powerful citizens, including utilities magnate Samuel Insull and Sears Roebuck chieftain Julius Rosenwald, into a shadowy organization dubbed by newsmen the "Secret Six." The Crime Commission and the Secret Six provided financial and political support to the Feds. The president had assigned the task of getting Capone to Treasury Secretary Andrew Mellon, who delegated the matter to Elmer Irey, his chief of Treasury intelligence. Formed in 1919, the Treasury intelligence unit had at first been used to police other employees of the Department of Treasury itself. Gradually the unit had begun to go after tax evaders. In 1927 when the Supreme Court rejected the contention of a South Carolina moonshiner that he could not be prosecuted for failing to pay taxes from an illegal business, a potent weapon was made available to attack organized crime.

President Coolidge had already authorized the intelligence unit to investigate the taxes of Chicago gangsters. Coolidge had also taken the step of naming an upstanding lawyer, George Q. Johnson, as the local U.S. attorney in Chicago. Not until Hoover gave his "Get Capone" order, though, did the drive really get under way. Mellon told Irey to give the case top priority. Whenever he went to the White House to toss a medicine ball with Hoover and his inner circle, Mellon explained, the president would ask, "Have you got that fellow Capone yet?" The shrewd, Washington-born Irey, who had become head of intelligence after long service as a postal inspector, believed there must be more than a sense of public duty accounting for the presidential interest in a bunch of Chicago gangsters. According to a rumor circulating around law enforcement circles, Hoover's anger had been piqued when Capone upstaged the president-elect at a Florida hotel. In his memoirs, Irey claimed that the story turned out to be false; he may not have cared very much about its truthfulness when he passed it along to his underlings. As any good law enforcement commander knows, nothing is calculated to make cops work harder on a case than their belief that the top brass have taken a personal interest in it.

Chamberlain, Loesch, Irey—all three played more pivotal parts in Capone's eventual defeat than Eliot Ness did. So did Frank Wilson, who was named to head the squad that Irey sent to Chicago. Wilson had hoped to follow his policeman father into law enforcement, but his eyesight was so bad he had been discharged from the wartime army as a menace on the rifle range. Treasury intelligence was not originally seen as a gun-toting outfit. Mostly the work entailed long hours poring over ledgers, preparing civil and criminal cases against tax evaders. When it came time to bring charges, the target of an investigation would usually come in with his lawyers and quietly surrender. Revolvers didn't become necessary until the unit began going after gangsters. Even then, Wilson usually left his weapon in a drawer at work. (Some of his colleagues suggested that the cheap smelly "ropes" he smoked were a guarantee that no one would come near him.) In Chicago Wilson and his team utilized their usual methods, developing informers, tapping phones, seizing books, and looking for weak points in Capone's empire. Lawyer and dog track operator Edward O'Hare—a business associate of the Capone gang—secretly gave information to the investigators.[1] Irey was also able to insert an undercover treasury agent, Mike Malone, into Capone's outer circle. Malone was an Irishman who looked Italian. To prepare for his assignment in Chicago he spent some time in Philadelphia with mob boss Boo Boo Hoff, developing a plausible history as a Philadelphia criminal. When he checked into the Lexington Hotel as Mike Lepito he aroused curiosity among some of Capone's followers, but like a good hoodlum he remained closed-mouthed when asked about himself. "Keeping quiet," Malone replied to a gangster who had inquired about his line of business. Later he became friendlier, admitting to being wanted back east

---

[1] His reasons remain unclear, though it has been speculated that he feared his association with Capone would stand in the way of his teenage son's ambition to be appointed to Annapolis. In World War II, the son, Edward "Butch" O'Hare, U.S. Naval Academy Class of '37, received a posthumous Congressional Medal of Honor for his exploits as a pilot in the Pacific. Chicago's principal airport, O'Hare Field, is named for him.

and dropping the names of some Philadelphia references. As expected, his room was searched and his contacts in Philadelphia checked. The Wanamaker department store labels in his suits and the previously alerted references gave him a clean bill of health.

The Secret Six decided they needed their own detectives and convinced Alexander Jamie, chief special investigator for the Chicago office of the Prohibition Bureau, to become their chief investigator. The Justice Department wanted a hand in the Capone investigation as well, and U.S. attorney George Q. Johnson took advantage of the Prohibition Bureau's 1930 transfer from Treasury to Justice to form a special ten-man squad of honest, hand-picked dry agents who would work directly for him. In his search for a man to head it, it was natural for Johnson to consult Jamie, since the Secret Six were financing much of the investigation and had clout at the White House. Jamie recommended his brother-in-law, a Prohibition agent named Eliot Ness.

Early accounts of the "Get Capone" drive deal almost exclusively with the tax investigation led by Irey and Wilson. It is rare to find even a mention of Ness in books about Prohibition-era Chicago by people who lived at the time, though his name does appear in old news clippings (it was a local reporter who coined the name "Untouchables" to describe the squad). Ness himself recalled his work as part of a two-pronged strategy: Treasury to investigate tax evasion and Justice to attack the booze racket, cutting off mob revenues and securing evidence to back up charges under the Volstead Act. The Prohibition Bureau had been raiding breweries and speakeasies for years, but the bootlegging business still flourished, and mob lawyers had become skilled in the art of concealing who really owned any particular joint. "We couldn't get enough evidence to convict Capone of bootlegging before a jury composed of my own nieces and nephews," Elmer Irey once said, explaining the focus on Capone's taxes.

Ness's contribution was to lead his team in a series of spectacular raids on breweries and drinking spots. Before departing on a mission, he would invariably tip off reporters and photographers. In addition to a penchant for publicity, he possessed an accurate sense of his own limitations and needs. Thus Ness chose to ally himself with a Chicago police detective chief,

William Schoemaker, who was both knowledgeable and straight. "Old Shoes," as he was known, was respected by gangsters because he was not on the take. Old-time Chicago detectives would recall the night when he dropped in unannounced at a mob dinner party, causing a score of guns to be dumped on the floor with a deafening clatter. Eyeing the assembled group, he paused, then muttered, "A fine congregation this is," and turned on his heel, leaving them to utter a collective sigh of relief. He kept Ness informed and lent help when necessary. Ness's memoirs present a picture of considerable gunplay, with foiled assassination attempts on him and his men, and hoodlums routed by judo chops, straight rights, and blazing machine guns. When the TV series about their work appeared, some of the surviving Untouchables protested that it had never been like that. But in their own memoirs Irey and Wilson also recalled assassination attempts and *mano a mano* encounters with the bad guys. None of the recollections are fully reliable, but they all capture an undeniable truth: Prohibition-era Chicago was a place where a lawman could easily get killed.

Law-abiding Chicagoans' fear of the Capone gang mounted when *Tribune* reporter Alfred "Jake" Lingle was shot dead at high noon while walking in the Loop in June 1930. At first it was believed he had been hit for writing about "Scarface." A gun dropped at the scene was eventually traced to the same dealer who had supplied the weaponry for the Valentine's Day Massacre. Yet according to his records, it had been purchased by Ted Newberry, boss of the Moran gang survivors. Meanwhile, questions about the victim began to pile up. Lingle had earned $65 a week, yet he had lived like a millionaire, maintaining a chauffeur and limousine and, in addition to his in-town residence, a vacation bungalow on the Indiana lakefront and a permanent room at the Sherman Hotel. Lingle had attributed his good fortune to a $50,000 inheritance from his father, but probate records proved that story false. An old Levee beat newsman and a friend of Jim Colosimo's, Lingle was actually a business partner of Police Commissioner Bill Russell. A few months before his death, he had lost $85,000 in the stock market crash, while Russell was rumored to have dropped $250,000. These revelations caused the commissioner to lose his job. When all the facts became known, officials and press alike backed away from the case. Eventually a

St. Louis Egan's Rat, Leo Brothers, was convicted of the crime but given a sentence of just fourteen years.

After his release from the Philadelphia jail and a sojourn in Florida, Capone returned to Chicago in the fall of 1930 to find the drive against him going full blast. Chamberlain had taken to drawing up lists of public enemies with the names of McErlane, Moran, and the O'Donnell clans. Capone was designated "Public Enemy No. 1." Loesch and Chamberlain persuaded a Chicago judge, John Lyle, to issue vagrancy warrants for the people on Chamberlain's lists. As a young man, Lyle had been a researcher for Chamberlain at the Municipal Voters League, and Loesch had been one of his law school professors. A former alderman, Lyle was an anti-Thompson Republican with mayoral ambitions of his own, and not averse to publicity. A Chicago detective swore under oath that the various hoodlums were "idle and dissolute," and the warrants were given to him for service. As a legal strategy it was not likely to lead to criminal convictions. If the vagrancy statutes were applied to anyone who was idle and dissolute, though not without money, a good many society folks would have been in Joliet Prison. The public enemy campaign did cause several hoodlums to leave town, however. More important, the name caught on, and time has shown that once a man becomes known as a public enemy, he is halfway to prison. That fall, as Capone and Jack McGurn were leaving a Northwestern University football game, four hundred booing students followed them to the exit.

While publicity helped, the real case against Capone was being made by the Feds. The income tax laws were still relatively new and no large body of cases had accumulated. Questioned by federal agents, Capone's attorneys conceded that he received substantial unreported income—even that he had never filed a return—and offered to settle his arrears. It was a damning admission. And there was more: a few years earlier, a group of irate citizens had set fire to a Capone gambling joint in Cicero and Al himself had shown up at the scene demanding entrance. "I own this place," he had loudly announced. Now the government had possession of the establishment's books and witnesses who remembered those words. In March 1931 Capone was indicted on tax evasion charges and 5,000 separate Volstead Act violations based on the raids conducted by Ness and his men.

Some government lawyers doubted that the tax case would stand up, and the Justice Department agreed to a plea bargain whereby Capone would get two and a half years in jail. It was a sentence Al could do standing on his head. But the deal was coldly rejected by Judge James Wilkerson. No one could bargain with justice in his courtroom, the judge declared. Capone was unconcerned. His underlings had bribed some of the potential jurors. But Treasury undercover agent Mike Malone got wind of this and alerted his superiors. When Judge Wilkerson was informed, he switched jury panels with another judge, set aside the bootlegging charges as so much eyewash, and moved ahead with the tax trial. The four assistant U.S. attorneys assigned to handle the case had plenty of evidence by now. Ed O'Hare had led them to a Capone bookkeeper whose records and testimony showed that Capone had earned a huge unreported sum of money. In contrast, the defense was poorly handled. As the centerpiece of their case, Capone's attorneys argued that his income was not as great as some witnesses claimed because he had lost a lot of money at the racetrack. One bookie took the stand to testify about a $60,000 loss that Capone had supposedly incurred in a single year. How could he be so sure of the amount? "My ledger showed that at the end of the season," the bookie told a very skeptical assistant U.S. attorney, Dwight Green, who then reminded him of previous testimony in which he had claimed he didn't keep any books. Capone was found guilty and sentenced to eleven years in prison. Tax convictions were also secured against his top lieutenant Frank Nitti (Nitto) and his financial wizard Jake Guzik, though they received shorter terms.

In May 1932 Capone was escorted to the Dearborn Street railroad station by U.S. marshals, federal agents, and fifteen carloads of Chicago police to begin the journey to the Atlanta penitentiary. In 1934 Capone was shipped back across the country to be among the very first inmates of a freshly opened maximum-security prison set on a bleak island in San Francisco Bay. Supposedly escape-proof, it was called Alcatraz.

Over the years, Capone would slowly lose his mind from the effects of venereal disease. Many of the reformers who helped put him in prison did not fare very well, either. The financial backers of the Crime Commission/ Secret Six found themselves in reduced straits or worse. The Crime Commission barely managed to keep its doors open and the reformers fell out among themselves. State attorney Swanson attacked the Secret Six for its use of shady private detectives, including one who was running a blackmail operation. Jamie accused Swanson's men of trying to wiretap him.

Many people have been credited with his downfall, but the man most responsible was Capone himself. His profile was too high, his methods too wantonly violent. The city was fed up with him. The business community also had a practical motive for taking action. Chicago was going to hold a World's Fair in 1933. Ostensibly scheduled to celebrate the hundredth anniversary of the city's incorporation, the fair was meant to provide a Depression-strapped town with a needed boost of morale and money. It wouldn't fulfill either aim if newspapers around the world kept reporting on Capone and his escapades.

In the end, Capone's removal from the scene amounted to no more than early retirement. Indeed, the government probably saved his life from lieutenants who recognized his shortcomings and were getting ready to take him out. When Frank Nitti came out of prison in 1932, the other gang leaders chose him to be Al's successor—supposedly a temporary appointment, although they all knew the big fella would never come back. The Sicilian-born Nitti had done some of the rough work for Capone, earning him the nickname "The Enforcer," but he was ten years older than Al and a much quieter sort. He moved into the executive suite in the Lexington Hotel and ran things in a low-key collegial fashion, holding the killings to a minimum.

Unfortunately for the mob in 1931 Mayor Thompson was defeated for reelection by Democratic party boss Tony Cermak. "Saving Tony" was known for his budget-slashing skills and looked like an ideal Depression mayor. One of his first moves was to cut police and fire salaries by 15 percent. As Thompson pointed out, though, when Tony had been president of the county board he had managed to save a $2 million fortune on an annual salary of $10,000. Nitti was unable to reach an agreement with Cermak, who preferred to deal with Ted Newberry, the latest head of the Moran gang. In

December 1932 a detective working for the mayor went to Nitti's office and shot and wounded him. His police partners pointed out that Nitti had offered no resistance, so the detective shot himself in the hand to make it look like self-defense. The other cops refused to go along with the story and the officer was fired. Rumor had it that Newberry had put a bounty on Nitti—a theory that gained plausibility three weeks later when Newberry himself was murdered by Nitti gunmen. The following month Mayor Cermak was shot in Florida while conversing with President-elect Franklin D. Roosevelt. He died after three weeks. Just nine days afterward the assassin, Giuseppe Zangara, was electrocuted. According to the accepted explanation, Zangara was a demented man who hated all rulers. But both Frank Loesch and Judge Lyle believed he had been recruited by the Capone gang. Cermak was known as an enemy of the mob and his killer had been put to death with breathtaking haste. Certainly, such a murder with such a denouement would have inspired ten books and half a dozen investigating committees if it had all happened a generation later.[2]

Cermak's departure, like Capone's, made for a smoother relationship between City Hall and the mob. The new mayor, Ed Kelly, was the operating head of the Metropolitan Sanitary District, a self-taught engineer. Under Kelly's stewardship the district's administration was anything but sanitary. Shortly after he assumed the mayoralty, it was revealed that Kelly owed $106,000 in federal tax penalties for unreported income earned while working at his previous job. Nitti found it much easier to do business under Kelly's administration.

Frank Loesch remained head of the Crime Commission until 1937 when, at age eighty-five, he retired. Henry Barrett Chamberlain stepped down as operating director in 1942. U.S. attorney George Johnson was given an interim appointment to the federal bench, but Roosevelt's incoming Democratic administration refused to recommend him for confirmation. Nor did it approve Judge Wilkerson's promotion to the federal circuit. Others fared better. In 1940, former assistant U.S. attorney Dwight Green was elected

---

[2]For the next generation, virtually everyone in Chicago believed the mob had set Cermak up.

governor of Illinois. Elmer Irey and Frank Wilson, respectively, became coordinator of all Treasury law enforcement and chief of the United States Secret Service. All, though, are largely forgotten. Only Eliot Ness's name is instantly recognized seventy years later. And his fate is the most poignant.

When Prohibition was repealed Ness was assigned to the Treasury's Alcohol and Tobacco Unit in Cincinnati, chasing moonshiners in the Kentucky hills. After a transfer to Cleveland, he became the head of a four-man office, and in 1935 his fortunes took an upturn. Only thirty-two years of age, he was selected by the city's Republican mayor, Harold Hitz Burton, to oversee the police and fire departments of America's seventh-largest city. As Cleveland's safety director, Ness cleaned up a corrupt police department and soon became one of the most popular figures in town. But he was less successful at solving a series of murders committed by the "Mad Butcher of Willow Run" who, between 1934 and 1936, cut off two dozen people's heads. Nor did he smash organized crime. In the 1930s, both Italian and Jewish Cleveland mobs were among the strongest in the country.

In Cleveland, Ness divorced his first wife and married a local artist. One night, after they had left a party together, his car skidded on a snowy street, striking another vehicle. Ness left the scene without identifying himself, though his license plate "EN1" was not hard to trace. A new mayor debated whether to dismiss him, and Ness found a face-saving reason to leave. America had just entered World War II and he resigned to become head of a federal team charged with cleaning up prostitution around military bases. The job gave him entree into Washington, D.C., social circles. Perhaps too much entree, because he soon divorced his second wife and married a third. At the end of the war, he obtained a well-paid job in the import-export business in New York City. In 1947, he answered a call from Cleveland Republicans to return to the city and run for mayor. He came over poorly on the stump, losing by a two-to-one margin. Not long afterward, his New York business folded. For the next ten years, he struggled to support his family while his health deteriorated. By 1956, he was living in the Allegheny Mountain hamlet of Coudersport, Pennsylvania, with his wife and eleven-year-old son. From time to time, he would reminisce about battling against Capone or cleaning up the Cleveland police force. Listening to a man with a lined face, slouched shoulders, a noticeable paunch, and a soft voice, the locals tended to be skeptical. He was in debt and his prospects were grim. His only money-making prospect was a book that a New York sportswriter was preparing about the Chicago days. In April 1957, shortly after Ness okayed the final galleys, he dropped dead at age fifty-four. Had he lived, he would have been both rich and able to enjoy the fame that came to him.

The man to whom Ness's name would be forever linked also died young. Released from Alcatraz in 1939, Capone settled down on his Florida estate. By then his mind was too far gone to pose any threat to law enforcement, or to his former associates in Chicago. After his death in 1947 at age forty-eight, his body was returned to Chicago for a quiet burial. Half a century later he remains a legend, though his reign had been relatively short and beset by troubles. Any objective evaluation of the man as a gang leader would judge him an example of what not to do.

8:

Lucky: The Rise and Rise of Charlie Luciano

According to Charlie Luciano, he was standing on a Midtown Manhattan street at six o'clock one October night in 1929 when three men with guns jumped out of a curtained limousine and forced him to get in. They sealed his lips with tape and drove him out to a deserted beach on Staten Island where they hung him by his thumbs from a tree, cut him with a razor blade, burned the soles of his feet, and beat him with their fists, feet, and gun butts until he passed out. He woke up around 2 A.M. to the sound of waves lapping on the shore. Managing to tear off the tape, Luciano staggered a mile until a policeman stopped him. Charlie offered the cop $50 to call him a taxi. Instead he was taken to a local hospital. When detectives questioned him later Luciano clammed up, saying he didn't know who kidnapped him and he would "attend to this thing myself."

Luciano's story raised eyebrows—not many people survived being "taken for a ride." His friends had already started calling him "Lucky," and this incident seemed to confirm it. The legend of Lucky Luciano was born. Everywhere he went his scars and permanently drooping left eyelid reminded people of his miraculous escape. It also made the slight, youthful-looking gangster appear more menacing. Among Italians, he acquired the same reputation as his boss, Joe Masseria: a man who could not be killed.

Lucky insisted that the reason he had been abducted and tortured was to get him to abandon his allegiance to Masseria. Of course, there were skeptics. Frank Costello always maintained it was a police strong-arm squad that picked up Luciano, working him over to find out where Legs Diamond was hiding. Cops, who knew the gangster well, speculated that the affair probably had something to do with his narcotics dealing. Whatever the truth, the legend invested him with a mythic quality. Lucky seemed fated to rise to the top.

Luciano was born Salvatore Lucania in Sicily in 1897. Either surname lent itself to the nickname Luc or Lucky. In 1907 his family emigrated to New York City, settling in a mixed Italian-Jewish neighborhood around First Avenue south of Fourteenth Street in the Lower East Side slums. He didn't like being called Sally and dropped Salvatore for Charlie. After spending a few months in a special facility for chronic truants, he dropped out of school at fourteen to go to work as a shipping boy in a hat factory earning seven dollars a week. According to him it was a job for a "crumb," a stiff who labored all his life with nothing to show for it. He quit, began hanging around poolrooms down on Mulberry Street, and soon was a member of the Five Points gang. In nearby Chinatown he was introduced to opium and liked it because "it did funny things to my head." He became a drug pusher and was arrested ánd sentenced to six months in a reformatory when he was eighteen. A short jail term could be a plus for a rising young gangster. It built character and provided higher education in crime. After his release he went back to the streets as a small-time dealer and petty criminal. In 1923 federal agents caught him in the act of delivering cocaine and opium to one of their informants. The Atlanta penitentiary beckoned, but Luciano traded up and led agents to a trunk full of heroin in a flat on Mulberry Street. Because Lucky talked, he walked. To save face, he told his hoodlum pals that a confederate had planted the trunk after he was in custody so that he could pretend to the Feds that he was cooperating.

Bootlegging and drugs brought Lucky into contact with one of his heroes, Arnold Rothstein. According to Rothstein's biographer, Lucky and Waxey Gordon convinced "The Brain" to enter the drug business. In turn, Rothstein taught Lucky management skills as well as a few social graces. When he advised him to get a genteel tailor and stop dressing like a Lower East Side hoodlum, Lucky indignantly replied, "What do you mean? My tailor is a Catholic." Under Rothstein's tutelage, the small-time punk decked out in garish purple shirts, white suits, and broad-brimmed hats was transformed into a Broadway fashion plate. The Rothstein milieu of guys and dolls appealed to Charlie, especially the dolls. He always seemed to have a beauty on his arm. The one thing he never mastered was speech—throughout his life he spoke in a raspy Lower East Side voice, with a slight trace of Sicilian. Even in polite company words like "broads" and "them guys" slipped from his lips. When a prosecutor asked him why he was carrying a shotgun in his car, he explained he was going hunting, "to shoot peasants."

To Rothstein and other mobsters Luciano was just a hired hand. So in 1927 when Joe the Boss asked him to be his top lieutenant in charge of Lower Manhattan operations, Lucky jumped at the chance. Masseria had moved to a swank penthouse in the West 80s overlooking Central Park where he threw lavish opium parties and posed as a retired gentleman. The growth of his empire left him with little time to personally supervise his old downtown stomping grounds. Luciano was tough, smart, and knew the territory. The bootlegging business compelled Italians to forge alliances outside their own community and Lucky got along well with up-and-coming Jewish hoodlums like Meyer Lansky (Suchowljansky) and Ben "Bugsy" Siegel. Auto theft was their entree to the big time: Siegel stole them and Lansky fixed them up for resale. From there it was a short step to trucking booze. Luciano was less trusting of the Irish, perhaps because so many he encountered were cops or criminal justice officials.

In choosing his new lieutenant, Masseria had to consider the possibility that Luciano might decide to move up by sending Masseria into early retirement, gangland-style. It was unlikely to happen anytime soon—the Boss controlled too many guns and had too many political connections—so Masseria took the risk. Luciano established his headquarters in Celano's restaurant at Kenmare and Mulberry Streets, near police headquarters. He formed a close alliance with a politician named Al Marinelli, who ran a garage across the street. Masseria stopped by regularly to keep an eye on things and remind people he was still the boss. As befit his new position,

Lucky moved into an expensive furnished apartment in the exclusive Murray Hill area and acquired a fleet of sleek black cars.

Around this time the man who would become Masseria's chief rival appeared on the New York scene—Salvatore Maranzano, a genuine Sicilian Mafia capo from Castellammare del Golfo on the northwest coast. He was part of the 1920s influx of mafiosi in flight from Mussolini's crackdown. Maranzano had a gravitas and an innate charm that made him the natural leader of the younger Sicilians who had fled to New York. These included Joe Bonanno, also from Castellammare; Gaetano "Tommy" Lucchese and Carlo Gambino from Palermo; and Joe Profaci from Villabate, east of Palermo. The first thing they noticed about Maranzano was his physical appearance. He was tall for a Sicilian and powerfully built, giving the impression that he could snap a man's neck with his fingers. But his greatest asset was his voice. According to Bonanno it was clear and pleasant with an "echo-like" quality. A former seminarian who spoke five languages and could quote the Latin poets, he held audiences in rapt attention. In New York he began producing false documents enabling more of his countrymen to enter the United States illegally, which paid well and supplied him with a growing body of retainers. With their support he planned to become *capo di tutti capi*—"boss of bosses" over all Italian criminals in the city and the czar of organized crime in general.

It was an impossible dream. In American cities various gangs had leaders, but there was no single overlord. Even the Italian mobs had no *capo di capi*. At the height of his power, Capone was competing with the Moran gang as well as Joey Aiello's Sicilian group. Masseria's hold over Ciro Terranova was tenuous and his relationship with Frankie Yale and his successors in Brooklyn was more of an alliance than a superior-subordinate one. Even Rothstein was not omnipotent, but his brains and status had guided the organized crime alliance, and with his death in 1928 the old system was ripe for an overhaul.

December 7, 1929, a date that would live in New York gangland infamy, was the day things began to change. That night the Tepecanoe Democratic Club held a testimonial dinner at the Roman Gardens up in the Bronx to honor its favorite son, city magistrate Albert Vitale. Ciro Terranova was the host of the affair and the attendees included a squad of his thugs. Also present were politicians, city employees, and a half-dozen of Vitale's fellow magistrates. The audience was enjoying a comedian's routine when seven masked gunmen burst in and started to relieve the guests of their money and jewelry and, in the case of a city detective and two court officers, their service weapons. Terranova made an appeal for ethnic solidarity, saying, "We are all *paisans,* here." It didn't work. When the uninvited guests departed Ciro opined they must have been "some boys from downtown around Kenmare Street," meaning Celano's restaurant, where Masseria and Luciano held court. Vitale told the city detective who had surrendered his piece to hold off making a report of the crime. Within three hours the officer's gun was returned to him. Word of the incident quickly leaked out and newspapers began to ask why cops and judges were socializing with gangsters. A former judge of the state's highest court, the patrician Samuel Seabury, was appointed to conduct an investigation. His probing disclosed some financial dealings between Vitale and Arnold Rothstein, and soon Vitale was a judge no more.

Everyone had a theory about the Tepecanoe holdup. A police inspector reported that one of the guests was a Chicago hitman and the whole affair had been staged to relieve him of a written contract in which Terranova had promised to pay $10,000 for Frankie Yale's murder. It was a dubious notion, since gangsters weren't in the habit of putting their names to written contracts. Besides, the murder was seventeen months old and the perpetrators, who had gone on to carry out the Valentine's Day Massacre, were now either dead or in hiding. The heistmen were not freelance amateurs—if so, they would have been hunted down and killed. Obviously some mob boss had sent them to embarrass Terranova and his supporters, making sure the press was informed. A showdown between Masseria and Maranzano was imminent, and putting heat on Terranova's group would reduce their effectiveness in the coming struggle. Nominally, Terranova was a Masseria ally, but his remark about guys from Mulberry Street implied that he thought they were Joe's men.

It is often enlightening to ask who benefits from a particular action. Lucky Luciano had already picked the eventual winner in the coming struggle—himself. Neither of the rival bosses appealed to the American-raised young gangster. Maranzano struck Lucky as pretentious, striding through Italian neighborhoods "bestowing blessings on the faithful like he was the Pope." In contrast, Joe the Boss was "first cousin to a pig." Watching the chief eat was always a trial for Lucky. Joe Bonanno likened Masseria at dinner to "a drooling mastiff."

The shooting started two months after the Tepecanoe affair. Masseria had his gunmen kill Guy Reina, one of his own sub-bosses, who he believed was about to defect. Masseria named a new leader but the Reina loyalists killed him. Around the same time Maranzano's men began hitting Masseria gangsters. During the conflict Maranzano cut a dashing figure, racing around in a limousine with a machine gun between his knees and two pistols and a knife tucked inside his coat. In contrast, Masseria tended to hide out as much as possible. At the height of the war, Luciano entered into discussions with the other side. When word got back to Masseria he approached Frankie Yale's successor, Joe Adonis, about eliminating Luciano. Lucky had already established a relationship with the Brooklyn gang and Adonis alerted him. In April, Lucky and Masseria drove out to Coney Island for lunch at one of the Boss's favorite restaurants, the Nuova Villa Tammaro. Masseria scarfed down a huge meal while Lucky tried to look away, perhaps comforted by the thought that it was the Boss's last supper. After eating the two men hung around to play cards until they were the only ones left in the place. Around 3:30, Lucky got up and excused himself to go to the men's room. Adonis, Bugsy Siegel, and two rising young hoodlums named Vito Genovese and Albert Anastasia burst in and began firing away. Masseria was hit five times and died quickly. Outside in the getaway car, Ciro Terranova became so flustered that he couldn't start the ignition and Siegel had to take over the wheel. The cops arrived to find Masseria still clutching the ace of diamonds and Lucky moaning, "Why would anyone want to kill poor Joe?"[1]

---

[1]Though the story of Lucky's reaction has been widely repeated, the newspaper reports failed to mention his presence. Some veteran reporters have claimed one of their number posed Masseria's body with the cards in order to make a compelling photo. Certainly it would not have been out of line with journalistic practices of the day. As late as the 1950s, some reporters were known to drop matchbooks from mob joints at the scene of gangland murders, pointing them out to detectives. The reporter could then file a story saying the cops had found a link between the victim and some organized crime figure. If the reporters didn't pull the stunt too often, the detectives usually went along with it.

The murder was followed by several meetings of Italian gang leaders. Maranzano proclaimed himself boss of bosses and parceled out fiefdoms; Luciano was given Masseria's downtown operations. The arrangements were confirmed with a three-day luncheon at the Nuova Villa Tammaro, attended by gang leaders from as far away as Chicago. Maranzano graciously accepted their cash tributes. He also quickly ascertained that a cabal of young gangsters under Luciano's leadership—including Adonis, Costello, Anastasia, and Genovese—was plotting to make his reign a short one. So he cast about for new allies. A baby-faced Irish hoodlum named Vince Coll had acquired a reputation as a ruthless and reckless killer, earning him the nickname "Mad Dog." The "Dog" was then in the midst of a war with one of his employers, "Dutch" Schultz (né Arthur Flegenheimer). Schultz was equally as crazy as Coll and had offered detectives at a Bronx police station $40,000 and a nice home in the suburbs for Mad Dog's murder. After Schultz's gunmen killed Coll's brother he had truly gone mad, attacking one of Dutch's joints in East Harlem in July 1931. The shots went wild: a five-year-old boy was killed and three other children wounded. Maranzano decided Coll was the man for the job of killing Luciano.

According to one account, Maranzano invited Lucky for a meeting at his Midtown office on September 10, 1931, where it was arranged that Vince Coll would murder him. It doesn't make much sense—Luciano was too smart to walk into an ambush. Actually, Maranzano had invited Coll to drop by to firm up plans for the hit. Coincidentally, Lucky planned his own attack on Maranzano for the same day, cleverly arranging it so that suspicion would be drawn away from him. A few weeks earlier he had been approached by some garment manufacturers seeking to enlist his services in fighting off Jewish racketeers led by Louis "Lepke" Buchalter and Jake "Gurrah" Shapiro. Luciano had no intention of going to war against the Jewish gangsters; instead he formed an alliance with them. He passed the supplicants on to Maranzano, figuring a strike against Lepke and Gurrah by the so-called capo di capi would cement his own alliance with them.

On September 10 Maranzano was working in his office, supplying half a dozen Italians with false IDs, when suddenly four "federal agents" arrived. Raids by the U.S. Immigration Service and other agencies were not uncommon and Maranzano invited them into his inner sanctum, expecting to pay them off. They turned out to be Jewish gunmen hired by Meyer Lansky, and when Maranzano realized their intent he began to raise a ruckus. The killers had planned to use knives—a Midtown office on a weekday was not a good place to start shooting—but the rugged old country capo put up such a fight that they had to shoot as well as stab him. As they were running away they bumped into Vince Coll and shouted that cops would be coming. Fleeing through nearby Grand Central Station, one of the gang managed to drop his gun in a commuter's coat pocket.

The scenario bore a strong resemblance to the Tepecanoe robbery in that someone arranged for third parties to do the dirty work so that he could pretend not to be involved. This time, everybody knew the someone was Charlie Lucky. Maranzano's death ended the so-called Castellammarese War. In a bid to win sympathy from his countrymen, Maranzano had claimed that Masseria had decreed a war of extermination against all Castellammare men, but it was essentially a power struggle among Italian gangsters.

Another war story is that after Maranzano's death, there was a purge of old-country "Mustache Petes" in which thirty to ninety Italian men across the United States were murdered within a 24- to 48-hour period by younger, more Americanized gangsters, an event that became known as the "Sicilian Vespers." The dubious notion of a mass purge is one of the foundations of the story of the American Mafia. Yet researchers who have scoured crime reports in American cities for the months following September 10, 1931, can only identify four or five victims whose deaths might have been related to the conflict in New York. As Lucky Luciano used to say, "Give me the names."

The first version of the story was provided by Richard "Dixie" Davis, once a lawyer for Dutch Schultz, and in 1940, at the time of his "revelations," disbarred and a convicted criminal. According to him, ninety men were killed nationwide (though a careful reading of Davis's account reveals that he was only relating what he had heard, not what he knew). A decade later Brooklyn assistant district attorney Burton Turkus repeated the story, dropping the number killed to "between 30 and 40." The account achieved widespread recognition when it was supposedly confirmed in 1963 Senate testimony by Joe Valachi, a low-level member of a New York mob family.

Most later accounts base their assertions on Valachi. Yet when questioned by the Senate, he could only cite four or five murders.[2]

At the time of his testimony, Valachi was a federal prisoner serving a life sentence. Nearing sixty, his only hope of release or transfer was making himself valuable to his captors. The Neapolitan Valachi had been recruited by Maranzano's men when they needed more guns during the war with Masseria. Though never anything but a minor figure in mobdom, he provided the Senate with a number of observations on how the Sicilian gangs were organized and operated, including supposedly inside accounts of top-level decision making. As Joe Bonanno observed, it was like a "New Guinea native who had converted to Catholicism, describing the inner workings of the Vatican." Much of what he testified to was clearly beyond his personal knowledge, yet he even introduced a new name for what had been variously called the Mafia, Black Hand, or Unione Siciliana. According to him it was really known as Cosa Nostra (Our Thing), though many veteran organized crime investigators had never heard of it referred to that way.[3] Scholars and journalists jumped on the bandwagon and words like don, caporegime, and family were used as though they were precise as military terms like general, colonel, or regiment.

In the 1930s some New York gangsters called their group family (*famiglia*). Others used *borgatta*, meaning section or neighborhood. Neither idea was unique to Italians—gangs like the Eastmans had adopted the name of their leader, while others such as the Five Pointers were identified by their geography. "Boss" was a business or political term. It was too corporate for Joe Bonanno, who was more comfortable calling himself the "Father" (not Godfather) of his group. Subordinate leaders might be called capos, captains, crew chiefs, or skippers. The counselor, or *consigliere*, position origi-

---

[2]Valachi also claimed the murder of Joey Aiello in Chicago on October 23, 1930, was part of the New York wars. As related in chapter 7, Aiello, the sixty-first gang murder victim in Chicago that year, had been on the outs with Capone since the time in 1927 when he had tried to set up an ambush on him.

[3]The term had previously come up on some New York wiretaps, but it seemed to be the equivalent of soldiers referring to "our outfit." In that sense it was not the formal name of a criminal organization any more than "outfit" was the name of the United States Army. Later it would come to be referred to as La Cosa Nostra, (The Our Thing), a term that made no sense.

nally started as an internal arbitrator, or ombudsman, and later became a kind of counselor to the family head. Even the widely accepted five-family structure of New York mobdom was not as clear as later accounts tend to make it. Cops and federal agents always tried to diagram the inherently loose arrangements into tight military-type organizations similar to the ones they worked in. The New York detective bureau had a chief and a deputy chief. The local FBI office was run by a special agent in charge (SAC) and an assistant special agent in charge (ASAC). It was natural for the cops and the FBI to assume that every mob family had to have a boss and underboss and a clear line of authority with specified duties. Yet Joe Adonis, never listed as head of a family, was the most important mob figure in Brooklyn. His power lay in his political influence. Albert Anastasia was underboss to Vince Mangano but ruled the important Brooklyn waterfront and handed out contracts to the killers who became known as Murder, Inc. Frank Costello, a member of Luciano's family who supposedly ranked behind underboss Vito Genovese, maintained his own independent enterprises, including thousands of slot machines scattered throughout New York City and later Louisiana.

The so-called Americanization of the mobs is another theory that doesn't hold up. In the immediate aftermath of Maranzano's death, Luciano convened a meeting of Italian leaders and announced there would be no boss of bosses. Maranzano's own group was split between Joe Profaci and Joe Bonanno in Brooklyn. A fourth group went to Vince Mangano (and would later be led by Anastasia). A fifth was given to Tommy Lucchese. An outfit across the river in New Jersey was assigned to Guarino "Willie" Moretti. Unlike Luciano and Frank Costello, who came to America as children, and Moretti, who was born in Harlem, Profaci, Mangano, and Bonanno arrived as adults and retained their old-country ways. Where Luciano and Costello dressed sharply and dined in fancy Midtown Manhattan restaurants, the Sicilians wore nondescript clothing and ate at one another's homes, feasting for hours on halibut, snapper, shrimp, clams, and lobster followed by platters of veal and filet mignon with pasta afterward. The meals were accompanied by copious amounts of wine and poetry recitations, joke telling, and toasts. Americanized values like Luciano's did not meet with approval from traditional Sicilians. According to Bonanno, Lucky was obsessed with money and overly influenced by his Jewish friend Meyer Lansky. Cultural differences were reflected in organizational ones. Men like Luciano and Costello tried to run their operations along corporate bureaucratic lines; Bonanno and his allies were clan chiefs who operated through kinship groups.

Jews played important roles even in the Italian hierarchy. Meyer Lansky and Bugsy Siegel were equal business partners of Luciano, as was "Lepke" (Yiddish for "Little Louis") Buchalter. In New Jersey another Jew, Abner "Longy" (as in tall) Zwillman, was on almost the same plane with Willie Moretti. Longy was one of the mob bosses who led the underworld's efforts to recover the kidnapped Lindbergh baby. Motives varied from sympathy for the family to a desire to gain favor with the authorities, but Zwillman's were more businesslike. The kidnapping had occurred in the heart of his territory, and in their search for the child police were stopping so many vehicles on the Jersey highways that Zwillman's beer trucks were significantly impeded.

Not all *borgatte* were equal. Wealthy Manhattan always had more status than the outer boroughs, so the premier leader of New York mobdom was Luciano. But he was the first among equals, not boss of bosses, as indicated when Lucky announced he did not expect any monetary gifts from other leaders. Cash tributes were peanuts compared to the wealth at hand from various rackets.[4] In the 1930s New York's harbor was the nation's leading seaport and the economic engine of the city's economy. Men like Luciano and Anastasia ruled a large portion of it. Manhattan's Fulton Fish Market handled the seafood supplied to New York homes and restaurants and was bossed by Joseph "Socks" Lanza, a Luciano capo. Louis Buchalter controlled the garment district, which produced 60 percent of the country's clothing, and Tommy Lucchese (known as "Three Finger Brown" because

---

[4]In nineteenth-century New York, *racket* was used in the Shakespearean sense to describe a noisy party. Since many were thrown to raise money for politicians, it began to take on the English legal meaning of a fraudulent scheme or unlawful business. In addition, to Italians the word racket sounded like *ricatto,* which in their language meant blackmail or extortion. In most of the country it was the criminal definition that prevailed, though even today in New York City the word is still used to describe retirement parties and testimonials.

of the two missing digits on his left hand) ran the kosher poultry industry in the most populous Jewish city in the world.[5]

In some ways the mob control structure of the 1930s was just an updated version of the traditional one. Lucky Luciano was the number one figure; Tammany district leader Jimmy Hines was Foley's political successor; Joe Adonis represented Brooklyn politics; and Meyer Lansky was the financial wizard, à la Rothstein. Anything important that needed to be done could be accomplished by agreement among those four.

Luciano lived like a prince, maintaining suites at the ritzy Barbizon Plaza and the even ritzier Waldorf Towers, where at the height of the Depression his annual rent was $9,600. Naturally, a man living in such surroundings did not want doormen or manicurists calling him Mr. Luciano, lest it upset his Park Avenue neighbors. At the Barbizon he was known as Mr. Lane, while at the Waldorf he was Mr. Ross. After his rise to the top no one ever called him Lucky in his presence. Among intimates he preferred Charlie.[6] Mr. Lane/Ross dined regularly at exclusive restaurants, sometimes in company with show business stars like Jimmy Durante, Frank Fay, and Ed Wynn. When he wanted some private relaxation he would slip into a Broadway moviehouse to watch a first-run feature. He took in the racing scene at Miami in the winter and Saratoga in the summer, hobnobbing with blue-bloods. When he called Polly Adler, then New York's most expensive madam, to have her send up one of her girls, he dropped the Lane/Ross pretense—every high-class hooker in New York knew "Charlie Lucky." His number one girlfriend was a beautiful White Russian dancer, Gay Orlova (née Orloff), whom he clothed in fox capes and diamonds. During his visits to Hollywood Lucky romanced movie star Thelma Todd until her mysterious suicide in 1935. The more traditional mobsters like Bonanno and Profaci had no objection to Lucky's whoring, but to them his permanent bachelorhood was another example of how the Manhattanites did not

---

[5]For similar reasons the nickname "Three Finger" had originally been applied to old-time Chicago Cubs pitcher Mordecai Brown.

[6]The same was true of most gangster nicknames. Owney Madden was only called "Killer" in the newspapers, and to address Ben Siegel as "Bugsy" was to ask for a bullet in the head.

behave properly (Frank Costello's childless marriage to a non-Catholic met the same response). Lucky claimed that he was likely to "end up on a slab," and didn't want to leave a widow. He also recollected that he and Frank Costello were the only bosses who "didn't think that there was some kind of Italian law that said he had to bang out a million kids." Perhaps his independence was part of what made him successful.

At the base of the mob pyramid were "the boys"—perhaps as many as 500 in Luciano's family and 1,500 more scattered through the others, counting some who were only loosely affiliated. Luciano made his boys dress as sharply as he did, telling them, "Leave them wide-brimmed hats to Capone and his Chicago guys." Becoming a "made member" could require elaborate initiations involving ceremonial drawing of the initiate's blood and swearing of oaths, and supposedly the membership books were closed after the early 1930s. The simplest way to find out if someone belonged to a group was to find out if the boss thought he did. The mobs did not pay a regular salary, nor were they like robbery or burglary gangs that split up the take so their boys had to scramble for their money. The advantages of belonging to an organized crime gang lay elsewhere. Membership provided political influence in case they got in trouble with the law—Luciano, especially, backed his boys to the hilt. It provided work in gambling, slugging for hire, and loan-sharking. Sometimes a hoodlum who impressed his superiors would be given a plum, such as a piece of a nightclub. His job would be keeping an eye on the place to make sure the employees did not skim money and rivals did not move in. If the joint had a chorus line, the overseer could help himself.

Lives of the low-level gangsters are not well documented. Though Joe Valachi's testimony about his superiors is suspect, his description of his own career trajectory is fairly typical of his type. Born in East Harlem, he went from a school truant to a petty criminal. At seventeen he was picked up in New Jersey carrying a loaded gun; in his late teens he was an active burglar and did a stretch in Sing Sing. After the 1931 wars he was a small-time gambler, sometimes in the chips, ending up a drug dealer. The pattern was the same everywhere. Young men who came out of mob-dominated areas such as East Harlem, the Lower East Side, Brooklyn's Williamsburg, or Chicago's

Lt. Joe Petrosino, commander of the NYPD Italian Squad. In 1909, he would be sent on a suicide mission into the Mafia's Sicilian stronghold. *Daily News*.

TOP: Don Vito Cascio Ferro, often labeled as the Sicilian Mafia's greatest leader. He may have been the one behind Petrosino's assassination. *Daily News*.

BOTTOM: A scene from the "Castellammarese War" of 1930: the bodies of two members of Joe Masseria's gang, ambushed by Salvatore Maranzano's gunmen outside a Bronx apartment building. *Daily News*.

TOP: Arnold Rothstein, the top figure in New York City organized crime for most of the 1920s and mentor to future bosses like Frank Costello and "Lucky" Luciano. *Daily News*.

BOTTOM: Dutch Schultz (Arthur Flegenheimer). Shown in 1935 with the admiring townsfolk of Malone, New York, where a sympathetic jury had just acquitted him of tax evasion. Three months later he would be murdered by rival gangsters. AP/Wide World.

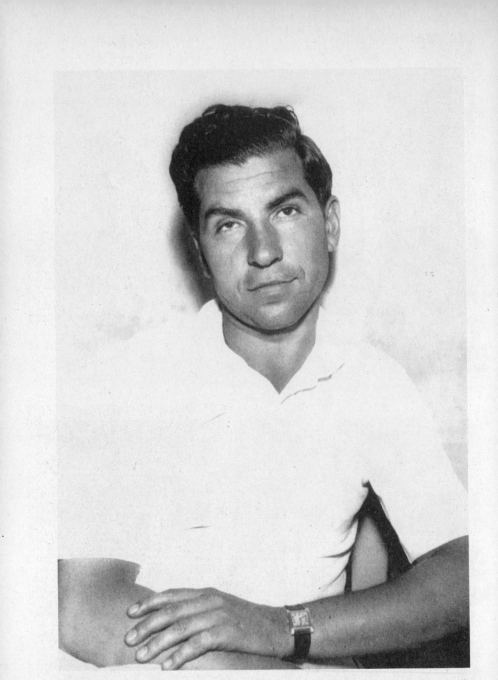

Charles "Lucky" Luciano. From 1931 to 1936, he was the biggest man in the New York mob world and even from prison and exile his influence remained strong. AP/Wide World.

The man who got Luciano. New York County District Attorney Tom Dewey (seated center) with his staff. Standing at left is Frank Hogan, who, after succeeding Dewey, served as district attorney for thirty-three years. AP/Wide World.

The scourge of the Levee, W. C. Dannenberg (seated) and members of his Chicago police Morals Squad, 1914. He raided so many of Colosimo's joints that the vice trust brought in hitmen to try to kill him. Chicago Historical Society.

"Diamond Jim" Colosimo (left), vice lord of Chicago's Levee district and friend of the elite. In 1920, when he refused to get into bootlegging, his lieutenants had him murdered. Chicago Historical Society.

Chicago detectives reenact the Valentine's Day Massacre of seven members of the Moran gang. Public outcry over the crime spurred the federal government to finally go after Capone. Chicago Historical Society.

Frank "The Enforcer" Nitti (center), Capone's successor as boss of the Chicago mob, 1933. That year, after a Chicago detective working for Mayor Cermak shot and wounded Nitti without justification, the mayor himself was assassinated. Chicago Historical Society.

Al Capone (in white hat) on the way to federal prison in 1931. Supposedly the most important gang leader in America, his reign in Chicago was short and troubled. AP/Wide World.

Elmer Lincoln Irey, head of Treasury Intelligence. He led the "Get Capone" drive and brought down other top mob bosses and corrupt politicians. AP/Wide World.

Secretary of the Treasury Henry Morgenthau Jr. (left) congratulates Frank Wilson on his appointment as chief of the U.S. Secret Service, 1936. Wilson had served as Irey's lieutenant in the "Get Capone" drive. Under Morgenthau's administration, the Treasury would relentlessly pursue organized crime and official corruption. AP/Wide World.

Joe Adonis, the mob's principal Brooklyn political fixer, 1937. He was so vain that he changed his name from Doto to Adonis. AP/Wide World.

New York City Mayor Fiorello La Guardia (left) displays some of Frank Costello's slot machines seized by the NYPD, 1934. AP/Wide World.

New York's ambassador to California and Nevada, Benjamin "Bugsy" Siegel (left), with movie star George Raft, 1944. AP/Wide World.

TOP: Vito Genovese, 1946. In 1937 he fled to Italy to avoid a murder charge. Brought back after the war, under military guard, he was set free when the chief witness against him was poisoned in jail. After Costello stumbled at the Kefauver Committee, Genovese moved to supplant him. AP/Wide World.

BOTTOM: The end of Siegel. When he was unable to account for the way he had handled their money, the commission bosses ordered him hit. AP/Wide World.

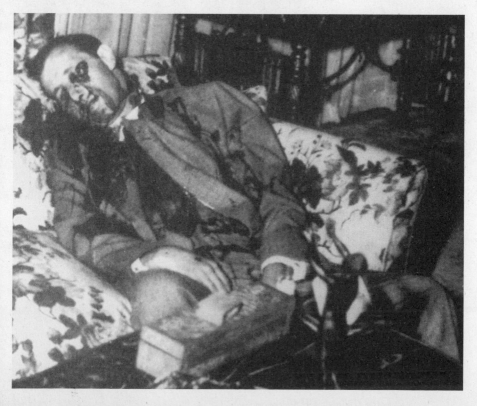

Mob "prime minister" Frank Costello testifying to a U.S. Senate committee, 1950. The following year when he appeared before the Kefauver Committee, he would not be so relaxed. AP/Wide World.

TOP: Johnny Torrio, 1936. So clever he was nicknamed "The Fox." He used the management skills he developed in Chicago to help create a national crime syndicate. AP/Wide World.

BOTTOM: Senator Estes Kefauver (standing) with Senator Charles Tobey on his right, being briefed by Federal Bureau of Narcotics commissioner Harry Anslinger on Kefauver's left. Anslinger would convince the committee that organized crime was dominated by the Sicilian Mafia. AP/Wide World.

TOP: Bugsy Siegel's mentor, Meyer Lansky. His financial acumen made him a major force in the national crime syndicate. *Daily News.*

BOTTOM: Owney "The Killer" Madden. After being exiled from New York, he transformed himself from the "Duke of the West Side" to the "Sage of Hot Springs," where he was always available to shelter and counsel mob figures. *Daily News.*

Near West Side, Cleveland's Woodlands district, South Philadelphia, or the North End of Boston had the best opportunity for making connections to become mob soldiers.

New York was too big for a single unified organization, and the post-1931 structure that developed with Luciano at its head was the optimum arrangement. It provided both concentrated power and dispersion, and as a result eliminated or subordinated all rivals and gave better access to politics. In both instances it benefited from its opponents' weaknesses. A few months after Maranzano's murder, Legs Diamond, who had survived four previous attacks, was surprised in an upstate hideout and filled with enough lead to guarantee he would not cheat death. Vince Coll was caught by Dutch Schultz gunmen in a drugstore phone booth—Owney Madden held him on the line long enough for the killers to get to the scene.

The Depression was a bleak time for Broadway nightlife. Many theaters and nightclubs went dark. Often it was mob money that kept places open. Even if a nightspot was not profitable, it provided a place for gang members to gather and enjoy the hot music and girls. Ritzy joints that catered to society were no different. The Stork Club and El Morocco ("Elmo's" to the elite) and many others had mob money behind them. The highest-paid entertainers performed at the Copacabana, which everyone knew belonged to Frank Costello. Willie Moretti's Riviera on the Jersey Palisades was just over the George Washington Bridge from Manhattan. Though the place ran gambling, it was even more noted for the quality of its entertainment. In the thirties, a skinny young kid from nearby Hoboken named Frank Sinatra made his career breakthrough there.

In the political sphere, the Seabury investigation that the Tepecanoe incident had launched was expanded into a general probe of municipal government. Many officials could not explain why their bank deposits were so large. The sheriff of New York County attributed his wealth to money that somehow came out of a marvelous tin box in his attic. The public was not amused by what was called the "the tin box parade." In 1932, when Seabury brought charges against Mayor Walker himself, Governor Franklin D. Roosevelt forced the mayor to resign. Downtown, Lucky Luciano decided it was time for an Italian district leader and he "persuaded" Harry Perry, one of the Sullivan clan by marriage, to step aside in favor of Al Marinelli. As a compromise the district was split in half and Congressman Christy Sullivan got the eastern portion and Marinelli the western.

At the 1932 Democratic national convention, Marinelli and Luciano shared a room at Chicago's posh Drake Hotel while they worked for the nomination of Tammany favorite son, Al Smith. Frank Costello and Jimmy Hines had a room in the same hotel and were pushing the candidacy of Governor Roosevelt, the eventual nominee. The arrangement was not accidental. Luciano didn't like or trust the Irish Hines, while Costello had hung out with Irishmen since boyhood days. The division between Luciano and Costello meant that it didn't matter which New Yorker won; whoever did would be grateful to at least one mob guy.

The Byzantine nature of New York politics was further revealed in 1933 when Joe Adonis of Brooklyn and the East Harlem mob supported anti-Tammany reformer Fiorello La Guardia in his successful run for mayor. East Harlem was La Guardia's base and the political bailiwick of his young protégé—some said the son Fiorello never had—Vito Marcantonio, who was on intimate terms with mobsters. In 1934 thirty-one-year-old Marcantonio won the seat La Guardia had previously held in Congress. The mobsters' support for La Guardia over Tammany was another hedge bet, but La Guardia's victory was mostly a negative for the gangsters. For eleven years hoodlum-hating Lew Valentine served as his police commissioner. Valentine constantly urged his cops to break gangsters' heads, an order La Guardia usually endorsed despite his civil rights orientation. Marcantonio's district in East Harlem and Joe Adonis's territory in Brooklyn didn't seem to receive as much police enforcement action, until Adonis supported La Guardia's opponent in the 1937 mayoral election—then the police came down on him so hard that he had to transfer his headquarters to New Jersey.

While La Guardia's behavior did not always square with good government notions, there was no doubt he was thoroughly honest (he lived in a modest East Harlem flat and died broke). As a practical politician he understood that to get elected, especially in a town where his Republicans were vastly outnumbered by Democrats, one had to accept the votes (but not the money) of individuals who might be less than saints.

Despite these realistic political accommodations, after he was sworn in as mayor La Guardia ordered the police to crack down on Lucky Luciano. A decade earlier Lucky had copped to a petty federal narcotics rap. In 1929 he had been lying half dead on Staten Island. By 1931 he had organized a mob structure in New York that would continue long after his own departure. Now, as far as the mayor was concerned, he was the "top gangster," a dangerous title, as Chicago's imprisoned Al Capone could testify.

9:   The Commission: The Mobs Go National

On December 5, 1928, when a force of detectives descended on the Statler Hilton Hotel in Cleveland and arrested twenty-three Italian mobsters from seven states, some cops and journalists declared the event to be a meeting of the "Grand Council of the Mafia." No one ever found out for certain what it was really about. One theory was that the group had assembled to discuss recent developments in the Unione Siciliana—the New York president, Frankie Yale, had been killed by Capone's men in July, and Chicago head and Capone appointee Tony Lombardo had been murdered by Joey Aiello's gunmen in September. A more prosaic explanation was that the meeting was a sit-down with local Cleveland bosses, who controlled the corn sugar essential to the distilling of whiskey. Of course, a meeting between consumers and suppliers of sugar did not have the same dramatic ring to it as one of the Grand Council of the Mafia, "the most secret and terrible organization in the world."

Cleveland had followed the usual pattern of big-city organized crime in the Roaring Twenties. After bootlegging king Tommy McGinty was sent to prison in 1924, an Italian gang headed by the Lonardo brothers, Joe and John, moved up. The Lonardos employed their neighbors in the Woodlands district to run stills that produced corn liquor. In 1927 both Lonardos were murdered by a gang run by Joe Porello, who took over the Woodlands operation. Access to Cleveland's corn sugar was one of the keys to control of the bootlegging industry, so Porello invited gang leaders from other cities to the meeting at the Statler. His leadership was being challenged by an Italian gang from the Mayfield Road section led by the Milano family, and Cleveland insiders believed it was the Milanos who tipped off the police to the meeting.

The official line put out by the police was that hotel employees had alerted them about suspicious men's comings and goings. It was a weak cover story. There was nothing unusual about the participants—cops and employees alike reported they were well-dressed, carried expensive luggage, and wore silk underwear and fine linens. The captain who led the raid said, "They looked like prosperous sales representatives." The hotel employees wanted no part of the affair. According to a hoary old rumor in law enforcement, a desk clerk was forced by police to knock on the door with the promise that he could jump out of the way before it was opened. Instead, the lead officers pushed him through as a shield against bullets. Cops also arrested the men who had not yet come down for the meeting. Others, alerted by the noise, managed to escape, as did those who were staying in other hotels.[1]

A Jewish group in Cleveland led by Morris "Moe" Dalitz was even stronger than the local Italians. Moe became part of Detroit's Purple Gang in the early '20s, when it was composed of Jewish gangsters led by Joe and Benny Bernstein, two of the admirals in the Great Lakes booze-hauling fleet known as the "Jewish Navy." Constantly at war with other gangs and each other, the Purples piled up an impressive body count and equally impressive headlines. Dalitz astutely divined that the Purples were too wild to last and moved to Ohio, eventually settling in Cleveland. By the early '30s, the Purples were virtually eliminated by rivals and the law, and replaced by Italians who were shrewd enough to retain the gang's name because of its terrifying

---

[1] Among those arrested was Joe Profaci of New York, who explained that he was there to expand the small olive oil importing business he ran in Brooklyn. Twenty-nine years later, when New York State troopers raided a gathering of Italian mob figures in the village of Apalachin, it too would be labeled "a meeting of the Grand Council of the Mafia" and Profaci would again be among those arrested.

reputation. In Cleveland, Dalitz formed a partnership with several other Jewish racketeers that continued for half a century, expanding to take control of gambling operations in Kentucky, Florida, and Nevada.

In 1930, Frank Milano invited Joe Porello and his bodyguard to a meeting at a Mayfield Road saloon. Both were murdered, and the Mayfield Roaders became the top Italian mob in town. When Milano retired to Mexico in 1935 he was succeeded by "Big Al" Polizzi, who had come to Cleveland from Sicily at age fourteen. Al continued the interethnic peace pact with Dalitz and company. From 1935 on Cleveland was governed by reform mayors who appointed tough lawmen like Eliot Ness. But Dalitz and Polizzi continued to operate. Ness's favorite Cleveland "untouchable" was a municipal police lieutenant. A few years after Ness's departure, it was revealed that the lieutenant had been on the mob payroll all along and he was sentenced to the state penitentiary.

The next national mob conference was in May 1929 in Atlantic City. Since it was multiethnic, it could hardly be called a meeting of the Mafia. This time it was under the protection of the local political boss, Nucky Johnson, so there was no need to keep it secret. In general things went smoothly: territories were allotted to bootlegging gangs; Arnold Rothstein's gambling operations were assigned to Frank Costello's friend, Frank Erickson; and Capone was persuaded to rusticate in a Philadelphia jail.

Some meetings were exclusively Italian or Jewish, others mixed. Luciano brought his friend Meyer Lansky to a small 1931 sit-down in Chicago where Luciano briefed his Windy City counterparts on the post-Maranzano New York scene, but Lansky had to wait outside the room. When he and Luciano returned to Chicago for a meeting at the Congress Hotel in 1932, Lansky was allowed in. Mayor Cermak and Frank Nitti were feuding, and after the meeting adjourned, Nitti, Lansky, Luciano, and two of Al Capone's cousins were arrested outside the hotel by local cops. The pinch was meant to embarrass the hosts.

The New York Jewish mobs had held their own exclusive meeting in 1933 at the Franconia Hotel on the Upper West Side of Manhattan. Despite the fact that Tammany Hall was still in control of the city, detectives from the Red Squad raided the place and arrested nine attendees, including

Bugsy Siegel, "Lepke" Buchalter, and his partner "Gurrah" Shapiro. Somehow the clever Lansky managed not to be there. Who sent the cops wasn't clear—it was the height of the Depression and New York was being swept by industrial violence involving both the communists and mobsters, so the Red Squad may have initiated the raid on its own.[2] Unconfirmed accounts claim that a grand conclave of mob leaders was held in New York's Waldorf Astoria Hotel in the spring of 1934. "Informed insiders" reported that it was presided over by Johnny Torrio and dominated by Luciano, Lansky, and Joe Adonis, with delegates coming from as far away as Minneapolis, Denver, New Orleans, and Los Angeles.[3]

The meetings were a natural manifestation of the interstate and corporate nature of organized crime, and by the mid-1930s a loose alliance existed that some referred to as a "syndicate." Largely composed of gangs in the Northeast and Midwest, it also extended to places like Florida, Louisiana, and California. At its core was a so-called commission, composed of the heads of the five New York "families" and four others. Two of the latter were also basically New Yorkers. Willie Moretti had left New York at age twenty-eight to run bootlegging, and later gambling, in northern New Jersey. And Stefano Magaddino had come to Brooklyn from Sicily just before the Fascist takeover. In 1924 he helped smuggle his cousin Joe Bonanno into the United States; by that time he had set up in Buffalo, New York, where eventually he became the head man.

Essentially, the commission was a consultative rather than ruling body. Its New York orientation meant it largely confined itself to parochial matters, maintaining peace between the more traditional leaders like Bonanno and Profaci and the Americanized Luciano, Costello, and Moretti. Its most significant accomplishment was putting a stop to internecine warfare and internal revolts. From 1931 to 1951 none of the six New York City area bosses were removed by rivals or members of his own family. The eighth seat on the

---

[2]In the '30s, the gangs did do some business with the communists. It wasn't for political reasons—most mob bosses had personal ideologies somewhat to the right of Herbert Hoover—but because communists controlled some unions. Later, anti-communist New Dealers would enlist the mob to help battle the Reds.

[3]The principal informant, Abe Reles, was part of the Murder, Inc. group, but he was only repeating what he had learned secondhand.

commission belonged to Cleveland, occupied first by Milano and then Polizzi. Chicago had the ninth chair, which was shared by two men.

By 1933 what Chicagoans called "the outfit" or "the syndicate"—meaning the local people, not national—had consolidated its position. On law enforcement organization charts and in newspaper accounts, Paul Ricca was usually listed as underboss beneath Frank Nitti. Paul had served time in Italy for murder under his given name of Delucia. When he arrived in the United States around 1920 at age twenty-three, he called himself Ricca. Just as taciturn and tough as Nitti, the two were basically equals, and either one could represent Chicago on the commission. Outsiders' confusion came from the newspaperman's habit of hanging nicknames on mob figures. Nitti was called "The Enforcer," and Ricca "The Waiter" because he supposedly had been one, though when anyone dared to ask him he would curtly declare, "I was the manager of the place." In contrast, Nitti had really been a barber, but enforcer sounded more powerful than waiter so to outsiders Nitti was officially the boss.

The Chicago mob was exceptionally multiethnic. Jake Guzik served as a lieutenant to Torrio, Capone, Nitti, and Ricca and was as much a part of the Capone gang as Big Al's brothers. Welshman Murray Humphreys—known as "The Camel," a play on another nickname, "Hump," and a nod to his favored camel hair coats—controlled labor unions and legitimate businesses, Bohemian Eddie Vogel took care of slot machines, and Irish crew chiefs like Danny Stanton and "Red" Fawcett (Forsyth) ran their territories in the same way as their Italian counterparts "Cherry Nose" Gioe, "Tough Tony" Capezio, and "Little New York" Campagna. Recalling the constant criticism directed against Colosimo, Torrio, and Capone for their involvement in prostitution, Nitti and Ricca had disengaged the mob from direct control of the sex business. The city's chief whoremaster was the Irish "Duke" Cooney of the First Ward. The principal figure in drugs was an Irish colleen, Kitty Gilhooley.

For the Chicago mob the pickings were especially good. The Century of Progress Exposition of 1933–1934 brought thousands of tourists to the city to be fleeced in the numerous mob-run nightspots, including some on the fairgrounds itself. In addition, there were an estimated 7,500 bookie joints in the city. The Chicago Crime Commission calculated that $20 million annually was paid to the police and politicians for protection. In 1950, when Mayor Kelly died, he left $600,000. However, his wife claimed at least $1 million more was missing from the safe-deposit box. The chief investigator for the state's attorney's office, police captain Dan "Tubbo" Gilbert, was a former labor union official and slugger with close ties to Democratic Party boss Pat Nash. He held his post for eighteen years, during which time he was virtually independent of his nominal superiors, the state's attorney, and the police commissioner. In the 1930s Gilbert was de facto controller of several powerful labor unions, a position akin to a later era federal monitor, though Tubbo operated on behalf of the outfit. By the 1940s he was known as "America's richest cop." In 1941 Jake Guzik's payoff list for suburban gambling fell into a reporter's hands. On it was a notation listing $4,000 a month to "Tub." When the *Chicago Tribune* suggested that it might refer to Gilbert, he protested that he was "Tubbo" not "Tub."

Mobs in cities that did not have a commission seat operated independently, but in certain instances the commission was able to lay down the law to them. In the 1930s, organized crime in Kansas City, Missouri, was dominated by an Italian gang, but was subordinated to an Irish-run political organization. The mob boss was Johnny Lazia, and Tom Pendergast was the absolute ruler and kingmaker of local and state politics. When Pendergast managed to wrest control of the local police from a state commission in 1932, Lazia was given a major share in the running of the department. Among his contributions to the public safety was the appointment of sixty ex-convicts to the force. With a mobster as de facto police chief, the city became known as a safe haven for wanted hoodlums from other jurisdictions.

In 1933 Johnny made a huge mistake that would draw the commission's censure. In June of that year the Bureau of Investigation, headed by the largely unknown J. Edgar Hoover, went after a bank robber named Frank Nash who had escaped from a federal prison in Leavenworth, Kansas. Nash was living unmolested in Hot Springs, Arkansas. Bureau agents were not yet full-fledged cops, so they enlisted the services of a tough Oklahoma police chief. Chief Otto Reed and two FBI men seized Nash on the streets of Hot Springs and rushed him out of town. Local police put out a kidnapping alert and set up roadblocks in an effort to save him, but they were too late. The arresting party boarded a train for Kansas City where FBI agents and local officers were to meet them and help escort Nash back to Leavenworth. When word went out in the underworld, Johnny Lazia recruited a three-man crew including bank robber "Pretty Boy" Floyd to rescue Nash when he arrived at Union Station. In the ensuing shootout, Chief Reed, an FBI man, two Kansas City detectives, and Nash were killed, and another FBI man and a bystander were wounded.[4] Word of the "Kansas City Massacre" roused public opinion against the wave of lawlessness sweeping the country. In the heart of the Depression, bank robberies and kidnappings (often carried out by unemployed bootleggers) had become common occurrences.

Lazia's folly got the attention of the national commission along with the earlier murders of Chicago reporter Jake Lingle and a Detroit radio journalist named Buckley, which had also created an outcry that was bad for mob business. In response to the unwelcome publicity the three episodes caused, the commission ruled reporters and cops would be off-limits. It further prohibited violence in resort areas—like Miami, Atlantic City, or Hot Springs—so as not to scare off tourists.

The pattern of organized crime in the South was different from the Northeast or Midwest. Dixie was traditionally more tolerant of vices like gambling than the puritanical North, but a certain gentility was required. When the powerful New York and Chicago mobs began to expand in the region during the 1930s, they had to proceed tactfully. Mayors, governors, and sheriffs had to be courted and catered to, and the machine guns left at home.

When Mayor La Guardia took office in New York in 1934, he declared war on Frank Costello's slot machines. So Frank shipped them to Louisiana. Later he would tell a federal grand jury that in 1935 he had made a deal with the czar of Louisiana, Senator Huey Long. When Costello's newly formed

---

[4]Lazia managed to conceal the killers until he could ship them out of town. Within a little over a year, Floyd had been killed by lawmen, another of the gang had been murdered in Detroit, and a third was captured and sentenced to death. Lazia was prosecuted by the Feds for tax evasion and was murdered by other gangsters in July 1934 while out on bail. His replacement, Charlie Carollo, carried on with the support of the Pendergast organization.

Bayou Novelty Company began to place slots in the state, Huey announced that the proceeds would go to a fund for widows and orphans. He kept his word—$600 out of the first $800,000 found its way to the purported beneficiaries, while $20,000 a month went to him. When Long was assassinated, one result was the temporary disappearance of Costello's slot machines.

Up the road from New Orleans—at least as viewed from a New York vantage—was Hot Springs, Arkansas, where Owney Madden ran gambling. Exiled to the South in the 1930s by the Italian bosses, he had married the daughter of the local postmaster and settled down for good, finally morphing into an elder statesman. Known as the "Sage of Hot Springs," he entertained and counseled mob figures from other parts of the country. After Costello's slot machines were banned in New Orleans, Madden brokered a meeting in Hot Springs between Costello's representatives and Huey Long's successors. There it was agreed a new corporation, the Pelican Novelty Company, would be allowed to operate slots in New Orleans under the joint direction of Costello's lieutenant, "Dandy Phil" Kastel of New York, and a Long machine wheelhorse.

Slots were always a target for the anti-gambling lobby. In New York, critics claimed gangsters forced small storekeepers to install them, though in the Depression many were happy to receive a weekly stipend from the mob. The most common image of slot machines was that of school kids losing their lunch money as they frantically fed the one-armed bandits, hoping for three cherries to come up. Mayor La Guardia loved to chop up seized slots while flash bulbs popped and newsreel cameras ground. To soften similar criticism in New Orleans, it was ruled that the machines would pay off in mints. The Louisiana Mint Company replaced Pelican Novelty, though winners were allowed to covertly exchange candy for money.

Hot Springs traditionally catered to an older crowd that came for lengthy stays, hoping the spa waters would improve their health. The new interstate highways now enabled others to go there for brief gambling visits, so the New York mob decided to invest in a country club and a casino where younger, more active patrons could play golf by day and gamble by night. The local politicians and lawmen were cut in for a healthy slice, and the citizenry was assured that the revenue from the new facilities would keep their taxes down. Directing operations from his headquarters at the refurbished Southern Club, Madden made Hot Springs a resort on a par with Atlantic City.

Miami had boomed in the 1920s land speculation and busted when a hurricane hit the area in 1926. In the 1930s the mob began to acquire control of local racetracks. New York's Big Bill Dwyer was placed in charge of Tropical Park. Chicago sent down Johnny Patton, its president for suburban vice operations, Moe Dalitz's Cleveland mob opened casinos in Broward County, and Owney Madden also managed to get a piece of the action. When an army sergeant named Batista seized power in nearby Cuba, Meyer Lansky went down to pay his respects. He obtained the wagering concession at the Hotel Nacional, which had more floor space for gambling than any place in the Western Hemisphere. During World War II, Batista faced unrest from his people and the hostility of the U.S. government. Interruptions to air and sea travel crippled the Nacional, and Lansky shifted his focus to Broward County. He also advised "The Sergeant" that it might be time for a vacation. Instead, Batista gambled on a free election, lost, and took up residence on the Florida coast not far from Lansky. The mob casino in Havana that Lansky and Dalitz had dreamed of was postponed until the dictator's 1952 return.

The growth and prosperity of the national crime syndicate caused people to wonder how small-time hoodlums and ex-bootleggers managed to do so well with Prohibition repealed and the country in the midst of a depression. Not only were they successful racketeers, some were owners of legitimate enterprises who rubbed shoulders with respectable businessmen and were deferred to by top politicians. The one or two grammar school kickouts who mangled the King's English and had extensive police records but who managed to rise to wealth and power could be attributed to innate brains and skill. The success of so many of their less-talented brethren raised other possibilities. One widely held notion was that such men were fronts and mobdom was run behind the scenes by respectable figures from the world of commerce and government. Many journalists and investigators looked for hidden Mr. Bigs who pulled the strings from their mansions and boardrooms.

In this vein, a Hearst reporter named Martin Mooney published a book

entitled *Crime Incorporated.* In it he described a meeting of the leaders of
New York City's mob world that he had supposedly witnessed. According
to his account, it was held in a Times Square office building and in atten-
dance were three important figures in local and national politics whose
names "if revealed, would shake every city in the country and topple scores
of state and national politicians." "The suave attorney who stood at one of
the windows looking down . . ." he reported, "held degrees from two of the
most esteemed of eastern universities." Another man was described as the
head of a business enterprise that was "considered one of the first half-
dozen in the East." Mooney's account was probably overly dramatic, but
some serious observers made the same accusations. Senator Royal Copeland
of New York chaired a 1933 Senate subcommittee that held hearings on
the crime problem. One of the witnesses, U.S. attorney George Medalie,
decried the relationship between organized crime and politics and offered
to name four major political figures in league with gangsters. Copeland
quickly declined the offer.

The New York judicial world included Martin Manton, the chief judge of
the U.S. Court of Appeals for the Second Circuit, which ranked just below
the Supreme Court. Long suspected of being on the take, he was nicknamed
"Preying Manton." Some of his decisions that reversed convictions of mobsters seemed incomprehensible. In 1939 he was caught taking a bribe and
sent to prison. Richard "Dixie" Davis was a graduate of Syracuse University
and Columbia Law School and he advised his client Dutch Schultz on many
a crooked deal from his plush office in a Times Square building. Businessmen who engaged in bootlegging during Prohibition were rumored to have
mob ties long afterward. Much has been written about Joseph Kennedy's
connections to men like Frank Costello. Some gang figures even referred to
the elder Kennedy as "Meyer Lansky with a Harvard degree." It is generally
accepted that Kennedy was involved in the liquor business both during and
after Prohibition. Like so much that is written about the family, however,
stories about other relationships with mobsters are difficult to verify.

The belief in a hidden Mr. Big who really ruled the mobs was in part a
class issue—how could immigrants or kids from the wrong side of the tracks
become so successful? Yet the differences between the twentieth-century

gang bosses and nineteenth-century robber barons like John Jacob Astor and Commodore Cornelius Vanderbilt are smaller than they might seem. Astor acquired his fortune furnishing Indians with liquor and cheating them out of their furs. He used the money to buy up Manhattan real estate, converting it into slum dwellings which were the spawning grounds for New York's gangs. In both businesses he bribed public officials. Vanderbilt, a simple, uneducated ferryboat man, used armies of gunmen to obtain concessions for his shipping company from Central American governments. Later he used the same tactics to gain control of American railroads. In subsequent years, when his fellow gangsters would complain about their bad publicity, Meyer Lansky would assure them, "Don't worry, don't worry. Look at the Astors and Vanderbilts, all those big society people. They were the worst thieves—and now look at them. It's just a matter of time."

Men like Torrio, Rothstein, Lansky, Luciano, and Costello possessed the combination of brains, daring, and ruthlessness required to succeed in certain types of businesses. Whether they could have succeeded in other fields is more problematic. When prison doctors gave Frank Costello an IQ test in the 1950s, he scored a surprisingly low 97. Yet clearly Costello was a very shrewd man. With their newfound wealth and connections the mob leaders were able to employ some of the best legal and financial talent, particularly in the Depression, when many professionals were not so choosy about where their fees came from. They also sought counsel from business and political friends. In the final analysis, elaborate theories of "Mr. Bigs" boil down to wishful thinking and flashy copy. The mob bosses appreciated expert advice in matters of law, finance, and politics, but they called their own shots.

By the 1930s the Italian gangs controlled or shared control of organized crime in most of the choice locations in the country. Even professional criminals such as robbers and burglars had to defer to them. Stickup men knew better than to rob a mob gambling joint or nightspot. The few who didn't were usually found in an alley or the trunk of a car. In some areas the mob collected what came to be known as "street tax" from thugs who made big scores; the practice was facilitated by organized crime's ability to launder money or dispose of stolen goods. In the 1940s Chicago mobsters negotiating with local cops to set up a gambling operation in Dallas stressed their ability to hold street crime down, arguing that the presence of organized crime would discourage punks from working the area. If some gun-happy hoodlum went on a spree, mob soldiers acting on information from underworld channels could quickly track him down.

At the same time the gangsters' power was often exaggerated, especially by those who opposed them. Lawmen, investigative journalists, and civic reformers sometimes acted as though the mobsters could always get away with murder, bribing, politically neutralizing, or intimidating officials right and left. Their claims actually enhanced mob power. If local racketeers controlled the mayor, governor, and police commissioner and could kill anyone with impunity, even the most courageous person would hesitate to oppose them. Yet, in Capone's Chicago, men like Frank Loesch or Henry Barrett Chamberlain were never harmed. During the twelve years La Guardia was mayor of New York, the mob had no clout at City Hall or the police commissioner's office, dampening the support of other political and police friends scattered around town.

In fact, the relationship of police, politicians, and organized crime was much more complex in those times than is usually portrayed. One of the best descriptions of real-world mob-government ties is contained in William H. Whyte's landmark sociological study, *Street Corner Society*. In the late 1930s, Whyte, then a graduate student at Harvard, set out to explore the social organization of a slum. The area he chose was Boston's historic North End ("Cornerville" in the study), a predominantly Italian district whose narrow winding streets heightened the native insularity of its residents. What Whyte did not know at first was that it was also the principal base of the Boston Italian mobs. Whyte had no grounding in law enforcement and was by his own account inexperienced and naive. Despite these shortcomings—or maybe because of them—he was able to win acceptance, and though analyzing crime was only a minor portion of his research, he was able to grasp the racket situation more clearly than many experienced lawmen or journalists.

Organized crime in Boston had followed the usual pattern. At the beginning of Prohibition a Jewish drug dealer, Charles "King" Solomon, became the city's principal bootlegger. In the early '30s two North End Sicilians, Phil Buccola and Joe Lombardo, began to emerge, though not without struggles against other Italians and an Irish gang, the Gustins. One North Ender told Whyte how in those days "there was plenty of action around here—shooting up and down the street, men riding in cars, standing on the running board, shooting. It got pretty hot." After the Gustins hijacked one of Lombardo's liquor trucks in 1931, he contacted their leaders and asked them to come and talk things over. When two of them arrived they were mowed down by machine-gun fire. In 1933 King Solomon himself was murdered by Irish gangsters. When Prohibition ended Buccola and Lombardo began to move into gambling.

Whyte described how the "Office" or the "Company," as the mob was known, organized local gamblers in a businesslike way and held violence to a minimum. To suppress competition, rather than resorting to guns the Office notified their police allies who raided competitors or simply told them to shut down. Once a taboo among gangsters, informing had become a necessary business practice.

Though the police were paid off, their response was dictated by their own organizational needs. It was in the interest of the cops as much as the racketeers to hold down violence. So special police squads composed of "untouchables" were assigned to carry out raids until the heat died down, whereupon they were reassigned to various department cubbyholes. And though they were not always popular with their fellow cops, they were a necessary part of the organization. As Whyte noted, if there were no Untouchables, when a crisis arose bringing corruption to the public's notice, the scandal might assume such proportions as to "threaten the prevailing system of police organization with destruction."

The police commissioner of Boston during Whyte's research was civilian Joseph Timilty, who had been appointed in 1936 by Massachusetts governor and archetypal corrupt big-city politician James Michael Curley. Timilty was also an intimate friend of Joseph Kennedy, a bitter foe of Curley's. During the seven years Timilty headed the police department, he was able to retain the confidence of both Curley and Kennedy, as well as a later Republican governor and Democratic mayor. The juggling act came to an end during a corruption scandal in 1943, when Timilty and other high-ranking Boston police officials were indicted (but not convicted) by a Republican state attorney general. Thus, police-political-organized crime alliances of the time were part of a complex system designed to maintain the equilibrium of all the groups involved.

By the end of the 1930s a list of the top dozen leaders of the national syndicate would have included Luciano (by then in prison); his successor Costello; Adonis, Lansky, and Siegel of New York; Nitti and Ricca of Chicago; Dalitz of Cleveland; and Moretti and Zwillman of New Jersey. Johnny Torrio and Owney Madden were the elder statesmen. All were millionaires, all were welcome in the best places, all had influence in legitimate worlds. Most had their best days still ahead. In the 1940s Costello would name the mayor of New York, Moretti would make the career of America's most popular entertainer, Lansky would come to control a small nation, Siegel would found modern Las Vegas, and Lansky and Dalitz would help make it a fabulous success.[5] When Costello told the Kefauver Committee a decade later, "I love this country," many people scoffed. Yet why not? America had been very good to men like him. At the beginning of the 1920s they were petty hoodlums confined to ethnic colonies in the big cities. Now they controlled an empire. In the 1930s they had fed their newfound wealth into a depressed economy, and in the 1940s some of them would come to believe that they were entitled to the same respect as other successful businessmen. In that hope they would be disappointed.

---

[5]It is generally accepted that it was Moretti's gunmen who "persuaded" bandleader Tommy Dorsey to release Frank Sinatra from his long-term contract.

10:   Racket-Busting: The Dewey Days

The plan had all the precision of a military operation. At precisely 9 P.M. on Saturday, February 1, 1936, 160 New York cops would simultaneously hit eighty houses of prostitution. Back then people still worked a six-day week; Saturday was the big night to howl; and the first of the month was a traditional payday: the whorehouses would be running full blast. To prevent leaks, the specially selected officers had not been told of their mission until 8 P.M., and none of them were from the vice squad or working with their usual partners. As a further precaution, they had been dispatched to neighborhoods away from their regular precincts. Not until five minutes to nine, when they opened sealed envelopes, would they even know their specific target. The envelopes contained orders to arrest every prostitute or madam present, to refrain from unnecessary conversation, and to take the prisoners to an out-of-the-way lower Manhattan police precinct by taxicabs that were standing by. After that, they were to be brought to the nearby Woolworth Building for processing by the special state prosecutor's office.

Seven months earlier, the governor had appointed a thirty-three-year-old lawyer named Tom Dewey to the post. Until shortly before the raids Dewey's office had been focused on an entirely different part of the underworld and a different mob boss—industrial racketeering and Dutch Schultz.

After Schultz was murdered in October 1935, Dewey had turned to building a case against Lucky Luciano for pimping, a crime that no one had heretofore accused him of.

Raiding whorehouses had not been a part of Dewey's original game plan. It was too reminiscent of old-fashioned moral reform. Dewey's mission was not to combat social evils but economic ones—industrial rackets. These went back to turn-of-the-century New York, when Monk Eastman and his boys slugged union organizers in the garment industry on behalf of employers, and sometimes employers on behalf of unions. In the 1920s gangsters working for Arnold Rothstein took control of labor-management relations in the industry New Yorkers referred to as "the rag trade." When he was killed, Lepke Buchalter became the top figure.

After the repeal of Prohibition ex-bootleggers turned to new sources of income, and industrial rackets became pervasive. The Depression exacerbated economic competition and tensions between workers and employers. Both labor and management used strong-arm men, but they were learning the hard way that bringing them in was easier than getting rid of them. The fortunate ones had only to accept racketeers as their partners, the less fortunate ended up working for them, and the truly unfortunate lost everything, including in some instances their lives.

Racketeering was built into many industries. The clothing business was a classic example. Made up of small shops with little capital, competition was fierce and public taste in fashion changed rapidly. Legitimate financial institutions were not disposed to lend money to manufacturers in so chancy a business. But gangsters with Prohibition wealth were—at exorbitant rates and for a piece of the profits. They also had a reputation for being good at collecting debts and eliminating competition by simple and direct means. Trucking was another highly competitive industry made up of small companies hungry for business, and trucks provided a way of controlling other industries dependent on the timely delivery of goods. A common tactic of industrial racketeers was the practice of organizing an employers association and forcing businesses to belong. At the same time, they took control of unions in the industry and then negotiated sweetheart contracts with the employers for a price. The workers might not like it, but in the Depression they had to accept low wages and union deductions without protest. The alternative was no job at all or a visit from some mob goons.

Racketeers generally had little to fear from the New York City prosecutors. Tammany's Jimmy Hines protected Dutch Schultz and Lucky Luciano through his control of the Manhattan district attorney's office; Joe Adonis of Brooklyn had similar power over the Brooklyn D.A. In 1935 a venerable criminal justice institution was used to upset the comfortable arrangements. The grand jury, a body dating to fourteenth-century England, was composed of private citizens summoned to determine if there was probable cause to bring a criminal charge against a suspect. Because they could compel witnesses and suspects to appear before them without lawyers, grand juries were a useful tool in conducting investigations. "GRAND JURY TO PROBE" was a familiar New York headline. When a judge granted a witness immunity, he could be held in jail for the life of the grand jury if he didn't talk. Grants of immunity were a powerful means of making small fish testify against big ones.

In Manhattan grand juries were often composed of solid citizens drawn from a list of individuals who volunteered to sit, on a part-time basis, for a month or so every two or three years. In theory a grand jury's authority was broad, but in practice they were run by the assistant district attorney assigned to shepherd them through their period of service. Occasionally the Grand Jurors Association, composed of former members, met and talked about frustrations, such as simply being a rubber stamp for the D.A. In March 1935 a grand jury was empaneled with Lee Thompson Smith, a real estate broker and president of the Grand Jurors Association, as foreman. Assistant district attorney Lyon Boston, the youngest lawyer on the D.A.'s staff, began the session by suggesting that the jury investigate the communists who had been active in fomenting unrest amid the industrial and political strife of the '30s. Though grand jury proceedings were supposedly secret, "Grand Jury Hears of Red Plot" would make a nice safe story that a Tammany D.A. could leak to the press. Assistant D.A. Boston, who gloried in the nickname "The Boy Detective," was raring to go, but Lee Thompson Smith and his fellow jurors had a different idea. They asked to investigate industrial racketeering. This was not a welcome topic. Hines would get upset and come down hard on Boston's boss, D.A. William Dodge. The young A.D.A. tried to deflect them, but the jury, aware of its legal powers, ordered him out of the room and petitioned the governor to assign a special prosecutor to work with them. It also ensured that its actions were made known publicly. In tabloid language, the jury had "run away." District attorney Dodge huffed, "I am the elected district attorney," and promised he would not surrender his power to a special prosecutor.

The ball was squarely in the court of Governor Herbert Lehman, a New York socialite and a principal in Lehman Brothers, an old-line Jewish investment banking firm. Lehman was known for his personal integrity and his antipathy toward Tammany. He agreed to appoint a special prosecutor and offered the job to four prominent New York lawyers of high standing, including some Republicans. All refused and urged him to name Dewey. The governor questioned his youth and inexperience, but the four were adamant, and Lehman reluctantly accepted their recommendation.

Thomas Edmund Dewey, the son of a newspaper editor in Owosso, Michigan, was a graduate of the state university at Ann Arbor who came to New York City in 1923 to study voice in a Manhattan conservatory and law at Columbia. He displayed more talent in the study of law than music, and after graduation went to work in a Wall Street firm. When the firm retained legendary trial lawyer George Medalie as a special counsel, Dewey was assigned to work with him. He so impressed the older man that when Medalie became the U.S. attorney for the Southern District of New York in 1931 he made the twenty-eight-year-old Dewey his chief assistant. After Medalie resigned, the district's federal judges invoked an obscure law to name Dewey U.S. attorney. In that office he prosecuted Waxey Gordon and Dutch Schultz on income tax charges. In 1934 President Roosevelt named a successor and Dewey went back to private practice. Medalie was one of the four lawyers that Lehman had offered to appoint as special prosecutor, and it was he who persuaded the others to back Dewey.

Most criminal lawyers were either steely, precise, no-nonsense types who devoured witnesses and overwhelmed juries with facts or ham actors who sought to sway judges and juries by emotional appeals, regardless of the facts. Dewey was a bit of both. Elmer Irey described how veteran IRS agents would present Dewey with what they thought was an ironclad case, only to have their evidence torn apart "with about a million questions, give or take ten." After which "wearily the agent would leave, determined to get more evidence. He got more, of course, and that is what Dewey wanted." To a casual observer, Dewey didn't appear dynamic. His conservative dress, neatly trimmed mustache, and aloof manner projected the image of a stodgy older man. When he rose to speak in a courtroom it was a different story. Employing the vocal techniques he had learned as a singer, Dewey could be soft and charming, winning a witness's confidence, and then quickly switch to a loud threatening manner. His cutting asides to the jury when he wished to discredit testimony or opposing counsel's arguments were accompanied by operatic gestures. While only about five-foot-six (he kept his height a secret) and of medium build, he dominated the courtroom.

His assistants were in awe of him. Dewey assembled a staff of twenty lawyers, all between twenty-five and forty, mostly products of Harvard or Columbia Law School, who were a mixture of Republicans, Democrats, and Independents. To support them he brought in accountants, office staff, and New York City detectives. The cops were picked for their youth, to screen out those who had been around long enough to learn bad habits, and relatively small size, which reduced the possibility that they would be identified when they worked undercover. Everyone hired was thoroughly investigated, warned not to frequent bars or racetracks, and impressed with the need for secrecy. To ensure the last, Dewey chose not to take space in the Criminal Court building or another government facility, places infested with political appointees. The sixty-story Woolworth skyscraper was a commercial building with eight entrances, including one that led straight into the subway. A complainant or witness could slip in unnoticed amid the office workers and visitors. As a further precaution, detectives were stationed in the lobby to spot known hoodlums who might be hanging around. Upon entering the prosecutors' offices on the fourteenth floor, visitors would find no waiting room where someone sent to spy on them could size them up or ask prying questions. Instead, a member of the staff escorted them to a private office where the blinds were always kept closed to prevent surveillance from adjacent skyscrapers. Even building employees were checked out by Dewey's investigators.

Dewey understood that as a special prosecutor he could not just make speeches and return a few indictments. To be judged successful he had to go after a powerful Mr. Big and bring him down, the way Treasury agents had done with Capone in Chicago in 1931 and Judge Seabury did with Mayor Walker in New York in 1932. Dutch Schultz looked like the best candidate, because he was as famous as Lucky Luciano and a lot more vulnerable. Where Lucky delegated, Schultz tended to micromanage. Dewey had already collected considerable evidence against him from the tax investigation cases. Born Arthur Flegenheimer in 1902, his nom de rackets came from a noted turn-of-the-century prizefighter in his native Bronx. In the late 1920s Schultz built a beer empire by employing violence notable even for that time. Everyone knew of his murderous feuds with Vince Coll and Legs Diamond. In the early '30s he became heavily involved in industrial racketeering. One of his lieutenants, Jules Martin (Megilowsky), opened up a cheap restaurant and then proceeded to form an employers group, the Metropolitan Restaurant and Cafeteria Association. Schultz's men also strong-armed their way into controlling two waiters unions. They forced restaurant employees to pay dues to the union while simultaneously warning restaurant owners that they had to join the association or risk strikes, picket lines, and stink bombs. Initiation fees in the association ranged from $5,000 to $25,000, plus heavy annual dues.

At about the same time, Dutch had taken over the lucrative Harlem policy racket, which grossed $20 million annually. Despite the big money, the business was a collection of small high-risk operations. A customer placed a bet on a three-digit number with any of 15,000 collectors who turned the slips in to "banks," most of them run by West Indians such as Henry Miro, "Spasm" Ison, Alexander Pompez, or the "Queen of Harlem Policy" Madame Stephanie St. Claire, who personally controlled thirty banks. The winning combination was determined by a daily number from a predetermined source, such as the tote board at a racetrack. With 999 possible winning combinations, banks paying out at the usual 600 to 1 to winners (minus 10 percent to the numbers writer) would make a profit, provided that too much money was not bet on a particular number. Like those who played the Italian lottery, numbers players consulted dream books, and on the day before Thanksgiving 1931, thousands put their money on a recommended number: 527. When it came up at a Cincinnati racetrack every Harlem banker took a beating. Spasm Ison was out $18,000; Alexander Pompez, $68,000. Schultz's lawyer, Richard "Dixie" Davis, convinced his boss that in its weakened condition the policy racket was ready for consolidation.

Davis made the necessary arrangement with Jimmy Hines to keep the police at bay, and Schultz's gunmen moved in. Henry Miro was told that henceforth he would have to pay $500 a week to the Dutchman, or else. After beatings and shootings he and others gave in. The only resistance came from Madame St. Claire, who went so far as to take out newspaper ads alleging a crooked deal between racketeers and politicians. But with no support from her peers, and facing both Schultz and the police raids Hines could order, she eventually fell into line.

If it hadn't been for Davis, Schultz would have been jailed the first time Dewey went after him. The son of a Romanian immigrant tailor, his nickname Dixie was a diminutive of Dick, not a reference to a southern heritage. His offices occupied an entire floor of a Broadway office building, he owned three homes, and he was always dressed in the most expensive clothes. Though married, Davis squired many young beauties, his main one being an ex-rodeo rider and Ziegfeld girl, flame-haired Hope Dare. Davis put on a good show at trials, but his success came from the fact that Jimmy Hines controlled the judges and prosecutors. As Dewey put it, Davis "shouted in court and whispered in the back rooms."

When Dewey indicted him for tax evasion in 1933, it looked like Schultz was finished. He went into hiding, surrendering the following year in Albany, New York. At his trial in upstate Syracuse, the jury could not reach a verdict. A retrial was moved to the little town of Malone, New York. Conviction seemed certain, but Dixie Davis figured out a slick strategy for his client. Abandoning his previous reputation as a tightwad, Schultz took up residence in Malone and began handing out money right and left. He sent flowers and candy to the local hospital and treated kids to sodas down at the drugstore. He picked up lunch and liquor tabs for people, always remembering to include a generous tip for the waitresses or bartenders. He hired the largest hall in town, threw a dance, and invited everyone in the community to come as his guests. Even his cheap suits helped his image. He looked like an ordinary guy, not the big-shot New York gangster the government claimed he was. In 1935, a jury acquitted him outright. The furious trial judge denounced the verdict, saying, "[It] has shaken the confidence of law-abiding people and obviously was based on some reason other than the evidence."

It didn't take Schultz long to go back to his old ways. Jules Martin, like everyone else, had assumed that the Boss would not return and began to siphon off some of the earnings from the restaurant racket. Schultz confronted Martin, shot him at point-blank range, and dumped his body in an upstate snowdrift. Another lieutenant, Bo Weinberg, had remained loyal while running Harlem policy for his absent boss, but that didn't stop Dutch from sticking a gun in his mouth and pulling the trigger during a petty quarrel in a West Side hotel room.

Schultz knew Dewey had him targeted. On one wiretap, detectives listened as Dixie Davis called to give his boss holiday greetings. "Merry Christmas, Arthur," Davis said. "Merry Christmas, Junior," Schultz replied. "And a Merry Christmas to those sons of bitches from Dewey's office who are listening in." To gain some breathing space he moved to Newark, New Jersey, out of the special prosecutor's jurisdiction. According to legend, Schultz decided the answer to his troubles would be to kill Dewey. He put the proposition to his fellow mob bosses. Luciano, Lepke, and Adonis refused approval, fearful of reprisals. Supposedly Schultz decided to go it alone. He ordered a surveillance placed on Dewey which disclosed that in order not to disturb his pregnant wife, Dewey left his apartment at Fifth Avenue and 96th Street every morning and went to a nearby drugstore, calling his office from a phone booth before having breakfast. The tailman even took his little boy into the drugstore and loitered unobtrusively to observe Dewey at close range, noting that his bodyguards waited on the street outside. A gunman already planted inside and armed with a silencer could kill the prosecutor and escape before the guards knew what was happening. The story goes that

48 hours before Dewey's murder was to take place, Luciano and Lepke got wind of the plan and ordered a hit on Schultz.

The rubout was one of the goriest of the age. On the night of October 23, 1935, Schultz was dining in Newark's Palace Chophouse with bodyguards LuLu Rosenkrantz and Abe Landau and accountant Otto "Abba Dabba" Berman, who handled the books for the policy racket. Two of Lepke's gunmen, Charlie "The Bug" Workman and Mendy Weiss, slipped quietly into the Chophouse. When they found Dutch's three lieutenants sitting at a table in the back room, Workman opened up with a .38 and a .45 while Weiss pulled a shotgun from under his coat and began blasting. Seven slugs hit Rosenkrantz, six found Berman, and Landau took three. Coming out of the men's room, Dutch was hit by shots from Workman and a wild one from Landau. He sat down heavily in a chair and slumped onto a table. Abe Landau began running after Workman with blood spurting from a severed artery in his neck, while Rosenkrantz attempted to follow him but quickly collapsed. Landau continued to run outside, still firing, then he toppled over. Mendy Weiss had jumped into a getaway car driven by a local hoodlum and the two raced off, leaving Workman to make his escape on foot.

Schultz lingered for twenty-two hours while a police stenographer took down his words. Some made sense, like "The boy shot me." "Please, John, did you buy the hotel" might have been addressed to the ubiquitous Johnny Torrio, who had been partners with Schultz in the bail bond business. But sentences like "No homo and popo" were incomprehensible. Some people found poetry worthy of Shakespeare in his babblings, particularly the line, "A boy has never wept, nor dashed a thousand kin." Dutch had not previously enjoyed a literary reputation. The vengeful Madame St. Claire sent a telegram to his deathbed that read, "Don't be yellow. As you sow so shall you reap."

It's a great yarn, but the story has many holes. Schultz was not a total fool; he had to realize that if Dewey were killed, there would soon be a replacement. Crack federal prosecutor John Harlan Amen was busy making antitrust cases against Lepke in the garment center and Luciano's man Socks Lanza in the Fulton Fish Market; already some observers had tabbed Amen as the next Dewey. The time line is also questionable. Two hours after the

Newark shootings, Schultz's chief enforcer "Little Marty" Krompier was ambushed and severely wounded in a Manhattan arcade under the Palace Theatre at 47th and Broadway. A double rubout across two states would have been hard to orchestrate with just 48 hours' notice. A slightly more plausible explanation was that Schultz had announced to Lepke and Luciano that he was converting to his wife's faith, Catholicism. Lepke did not object to his religion losing a follower or Luciano to his gaining one, but when men like Dutch make sudden life changes, especially by embracing a faith in which confession is an integral part, it raises questions as to whether the convert is thinking of making a clean breast of his sins to a man like Dewey. Whether he died for them or not, Schultz received the rites of the Catholic church and was buried in Heaven's Gate cemetery.

It is far more likely that the murders were carried out to rid the mob world of an unstable character who constantly drew unwelcome attention. This scenario becomes even more compelling when you consider who benefited the most from the killing. One was Lucky Luciano, who split Dutch's holdings with Lepke. Luciano's capo "Trigger Mike" Coppola from East Harlem was assigned to control policy, with his black top lieutenant Ellsworth "Bumpy" Johnson functioning as the middleman between the East Harlem Italians and the Central Harlem blacks.[1]

The fact that Schultz's killers were Lepke's gunmen was in line with Lucky's usual practice of having the hit carried out by a third party. Despite his attempt to remain above the battle, the publicity from the shooting caught up with him. While newspaper accounts mentioned that "Lefty Buckhouse" (Lepke Buchalter) and "Charles 'Buck' Speigel" (Benjamin "Bugsy" Siegel) were in on the takeover of Schultz's operations, they clearly identified Charles "Lucky" Luciano as the top figure. The management of the Waldorf Astoria asked "Mr. Ross" to vacate his suite.

---

[1]Enforcement was part of Bumpy's duties and he was much feared, but he was more than just a slugger. Of medium height and husky, his nickname came from a bump on the back of his head. Though he never went beyond the fourth grade, he was an avid reader and chess player. Many of his fellow hoodlums called him the "Professor." The handsome and charming Bumpy was also popular outside Harlem. Columnists sometimes mentioned him, and chic ladies enjoyed his company. For a time one of his girlfriends was the editor of a top magazine.

Now Dewey's office had to find a new Mr. Big. The logical replacement was Luciano—exactly the reason Meyer Lansky had urged Lucky not to kill Schultz. The question for the prosecutor's office was how to proceed. One way was to laboriously build up a state tax evasion case with charges that might have brought Lucky a couple of years in prison at most. Another was to try to convict his subordinates of racketeering and get them to turn against Luciano, but usually only the threat of the electric chair could convince capos to talk. Luciano's organizational structure contained many levels and it was unlikely that the smoke from a hitman's pistol would ever drift all the way to the top.

It was Eunice Carter, a black lawyer on Dewey's staff, who provided the solution. Carter had previously practiced in the women's court where prostitution cases were heard, and in the last couple of years she had begun to notice that a group of girls always had the same bondsmen and lawyers. Dewey authorized her to place wiretaps on brothels and assigned additional detectives to the investigation. Gradually, they began to learn about "the combine." At its heart were four bookers who moved 2,000 girls through some 300 whorehouses. A booker scheduled a girl into a different madam's house each week, where she worked a twelve-hour shift with only one day off in seven. The average girl earned about $300 a week. Half went to the madam, plus $25 for meals and $5 for a weekly medical exam. That left the girl little more than $100 to bring home to her pimp. In addition to regular payoffs, the madams had to kick in $10 of their share to a fund the combine maintained to pay bail bondsmen and lawyers. The system was run by "Little Davey" Betillo and "Tommy the Bull" Pennochio, both associates of Lucky Luciano. A few years earlier they had begun to move in on independent bookers and madams, forcing them to work for the combine. Those who refused were beaten or threatened by mob heavies like Ralph Liguori, who freelanced as a stickup man. Others gave in when Davey or the Bull dropped Luciano's name. By the mid-'30s, bookers, madams, and pimps had to pay off the combine.

When a Boston pimp named Dan O'Brien came down to get in on the lucrative New York trade, he made straight for Jamison's, an ordinary bar and grill on 57th Street west of Broadway where the combine bosses hung out. After a few visits he got into conversation with a swarthy hoodlum who called himself Jimmy Fredericks (Fredericio). O'Brien was vague about his activities and did not object when occasionally someone would pat him on the back or help him with his coat, subtle frisks to determine if he had a gun or a microphone on him. After an interval he revealed that he wanted to set up a stable of prostitutes. Fredericks warned him not to try to do it independently because "Lucky did not allow it." While O'Brien was negotiating he made a faux pas, assembling a group of cheap Hell's Kitchen whores and bringing them into Jamison's for a drink. The reception he got was icier than if he had taken them to a society tea dance at the Waldorf. Fredericks told him, "If Tommy [Pennochio] was here he would break your head." In La Guardia's New York, even the combine had to fear that some honest vice cop might walk in and bust the joint, leading to a license revocation. O'Brien beat a hasty retreat all the way to Dewey's office where, under his real name, Harold "Dan" Danforth, he worked as a criminal investigator. When a police inspector heard the story, he warned Danforth's bosses, "This young man is going to get himself killed." The whorehouse raids were imminent, so Danforth was ordered to lay low for a while.

The police teams moved in on schedule, hitting brownstones and flats in respectable, even deluxe, apartment buildings. At forty-one of the spots, the occupants were surprised. A *Daily Mirror* writer reported, "Half-naked women shrieked. Gangsters reached for guns, terrified patrons for clothing. Madams rushed frantically for hidden exits." It wasn't actually that exciting. Anyone reaching for a gun would have landed in the morgue. Mostly, the madams began their usual dickering—"Can't this be squared?" "Let me call my lawyer," etc. In all cases, the answer was "No." Thirty-nine of the places were empty. Since recent surveillance by Dewey's investigators had confirmed they were operating, they had obviously been warned. Some people blamed it on police leaks, but it was probably a result of a decision Dewey had made to seize Pennochio, Betillo, and fourteen other managers of the combine the previous evening. They were being held incommunicado, but doubtless their sudden disappearance set off alarms among some madams and made them cautious about opening shop.

When the prisoners arrived at the Barclay Street entrance to the Wool-worth Building, they were taken by freight elevator to the 13th floor. Some-one on Dewey's staff had foreseen the possibility that an extra floor would be needed and deliberately rented the 14th, knowing that in the midst of a depression, with buildings half full, the unlucky 13th would always be empty. Despite orders to lie low, Dan Danforth slipped into the building to watch the arrival of the prisoners. Years later he recalled the scene: "Sleek-haired pimps with their harlots; tough gangster's molls, dyed blondes, redheads, young, old, sick, bored, weeping, bewildered, many of them dis-eased, herded down the marble halls." When a superior spotted Danforth he ordered him out of the building.

By midnight, nearly one hundred women, variously and colorfully dressed, were sitting or standing around as though at college registration. Tough madams like "Polack Frances," "Sadie the Chink," "Six Bits," "Jenny the Factory," and "Cokey Flo" waited with their girls to be interviewed by Dewey's assistants. The D.A. himself walked around like a dean greeting the freshmen. A pert blond hooker named Nancy Presser recognized him, say-ing, "So you're Dewey. Run along, Boy Scout, and peddle your papers." She was a little mixed up from the excitement: Boy Scouts typically helped old ladies across the street. When "Fancy Nancy" had come to New York at fourteen, she worked for a while as an artist's model before becoming a high-priced call girl favored by top mob guys. Now at twenty-seven, her looks were gone and she was the sweetheart of the petty thug and combine enforcer Ralph Liguori.

The girls were familiar with arrest procedures. A bail bondsmen would soon arrive and put up $300 apiece to obtain their release pending trial. A lawyer had tutored them on what to say in court. "I am from out of town, Judge, I was just stopping by the apartment to see a friend when the police came in and arrested everyone. Please let me go back home to my sick mother in Ashtabula." Magistrates dismissed the cases or gave the girls small fines, for which they could expect a payoff of $25 a head. If the heat was on and acquittals not easy to come by, the bail bondsman would tell the girls to get out of town and, "Don't come back until you're old and gray." Not this time. Dewey secured bail of $10,000 each, ensuring that the girls and madams would remain locked up while his assistants grilled them and collected further evidence.

Pinning the combine to Luciano was a real challenge. The man had been a dope dealer, gambler, bootlegger, and murderer, but never a pimp. Money was rolling in from his other enterprises—why would he want to get into prostitution? The question has people arguing his innocence to this day. The prosecution's theory was that since Luciano was the top organized crime figure in Manhattan, a vice ring could not operate without his approval. To convict, the state would have to prove that he was in ultimate control of the combine. Dewey's interrogators used good cop–bad cop methods to persuade some of the prisoners to cooperate. The chief shepherd of the girls was assistant district attorney Frank Hogan, a young Irish-Catholic from Connecticut who had lettered in football and baseball at Columbia. Under "Father Hogan's" direction, girls lodged in the Manhattan House of Detention for Women were sometimes taken out to movies, bought ice cream, or given pairs of stockings. Male prisoners like the bookers were threatened with long prison sentences. Luciano's hoods could also play hardball. On several occasions the jailed girls heard rough voices from the adjacent elevated tracks calling to them to keep their mouths shut. Eventually three of the bookers, some madams like Cokey Flo Brown, and prostitutes including Nancy Presser decided to testify. Presser's boyfriend Ralph Liguori and bosses like Betillo and Pennochio kept their mouths shut.

In April 1936 Luciano and fifteen of his associates were indicted on charges of compulsory prostitution, in Lucky's case, on 99 counts.[2] Lucky decided that he needed a vacation in Owney Madden's Hot Springs. A fugitive warrant was forwarded from New York City; Luciano was arrested and then released on a piddling $5,000 bail. With the authority of the governor of New York behind him, Dewey demanded that the attorney general of Arkansas "render" (return) the fugitive. Luciano was moved into the local jail while lawyers debated. Madden mobilized enormous political pressure to keep Luciano from being extradited, but the story was making national

---

[2]Previously, under New York law, each of the charges had to be tried separately, but Dewey had gotten the Albany legislature to change the law, permitting offenses to be joined.

headlines. The Arkansas attorney general sent state troopers with machine guns into the jail to seize Lucky, bring him to the state capital, and turn him over to New York detectives.

Luciano's trial strategy was to deny he knew any of the people who claimed they were present when he discussed combine business with defendants like Betillo or Pennochio. Unfortunately for him, hotel employees testified that they had seen the defendants in Lucky's suite at the Waldorf. To make it harder for the witnesses to identify them, the defendants began to change their appearance every day, behavior not unnoticed by the jury. Phone records from the Waldorf and Lucky's downtown headquarters at Celano's restaurant confirmed many calls to and from the bosses of the combine. Nancy Presser's testimony struck an especially low blow: not only did she describe visiting his place on business and overhearing incriminating conversations, she claimed he was frequently unable to perform in bed. For the rest of his life he maintained that "ugly broad" had never been in his apartment. All sixteen defendants were convicted, Lucky on 62 counts. Presiding judge Philip McCook, who was specially assigned to Dewey's cases, gave Luciano 30 to 50 years; Betillo, 25 to 40; and lesser figures like Ralph Liguori, 7½ to 15. Luciano was incarcerated far upstate in Dannemora, the Siberia of New York's prison system. Despite later recantations by some of the state's witnesses—including Nancy Presser, who said her testimony was scripted—the judgment was affirmed by the higher courts. Lucky maintained his innocence but did concede, years later, that he knew Betillo and Pennochio had used his name to muscle in on prostitution. Because it was such a petty thing and he was not personally involved he thought he could never be charged. Fifty-year sentences were not the norm for convicted pimps, and it is clear that Lucky was sentenced, in large part, for the other things he was thought to have done. It was the penalty of fame. Al Capone had gotten eleven years for income tax violations at a time when the usual sentence was two.

When Dewey was nominated in 1937 for district attorney by the fusion coalition that backed Mayor La Guardia for reelection, both men were victorious. Dewey fired 61 of the 64 assistant district attorneys who had been on Dodge's staff, and secured a corruption indictment against Jimmy

Hines for receiving payoffs from Schultz's policy operations. The judge was Ferdinand Pecora, a longtime Tammany assistant district attorney. Hines's defense attorney was Lloyd Paul Stryker, one of the most eminent lawyers of his day. During the trial, Dewey cross-examined ex-A.D.A. Lyon Boston, asking him, "Do you remember any testimony about Hines and the poultry racket?" Stryker demanded a mistrial, declaring the question implied the defendant was guilty of crimes other than those for which he was being tried. Pecora granted the motion over Dewey's vociferous protests and the case sparked widespread controversy over the legitimacy of the ruling. For Dewey it was only a temporary setback. At a second trial Hines was convicted and sentenced to four to eight years in prison.

Dewey's efforts against organized crime were the most successful since the federal "Get Capone" drive. But he was no more effective in breaking the mob's grip on New York than the Capone prosecutors were in destroying the Chicago syndicate. Though the restaurant industry was cleaned up, the mob was not forced out of lucrative areas like the garment center, the waterfront, or the Fulton Fish Market. Policy in Harlem continued to flourish. Dewey's attacks on Hines were devastating to Tammany, but the organization was already a shadow of itself. The Manhattan base had shrunk from over half of the population of New York City in 1900 to less than one-quarter. The loss of City Hall and its vast patronage had put the organization on a starvation diet. In jailing Hines, Dewey was actually clearing the way for Luciano's ultimate successor, Frank Costello, to become the backstage ruler of Tammany.

Luciano's rise (and Adonis's role in Brooklyn) was the final blow to the old order that had begun with Rothstein's ascension to middleman between Tammany and the gamblers twenty years earlier. New York politicians no longer had the power to control mobsters; instead, it was the reverse. This was different from Chicago, where the Democratic machine had actually gained power in the years after Prohibition and was now stronger than the gangsters at least most of the time. The new power did not go to Frank's head; he was careful to show respect to Lucky up in Dannemora and retained the wise counsel of Meyer Lansky.

Dewey's writ ran only in Manhattan, so the political leaders of the other four boroughs were essentially beyond his reach. The most solid long-term accomplishment of the Dewey days was the removal of the New York County district attorney's office from political control. For the remainder of the century and beyond, the post would be occupied by two distinguished figures, Frank Hogan (1942–1974) and Robert Morgenthau (1975–to date).

The civic reform forces did attempt to expand their scope beyond Manhattan. In the fall of 1936, Lee Thompson Smith and some of his fellow runaway jurors who had been responsible for Dewey's appointment as special prosecutor formed a citizens' crime commission to support him and to serve as a watchdog over criminal justice city-wide. The chairman of the group was copper heir and former ambassador Harry Guggenheim, and outstanding figures such as former U.S. attorney George Medalie were appointed to the board. Mayor La Guardia joined them at their initial press conference to offer his support, though he became less friendly when the Crime Commission began criticizing the city administration. In 1938 the commission launched a case-fixing investigation in the office of Brooklyn district attorney William Geoghan and requested that a special prosecutor be appointed. Again Governor Lehman acquiesced and appointed John Harlan Amen, who by that time had convicted Lepke and Lanza. Amen's investigations over the next four years would result in one assistant district attorney being sent to Sing Sing and two others disbarred. He also uncovered a corrupt bail bond system, an abortion conspiracy, and gambling payoffs to police officers. Because he was only a special prosecutor, Amen could not achieve the same kind of results as Dewey, and given the power of the local political organization, he had no chance of becoming the elected D.A. of Brooklyn.

In an era when crime stories filled the papers, airwaves, and movie screens, Dewey inspired several films and a radio series, *Mr. District Attorney.* He was a national hero. In 1938 he lost a close race for governor to the popular Herbert Lehman, but it was one of those defeats where the loser's star rises even higher, and Dewey was widely discussed as the Republican nominee for president in 1940.[3]

---

[3] Another transplanted midwesterner, Wall Street lawyer Wendell Willke, was enjoying an equally mercurial rise. At the 1940 Republican Convention in Philadelphia Willke managed to beat Dewey for the presidential nomination.

Dewey was elected governor of New York in 1942 and received the Republican nomination for president two years later. No one expected him to defeat Roosevelt in the midst of a war, so the loss did not damage his chances next time around. In 1946 he stunned his former supporters by releasing Lucky Luciano, then in the tenth year of his sentence, on condition that he be deported to Italy. Despite the accusations by his fellow bosses that Lucky was too American, he had never bothered to acquire United States citizenship. Dewey's explanation was that Luciano had been helpful during World War II in preventing sabotage on the New York waterfront and providing information to American forces invading Sicily. Ever since then there had been assertions that payoffs were made to secure the release or that Dewey was tacitly admitting Lucky had been framed—perhaps both. Lucky's alleged memoirs even claim that Judge McCook visited the gangster in prison and fell on his knees to beg forgiveness for sentencing him on trumped-up charges. Dewey himself admitted when he released Luciano that "the actual value of the information [he] procured is not clear."

No evidence has ever been presented that New York mobsters intended to carry out harbor sabotage. When the giant French liner *Normandy* was gutted by fire in February 1942 while it was being fitted as a troop ship at a West Side pier, it was rumored that it was a message from the mob to the authorities not to bother the waterfront rackets. Investigation disclosed the fire was started accidentally by a workman. In 1951, the Kefauver Committee concluded there was no reason to believe that Luciano had furnished any wartime services worthy of a gubernatorial commutation. Whatever the explanation, by 1946 Dewey had transformed himself from racket buster to politician, and in that capacity his interests were better served by a free Luciano 3,000 miles away than one carrying on a high-powered campaign to obtain release from a New York State prison cell.

Luciano's departure was an event Dewey would have railed against had he still been a prosecutor. Gangs of longshoremen armed with bailing hooks formed lines to keep reporters away from the *Laura Keane* while mobsters were allowed to go aboard the ship and pay their respects. Luciano did not stay long in Italy. Within a short time he slipped into Cuba and began to set up a headquarters while planning his reentry to the United States. When news leaked out, the U.S. government demanded that the Cubans order him out of the country. Luciano spent the remaining sixteen years of his life in Italy where the Federal Bureau of Narcotics claimed he directed an international drug ring. According to historian Luigi Barzini, he was laughed at by genuine Italian mafiosi, who constantly cheated him.

In 1948 Dewey's sure-thing presidential candidacy was upset by Harry Truman. The 1997 movie *Hoodlum* featured scenes of Dewey receiving bribes from Schultz and Luciano, a canard that would have brought a storm of criticism a generation earlier. By 1997, the three-time governor and twice presidential candidate had become such an obscure figure that the calumny passed without notice.

11: The Feds: Assessing the Menace of the Mafia

They were two of the most powerful and famous men in America, one a journalist, the other a cop. On the night of August 24, 1939, they were trying to pull off a headline-making coup. Sitting in his car at 23rd Street and Madison Avenue was Walter Winchell, the country's premier gossip reporter. His column appeared daily in 1,000 newspapers. A plug from him could make a book into a bestseller, turn a routine Broadway musical into a smash hit, or send a stock soaring. The rich and famous hired press agents to get them a mention in Winchell's column—or to keep them out of it. Sitting alone in an official car six blocks away was J. Edgar Hoover, head of the FBI. In the past six years, he had literally shot to fame as his G-men mowed down colorful, high-profile public enemies like John Dillinger, "Pretty Boy" Floyd, "Baby-Face" Nelson, and Ma Barker, or jailed the likes of Alvin "Creepy" Karpis and Thomas "Machine Gun" Kelly. The resulting headlines made Hoover a national hero and brought him the kind of power that made people hesitant to cross him.

Over the past few years, Winchell and Hoover had become close associates (the relationship was too utilitarian to describe them as friends). Hoover's Bureau fed Winchell tips, while Winchell praised Hoover and introduced him to New York nightlife. Their favorite haunt was the Stork Club, though both knew that owner Sherman Billingsley was an ex-bootlegger and that Frank Costello had once been a silent partner. Hoover continually wrote articles and made speeches decrying the breakdown of American morals, yet he loved to play the horses and never hesitated to accept Winchell's tips, despite the insiders' claim that the source of the columnist's information was often Costello.

Their mission that August evening was to put handcuffs on Louis "Lepke" Buchalter, the most wanted man in America. Hoover's presence was largely a publicity stunt to deflect the criticism that he had sidelined his Bureau in the fight against organized crime. The FBI had less claim on Lepke than other law enforcement agencies. District attorney Dewey wanted Lepke for racketeering and murder, and the Treasury's Federal Bureau of Narcotics had developed a major drug case against him. All the FBI had was a technical charge of unlawful flight to avoid prosecution after Lepke jumped his paltry $3,000 bail on an antitrust conviction that had netted him only a two-year sentence. And even that had been thrown out by corrupt Federal Appeals Court judge Martin Manton, who ordered a new trial. Since 1937 Lepke had been hiding out across the river in Brooklyn under the protection of Albert Anastasia. Neither Winchell, with all of his sources, nor Hoover's vaunted Bureau was able to find him. Instead Lepke had arranged to surrender as part of a deal, or as he would find out later, a double-cross.

When Dewey indicted Lepke and his partner "Gurrah" Shapiro for racketeering in the bakery industry, he began poking around some murder cases that might be laid at their door. Lepke decided to go on the offensive and told Anastasia to have his hired guns, shortly to be known as "Murder, Incorporated," get rid of any possible informers. When a Lepke lieutenant who had been shipped out of town got lonely for his family and came back, a bullet from one of Anastasia's shooters got him in the neck. It didn't kill him, but it did loosen his tongue, and he gave Dewey's investigators information that led to a murder charge against Lepke.

The hunt was big news and an army of detectives searched high and low for the fugitive without success. Then in July 1939, Anastasia's gunmen killed an innocent citizen, mistaking him for a stoolie they were after. The outcry was enormous. Acting for the mob commission, Frank Costello decided that it was time for Lepke to come in from the cold. The mobsters contacted Winchell, who they knew was friendly with Hoover, and offered a deal whereby Lepke would surrender to the Feds and be given a stiff sentence on narcotics charges, keeping him away from Dewey and the electric chair. Winchell began broadcasting appeals to Lepke to "come out, come out, wherever you are." A meeting place had been arranged. At 10 P.M. Lepke walked up to Winchell's car and introduced himself. Winchell drove him to 28th and Fifth and introduced him to Hoover. "How do you do?" said Hoover. "Glad to meet you," answered Lepke. "Let's go." A few months later he was sentenced to twelve years, and for the next three years there would be a tug of war between the Feds and the state of New York over his custody.

During the hunt for Lepke, the name that had struck the most fear in New York mob circles was Dewey, the man with tickets to the electric chair. Gangsters trafficking drugs also respected the Bureau of Narcotics' ability to secure long prison sentences. The FBI was largely irrelevant to mobsters. Hoover's participation in Lepke's surrender was an easy way to earn plaudits for fighting the racketeers without having to get involved with the seamy world of organized crime.

Comprehending Hoover's laissez-faire attitude toward the mobs requires an understanding not only of the man but of his organization. When he took over the Bureau in 1924, it was already sixteen years old and had yet to distinguish itself. Theodore Roosevelt had created it after Congress sought to punish the Secret Service for its investigation of land fraud that led to the jailing of a U.S. senator.[1] Having originated as a retaliatory strike rather than a necessity, it lacked a unique mission—a dangerous situation in federal law enforcement where the key to an agency's survival was to have a definite task to perform. The Secret Service protected the national currency, customs prevented smuggling, and the postal inspectors investigated thefts or frauds involving the U.S. mail. In 1910 the passage of the White Slavery, or Mann,

---

[1] Prior to 1908, the Treasury loaned Secret Servicemen to other government agencies to conduct criminal investigations. It was William Burns, star of the Service, who nailed Senator John Mitchell of Oregon by using tactics that drew much criticism. When Congress refused Roosevelt's proposal to create a general investigation bureau within the Justice Department, the president established it by executive order.

Act provided the Bureau of Investigation with a focus. The statute forbade the interstate transportation of a female for immoral purposes. Most people assumed that it applied to commercialized vice, not private conduct. President Taft's attorney general, George Wickersham, had specifically cautioned that federal courts should be careful to avoid "ordinary criminal cases which should be dealt with by local tribunals." His instructions were quickly forgotten and the law would be broadly enforced whenever it was politically advantageous to do so.

In 1913, President Woodrow Wilson appointed former congressman Anthony Caminetti to be the United States commissioner of immigration. He was known as a strong supporter of law enforcement and during World War I and the postwar Red scare he would be criticized by leftists for his hard-line law and order views. But with all that yet to come, all the anti-immigrant forces could see was that an Italian had been placed in charge of keeping undesirables out of the United States. Caminetti's son Drew, a young married man, had a girlfriend he occasionally took from Sacramento to the resort town of Reno, Nevada. Shortly after the elder Caminetti took office, Bureau agents arrested the younger one and charged him with violation of the Mann Act. He was convicted and sentenced to 18 months imprisonment. On appeal, the U.S. Supreme Court upheld the application of the law to private conduct. Jack Johnson, the first African-American to become heavyweight champion, was arrested for traveling interstate with his white girlfriend and had to leave the country to avoid imprisonment. Instead of going after pimping rings, the Bureau's best-known cases were made against prominent members of ethnic and racially disfavored groups engaging in consensual sexual conduct.

Because federal law enforcement was spread so thinly across the country, to some extent it was necessary to concentrate on high-profile offenders to deter ordinary violators. In the 1920s, Elmer Irey's Treasury intelligence unit went after prominent movie stars such as Charlie Chaplin and Tom Mix for not paying their income tax, because they knew cases involving screen idols would make front-page news. But the targets were picked because the dollar amounts were significant and their profiles were high, not because of their race or ethnicity.

During World War I the Bureau of Investigation issued credentials to 250,000 volunteer sleuths, some of whom acted as vigilantes against antiwar activists, or used heavy-handed tactics against Americans who committed technical violations like leaving their draft cards at home. From 1919 to 1920, the Bureau conducted widespread roundups of aliens and radicals in so-called Red raids, followed up by deportations. It was these activities that first brought J. Edgar Hoover to notice. Born into a family of Washington civil servants, Hoover earned a law degree from George Washington University and joined the Department of Justice as an attorney in 1917. His arrival coincided with the onset of the world war and the twenty-two-year-old was assigned administrative duties dealing with aliens. Afterward he was placed in charge of the general intelligence division, which dealt largely with domestic security. In both positions he was an office administrator, not a field operative. Even as head of the FBI it was not until the mid-'30s that he personally made an arrest.

In 1921 the Harding administration replaced Director William Flynn with William Burns, and Hoover's division was moved into the Bureau of Investigation, where he was named assistant director. After it was discovered in 1924 that Burns had sent agents to investigate critics of the Harding administration during the Teapot Dome scandal, he was dismissed by incoming U.S. attorney general Harlan Fiske Stone. Elmer Irey was the favorite to replace him, but Stone turned for advice to former Secret Service agent Larry Richey, who was then the top aide to Secretary of Commerce Herbert Hoover. Richey recommended his daily luncheon companion, J. Edgar Hoover.

The end of the war and the declining threat from the Reds left the Bureau short of missions. When Congress made the interstate transportation of a stolen car a federal crime in 1919, jurisdiction was assigned to the Bureau of Investigation. Recovering a citizen's vehicle did not carry the same emotional impact as protecting one's daughter from being kidnapped and placed in a whorehouse, but it did give the Bureau a popular task.

While bootlegging gangs shot up the streets of American cities, bribed police and prosecutors, and took over whole communities, Hoover's Bureau spent most of its time on relatively unimportant crimes. The director's usual response when challenged about his failure to move against racketeers was that mob activity was local and did not fall within the purview of federal laws that his Bureau was authorized to enforce. This explanation was somewhat disingenuous. When the governor of Louisiana asked for federal assistance against the Ku Klux Klan, the Bureau turned over evidence to local authorities and brought a Mann Act prosecution against a Klan leader, when it was unable to make any other cases under federal law. Mob bosses like Capone were involved in prostitution and many of them took their girlfriends across state lines, but Hoover did not pursue that avenue of inquiry.

When undercover agents alerted the Bureau to a communist meeting being held in Bridgeman, Michigan, agents raided the gathering and seized records. There were no applicable federal statutes under which the communists could be tried, so the Bureau turned over the evidence to the state for prosecution under Michigan sedition laws. Similarly, the Bureau could have gathered evidence of murders, bombings, and hijackings committed by bootlegging gangs and furnished it to state prosecutors. If there was a will, a legal way could have been found. Hoover's Bureau owed its existence to Congress's desire to punish the Secret Service for stepping on political toes. The Prohibition Bureau was shot through with corruption. So Hoover had no appetite for investigating bootlegging or other rackets that might tempt his agents with bribes or bring down the wrath of politicians who were paid off to protect mobsters.

The onset of the Depression and the end of Prohibition produced criminals who roamed from state to state, robbing, kidnapping, and killing. Only the federal government was in a position to go after gangs pulling a holdup in Oklahoma on Monday, another in Iowa on Wednesday, and killing a policeman in Minnesota on Friday. Hoover's agents were not really full-fledged cops—their authority to carry guns and make arrests was severely limited— but they were the most readily available force. In 1933 Congress gave them the responsibility for enforcing new federal laws against interstate crime.

The Bureau's exploits against "public enemies" like Dillinger and the other small-time hoodlums made "G-men" a household word and won Hoover praise from attorney general Cummings and President Roosevelt. In 1935, his agency was formally designated *The* Federal Bureau of Investigation, indicating it was the primary government law enforcement agency. The next year when some U.S. Secret Service agents opened a quiet investigation of a case where FBI agents had shot an unarmed man, Hoover's protest led to demotion of the men involved, one of whom was assistant director of the service. Hoover's Bureau clearly occupied a higher position than other federal investigators. But organized crime was still not on the FBI's agenda.

The agency that did attack mob bosses was the Federal Bureau of Narcotics under Commissioner Harry Anslinger (predictably known in the underworld as "Asslinger"). Like Hoover, Anslinger had not set out to be a cop. Born in 1892, he had grown up in a Pennsylvania Dutch family. During his early teens the Commonwealth of Pennsylvania was engaging in its great anti-Mafia drives and Anslinger attended the trial of a local capo charged with shooting an Italian laborer who refused to pay extortion money. While young Harry watched, the defendant threatened the victim in open court, causing him to clam up. "Such was my first encounter with the transplanted brotherhood," he wrote over forty years later. After attending Penn State he landed a State Department job during World War I, performing intelligence work in Europe. After the war he became a vice consul and continued in European posts. Later he was assigned to the Bahamas, where he attempted to persuade the local authorities to stop the liquor trade that was supplying the East Coast rum fleets. The island was growing rich from it and Anslinger did not succeed. Frustrated, he transferred to the U.S. Treasury's foreign interest section and was named commissioner of the newly formed Bureau of Narcotics in 1930.

Treasury's Narcotics had much the same origins as the Justice Department's FBI (and the Prohibition Bureau), all growing out of early-twentieth-century crusades against drugs, prostitution, and liquor. Each had to overcome the congressional reluctance to pass laws that might infringe upon states' rights. The Mann Act was the first to be enacted, aided by lurid tales of white slavers. Drugs were a harder sell. At the beginning of the twentieth century, there was considerable debate over the use of opium and its derivatives and the products of coca leaves. Some physicians attested to the miraculous medicinal effects of these substances; others argued they had deleterious effects. As Dr. David Musto has written, "Cocaine and heroin were both introduced from excellent laboratories by men with considerable clinical experience who judged them to be relatively harmless; in fact, to be possible cures for morphine and alcohol addiction."

Gradually the drug opponents won out, helped in no small measure by the fact that narcotics addicts and peddlers seemed to be disproportionately drawn from blacks, Asians, and southern and eastern Europeans.[2] Some claimed that cocaine turned African-Americans into criminals or made them rebellious. The association of West Coast Chinese with opium provided images of yellow men corrupting whites, particularly women.

Early in the century a number of treaties were signed that outlawed drug trafficking, and in 1914 Congress passed the Harrison Act forbidding the sale and possession of nonmedicinal drugs. Policing was originally assigned to a small narcotics section within the Internal Revenue Service, and early enforcement was tentative. Many people doubted the law's constitutionality. Others assumed drug users were safe as long as they obtained a doctor's prescription, and there was no shortage of physicians ready to write them. In 1921, the U.S. Supreme Court not only found the act constitutional, but held that under its provisions doctors could write prescriptions only for specific medical reasons, not just to maintain the addict. When the Volstead Act took effect, narcotics enforcement was assigned to a section within the Prohibition Bureau. In the 1920s, under the leadership of Ohio pharmacist Levi Nutt, narcotics agents conducted roundups of addicts and engaged in vigorous drives to close drug treatment centers and generally make life difficult for doctors and pharmacists. Between 1918 and 1925, the annual number of federal drug arrests rose from under 1,000 to over 10,000.

In the mid-1920s Arnold Rothstein had entered the drug business in a big way, for the same reason more conventional bankers expanded their loan portfolios—he wished to remain a major player. Bootleggers were raking in money. With their wealth, some might seek to displace Rothstein as the

---

[2]One of the reasons that Prohibition came into effect last was that liquor's users and distributors were more likely to be northern Europeans. Even then, a constitutional amendment was required to make Prohibition a law.

underworld's leading financial power. Drugs offered fabulous returns on small investments. A pound of raw opium could be purchased for $1,000 and refined to produce $150,000 in profit. Drug deals would generate enough income to keep Rothstein's bankroll the biggest in the New York underworld. He dispatched agents to Europe and Asia to buy opium and smuggle it into the United States. The volume of his business is suggested by the fact that after his murder, information seized by federal agents enabled them to recover $2 million in drugs from a Forty-second Street hotel, $3 million more being transported into New York on the Twentieth Century Limited, and $4 million waiting to be picked up at Manhattan piers. The investigation also disclosed that Rothstein had retained Levi Nutt's son and son-in-law in various matters and had given the son a loan. Nutt was removed as head of the narcotics section and assigned to supervise a small alcohol tax unit in Syracuse, New York.

Due to the Rothstein scandal and the efforts of the socially prominent and politically powerful Mrs. Hamilton Wright (whose father and three brothers had represented four different states in the U.S. Congress), the narcotics section was made an independent agency within the Treasury and Anslinger was named to head it. Hard-driven in crusading for vigorous enforcement, Anslinger was also as good a bureaucrat as J. Edgar Hoover. He seized on the mission of fighting drugs via law enforcement and strongly resisted sharing his turf with other agencies or yielding to those who advocated alternative methods of combating drugs, such as treatment. He did learn from the Prohibition Bureau's failures, warning his agents to "discontinue investigating the corner drugstore and family doctor and get after the smugglers and racketeers." With a force of no more than 180 agents, his Bureau was able to make arrests of a number of drug importers and dealers while carrying on an extensive public relations campaign about the menace of narcotics. The 1936 movie *Reefer Madness,* destined to become a camp favorite on college campuses, was the Federal Bureau of Narcotics' serious attempt to establish a link between a few puffs of marijuana and a life of crime and degradation. In 1937, Anslinger helped to secure enactment of a federal law outlawing the possession and use of cannabis. Still mindful of Prohibition mistakes, he ordered his agents not to take marijuana arrest cases into federal court, but to turn them over for prosecution by state authorities. Public opinion was strongly anti-drug and Anslinger was praised by civic groups and the media. Franklin Roosevelt's feelings about narcotics were made clear by the president's secretary, who warned Anslinger that were he to send Roosevelt a recommendation for clemency for a convicted dealer, he should attach his own letter of resignation.

In some ways the FBN was a mini FBI, but its agents and their methods were quite different. FBI men were drawn from Middle America backgrounds and spent most of their time conducting interviews and filling out reports. Narcotics agents were more likely to be urban ethnics (even blacks or Asians) and they often worked undercover, sometimes posing as criminals. Robberies or kidnappings were assigned to FBI men after they had occurred, while narcs had to find violations and make their own cases. Hoover disapproved of undercover tactics, suspecting that agents who hung around with shady characters were likely to go bad themselves, bringing disgrace on the Bureau and its director. Hoover covered his own stern inner core with the image of a courtly southern gentleman. Anslinger spoke and acted in the rough and direct way of the Pennsylvania coal mines. One reporter described him as "a man whose eyes seem to be cataloging you—your features, build, clothes," in the intimidating way cops did with suspects.

One of Anslinger's top narcotics agents was Charlie Siragusa, whose grandfather had been killed by mafiosi in Sicily. Growing up in the Bronx, Charlie watched with disgust as Italian hoodlums drove around in shiny cars wearing sharp suits and acting as if they owned the world. He decided to become a cop at a young age, specifically one who fought against mob guys. In 1939, he was appointed an agent of the Bureau of Narcotics. Because of his mastery of Sicilian and other languages and his ability to talk and dress like a gangster, he was frequently employed in undercover work. In his first five years of service, Siragusa averaged about two hundred arrests a year.

In 1937, a Sicilian named Nicola Gentile, acting as liaison between Italian and American drug dealers, was arrested in New Orleans. "Zia Cola" (Uncle Cola) was a man with many connections. On his person was found detailed information on U.S. narcotics dealers, including Nick Impostato of Kansas City. Nick left Sicily because of Mussolini's crackdown on the Mafia, and in Kansas City he became a hitman for Johnny Lazia, rising to become underboss of the local narcotics operation. The Federal Bureau of Narcotics investigation led to Tampa, Florida, where locals received smuggled drugs from Marseilles via Havana and shipped them to Missouri. Arrests were made in both states.

Siragusa and other agents worked the case hard. When some of the lower-level members assembled in a Kansas City hotel, the agents bugged the room. One of the arrestees was Carl Caramussa of Kansas City. In 1919, his eleven-year-old brother had been shot and killed by a mob hitman named Paul Cantanzaro, who beat the rap by threatening witnesses. Twenty-two years later, Caramussa and Cantanzaro were working in the same drug gang. Facing the federal charges, Caramussa decided to turn government witness. When Caramussa told his story on the stand, Cantanzaro's threatening gestures got him ejected from the courtroom. The defendants were convicted and Caramussa was released as a reward for his cooperation. He changed his name and moved to Chicago, but one day in 1945 he came out of his house to find a flat tire on his car. His family, anxious to pile in and go to an anniversary party, waited on the porch while he changed it. Caramussa was either not aware or had forgotten that flattening tires was a classic hit setup. A car rolled by with a shotgun poking out the window and the informer's head was blown off before the eyes of his horrified family.

According to Anslinger, after Lucky Luciano was deported to Italy he became head of an international drug smuggling ring. Charlie Siragusa was assigned as head of the FBN office in Rome, where he spent most of his time harassing Lucky. Asked what he would like most in the whole world, Luciano replied, "Siragusa in a block of cement." The smuggling activities of some of the American gang bosses and their links to Italian drug sources led Anslinger's Bureau to believe that the Sicilian Mafia controlled the international drug trade and dominated American organized crime. While J. Edgar Hoover was denying any links among American organized crime groups, Anslinger believed they were part of a vast international conspiracy directed from abroad.

It was not surprising that an agency would put its own particular mission at the center of law enforcement's big picture. The more important its task seemed to the public, the more likely it was that the agency would obtain additional resources and sustain high morale in its workforce. The prestige would give its director more power. But one problem for the FBN was that gambling, not drugs, was the syndicate's principal profit center. Another was that some drug smugglers, such as Lepke's gang, were not Sicilians. In 1935 Lepke had set up his own international ring. His agents purchased pure heroin in China and stored it in trunks on ocean liners bound for Marseilles. At Marseilles the trunks were transferred to Cherbourg where they were put aboard luxury liners bound for New York, such as the *Queen Mary* or *Aquitania*. On arrival, Lepke's men paid customs inspectors $1,000 to obtain baggage clearance stamps. Over a two-year period, the ring managed to smuggle heroin worth $10 million on the street into the United States. Then in 1937 the girlfriend of one of his smuggling crew—angry with her two-timing boyfriend—informed on him to the Bureau of Narcotics. Some members of the gang were arrested and, facing stiff sentences, talked.

By the 1930s American law enforcement was so fragmented that none of its various parts were able to grasp the big picture. Treasury alone had five major enforcement divisions: the Secret Service, Intelligence, Alcohol Tax (the residue of the Prohibition Bureau), Narcotics, and Customs, whose work was supported by the U.S. Coast Guard, another arm of the Treasury. At many U.S. border posts, customs inspectors stood next to immigration inspectors—then part of the U.S. Department of Labor—the former concerned with property and the latter with persons. If the two foot soldiers, customs and immigration officers, got into a dispute and their bosses could not resolve it by negotiation, the only superior with authority over both was the president of the United States.

In 1936 Secretary of the Treasury Henry Morgenthau undertook a major step to remedy the problem of divided authority. He proposed to combine all the Treasury enforcement agencies (except the Coast Guard) into a single force, with Elmer Irey as the chief. J. Edgar Hoover had no desire to see such an agency created. Irey would be commanding 2,500 agents, triple the force Hoover had at the time. In addition, the Bureau had disliked Irey since his arrival on the scene in 1921. "Irey of Intelligence, what a misnomer,"

William Burns once declared. J. Edgar Hoover would never forgive or forget that Irey had almost been named head of the FBI in 1924. Irey had never been afraid to go after organized crime. In 1935, his intelligence agents received a tip that a New York liquor-importing business was secretly owned by Johnny Torrio. Agents sent to check the place noticed that a man named J. T. McCarthy seemed to be in charge. An agent brought in from Chicago identified J.T. as Johnny Torrio. Capone's conviction had inspired Torrio and other mob bosses to keep their taxes aboveboard for a while, but now he was back to cheating. With the agents closing in, he applied for a passport to visit Italy, but the T-men blocked it and brought a case against him that resulted in Torrio receiving a two-and-a-half-year prison sentence.

As head of a combined force, Irey would have had the support of a boss equally willing to take on organized crime and corrupt politicians. Henry Morgenthau Jr., scion of a New York City banking family, was publisher of a national agricultural journal and a commercial farmer in Dutchess County, New York. There, he developed a close friendship with one of his neighbors, Franklin Delano Roosevelt. In 1933, when FDR became president, Morgenthau was appointed to a financial post in the Department of Agriculture. The following year he was named secretary of the Treasury.

Congress was still fearful of conferring too much authority on federal law enforcement. Secretary of State Cordell Hull, an ex-senator from Tennessee, was brought in by his former colleagues to testify that under existing treaties, the Bureau of Narcotics had to be independent. The Senate killed the reorganization plan, but Morgenthau refused to accept defeat and named Irey coordinator of all Treasury law enforcement.

Morgenthau took a strong personal interest in law enforcement matters. When a corruption scandal occurred in the Buffalo customs office, he called in the Service's deputy commissioner for enforcement and ordered him to clean up the situation or be fired. The thirty-year career employee had actually been waiting for such an order and he moved vigorously to get rid of the bad apples. Impressed, Morgenthau gave customs increased responsibility in stopping narcotics smuggling and designated it the department's liaison with the State Department in place of the Narcotics Bureau. To discourage drug shipping on ocean liners, Morgenthau urged U.S. lines to emulate their Canadian counterparts and fire the entire crew of any ship on which contraband drugs were found. He also put T-men aboard the vessels.

Morgenthau believed in joint task forces, a practice resisted by turf-conscious bureau chiefs. He sent customs agents to the West Coast to work with the Bureau of Narcotics in breaking up drug rings headed by Asian kingpins. In Seattle, a Japanese national named Yamamoto was head of a group that received and distributed manufactured drugs from Japan without interference from the local police, who were on his payroll. In Portland, Oregon, Low Kim Yuen directed a chain of Chinese opium joints extending up and down the West Coast, including one across the street from Portland police headquarters. Yuen did not have to worry about any trouble from the police—he usually selected the vice squad in his cities. When the T-men began to close in on Yamamoto he returned to Japan, while Yuen jumped bail after being indicted and fled back to China. Both operations provided more proof that the Sicilian Mafia was far from alone in the drug business.

Morgenthau also turned Irey loose on corrupt politicians like Huey Long of Louisiana and Nucky Johnson of Atlantic City. Long was murdered before an indictment could be bought against him, but cases were prepared against the mayor of New Orleans and other Long henchmen. The local U.S. attorney, a political appointee, did not press charges, so the T-men filed civil suits and were able to collect six-figure fines. In the Atlantic City investigation, T-men counted the number of towels in local whorehouses in order to calculate how many customers the girls served and thereby determine the amount of illegitimate income that was flowing to Johnson. After three trials over five years, Nucky was convicted and sentenced to ten years in prison.

Morgenthau did not spare loyal Democrats. His instructions to his subordinates were, "Let the chips fall where they may." Missouri boss Tom Pendergast ran up impressive city and state vote totals for the party while his administration did business with Charlie Corallo, boss of the Kansas City underworld. Gambling ran wide open, nude waitresses served lunch in the 12th Street dives, and drug and prostitution rings flourished. As Elmer Irey noted, "You could buy all the morphine or heroin you could lift in Kansas City; and the man who wanted to keep his job as a police captain . . . had better keep his prostitute file correct and up-to-the-minute so Tom's machine would be certain that no girl practiced her ancient art without paying full tribute."

Pendergast's machine made the career of Harry Truman. During World War I, farmboy Truman had commanded a field artillery battery in France that was full of tough kids from Kansas City who hit it off with their captain. After the war Truman opened a haberdashery shop in Kansas City. When it went bankrupt, his friends persuaded the machine to elect him county judge, an administrative post equivalent to county supervisor in other jurisdictions. Though personally honest, Truman had to hire some patronage employees whom he later described as "no-account sons of bitches" and award contracts to the party faithful. In 1934, the Pendergast machine elected him to the U.S. Senate. Irey's T-men managed to make tax cases against Charlie Corollo, Boss Pendergast, and a number of machine stalwarts. In 1939 Pendergast was given fifteen months in jail and Corollo got eight years. An uprising of voters removed the Pendergast organization from office and the police department was returned to the control of the state.

Some politicians did not like Morgenthau's policies, but he was too high up and too close to Roosevelt to be pushed around. While Morgenthau backed Irey to the hilt, a coordinator was not the same as a chief. He could only suggest, and could not move agents from one bureau to another. Had the reorganization plan gone through in 1936, Morgenthau and Irey's unified agency would have had nine years to develop cases against mobsters and their political protectors. When Truman became president in 1945, he decided to dispense with the services of both men, as well as the U.S. attorney who prosecuted Pendergast. Despite thirty-nine years of government service, Irey did not even receive the customary presidential letter congratulating retiring federal bureau chiefs. Within a short time the Internal Revenue Service was honeycombed with corruption.

J. Edgar Hoover was in no danger of being fired—his prestige had increased because of the FBI's generally good record during World War II. Hoover had avoided the World War I mistake of giving badges to volunteers. He also tried to prevent the removal of Japanese-Americans from the

West Coast, vouching for their loyalty. It was one of the few administrative wars he ever lost. Opposition led by California attorney general Earl Warren carried the day and the Japanese were put in concentration camps.

By 1946, Hoover's FBI was generally considered to be the most honest and efficient law enforcement organization in the United States. Compared to local police departments his agents were models of professional behavior. They did not employ physical coercion against suspects and routinely issued warnings against self-incrimination before conducting criminal interrogations. The crime lab services and training programs the Bureau offered to local police departments were superior to those provided by any other agency. Hoover was not without his critics. Some complained about his penchant for keeping the spotlight focused on himself and stealing credit for cases such as the Lepke surrender. Even Hoover's many supporters had to concede his low tolerance for advice or criticism. The most serious complaint was that he investigated individuals because of their beliefs rather than their criminal actions. But prior to the 1960s, most of those investigations were authorized, at least tacitly, by the president or attorney general of the day.

Why did Hoover keep his Bureau on the sidelines of the fight against organized crime? Fear of blackmail or his personal corruption have been offered as explanations. These are unlikely. Rumors abound, but if anyone had anything concrete on him, it would certainly have been revealed long ago. In the 1950s, some NYPD detectives attempted to discredit Hoover by conducting surveillances of him during his frequent visits to New York. One of their spies was the doorman at the Stork Club, an ex-cop. They turned up nothing. Hoover's betting at racetracks was legal and a common practice among respectable citizens. The best explanation for Hoover's reluctance is that he wanted to play it safe. When the FBI was small and weak, Hoover's fear of scandal or political retaliation was probably well founded. After Hoover had achieved the power to defy his critics, his position may still have been smart from a bureaucratic perspective, if indefensible from the standpoint of the public interest.

Having reached the pinnacle of success in the postwar era, Hoover saw no reason to take on organized crime. Neither did his bosses, the various attorney generals and President Truman. Fighting the new "red menace" provided a sufficiently attractive mission for the FBI. In 1946 the New York office had four hundred agents assigned to investigating communists and five working on organized crime. Had Hoover reassigned two hundred agents from Red squads to Mafia squads, the historical judgment on his directorship might be much more positive.

12:   Overreaching: Hollywood and Detroit

Over the years, Hollywood has made a great many movies about ordinary Joes whose lives are changed by unexpected windfalls. A real-life version of this tale began in Chicago in March 1934. In time, it would have a profound effect on Hollywood itself. It started when two minor Chicago hoodlums named Morris "Willy" Bioff and George Browne got their hands on $16,000—a small fortune at the height of the Depression. To celebrate, they decided to treat themselves to a blowout at a fancy restaurant. The place they picked was the 100 Club in the heart of the glitzy Near North Side nightlife district, run by a Capone gang member named Nick Dean.

The 100 Club was not a dive, and Bioff and Browne were not the type of customers Dean encouraged to patronize his place. Willy Bioff was basically a pimp. His formal education ended with third grade and his real one began on the mean streets of the West Side slums of Chicago. Short and muscular, at seventeen he became chauffeur and bodyguard for an Irish political boss who doubled as head of the local Teamsters Union. When he was nineteen, Prohibition went into effect and Willy tried his hand at driving a beer truck. It wasn't much of a job, so he took up pimping. When approaching a potential customer, his opening spiel was usually to offer sex with "my fourteen-year-old sister who has only done it with two boys in her class, never a real man." It worked often enough, though the customer would usually find the fourteen-year-old was closer to thirty, had known plenty of real men, and bore scant familial resemblance to Willy. Eventually, Bioff became the male madam of a six-girl whorehouse on Halstead Street in a cheap West Side vice district. In 1922 he was arrested, convicted, and sentenced to six months in jail for pandering. He appealed and the court upheld the sentence, though he never went to jail and the criminal justice system did not pursue him; it even returned his bail money. Somehow, between his conviction and the system's lapse of memory, Willy had acquired some clout. Through the 1920s, Bioff was a small-time pimp and labor slugger. In the early '30s, he attempted to organize the city's kosher butchers in a price-fixing scheme, but the Depression was not an ideal time to try to maintain artificially high prices.

His career in the doldrums, Willy took up with George Browne, business agent for Local 2 of the stagehands' union. George got his job by beating his predecessor over the head with a lead pipe until he resigned. Now his opponent in the upcoming union election was his own brother-in-law. Afraid that his taking a pipe to his in-law would upset the family, he got Bioff to do it for him. Browne, too, was experiencing hard times: 150 of his 400 members had been laid off and the rest had received a 20 percent pay cut. George had a reputation as a crazy drunk. It was claimed that he drank one hundred bottles of imported beer every day and would wander around town under the influence, poking his nose into saloons, waving a gun, and asking, "Does anybody in here think he's tough?" Although both assertions are probably exaggerated, it's clear that Bioff had to supply both the muscle and the brains for the duo.

To aid his members, Browne had opened a small soup kitchen across from City Hall. Working stagehands were required to buy two tickets at 35 cents each, one for their own use and one to be given to an unemployed colleague. The price even left a little money for Browne to make a profit. Bioff suggested that they hit up some politicians for donations. With the $2,000 they received they upgraded the kitchen: in addition to offering soup and sandwiches for the members, Messrs. Bioff and Browne provided free help-ings of roast beef, chicken, lobster, and other delicacies to politicians, cops, and journalists in a newly installed side room. In addition, when stars like Al Jolson or Eddie Cantor came into town they were dragooned into entertain-ing at lunch. Celebrities who refused were likely to find that a mechanical problem prevented the stagehands from raising the curtain on time for their shows.

Bioff persuaded Browne to go to Barney Balaban, head of the Balaban & Katz theater chain, an affiliate of Paramount Studios, and ask him to restore the 20 percent pay cut. Balaban refused, but offered to give $150 a week for the soup kitchen. Bioff and Browne countered by demanding a $50,000 lump sum payment, which was eventually negotiated down to $20,000. Bioff knew Balaban had powerful Hollywood connections and might "yell cop-per," and the Capone trial had made Chicago gangsters wary of the IRS. So Bioff and Browne had Balaban make out a check for "legal services" to a lawyer friend, who deducted $4,000 to pay the taxes plus a small fee and gave the boys the rest to split. Willy put his share directly in his pocket, but Browne had an obligation to his members. He contributed $5 to purchase two cartons of soup for the kitchen.

The night Bioff and Browne were celebrating at the 100 Club, Nick Dean was entertaining his pal Frankie Rio, former bodyguard to Al Capone. When Dean saw Bioff and Browne feasting, he muttered, "Where did the pimp and the stupe get the dough?" "Let's ask them," Rio volunteered, and the two walked over and patted Browne on the shoulder. Asked about the source of his money, Browne muttered something about gambling winnings and told Willy that it was time to leave. The next day, Browne got a call from Rio telling him to meet him at the corner of 22nd and Michigan, adjacent to the Capone gang's headquarters. Fearful, Browne called Bioff, who volun-teered to accompany him. When they arrived, Rio and another Capone muscleman, Ralph Pierce, were waiting in a car. "Brownie," as they called him, was ordered to get in. Eyeing Bioff, Pierce said, "Who invited you, Willy—screw [take off]." For two hours, Browne rode around Chicago with the two hoodlums as they interrogated him about whether Willy was trying to muscle in on the union and how they had gotten so much money. Going for a ride with Capone gangsters was known to have been the last act of many men, and George held nothing back. Finally satisfied that he was telling the truth, they dropped him off, saying that he would hear from them.

A series of negotiations followed until Bioff and Browne ended up at a house in the western suburbs where they were confronted by Frank Nitti, Paul Ricca, and their lieutenants. Also present was New Yorker "Lepke" Buchalter. The mob was then in the process of taking over unions and Bioff and Browne were informed that they now had new partners who would expect 50 percent of the take. The two asked for a moment to confer privately. "Sure," Nitti told them, but the proposition was still going to be the same. Frank must have been in a good mood that day—his usual line to a recalcitrant union head was, "How would your wife look in black?" Faced with the inevitable, Bioff and Browne gave in. The deal had its consolations. Browne had run for president of the International Association of Theater and Stage Employees (IATSE) in 1932, but lost because the eastern locals did not vote for him. Nitti told Browne that he should run again at the convention in Louisville to be held in 1934. Lepke, he explained, would talk to Lucky Luciano and ensure that the eastern bloc voted correctly. A wounded Lepke protested that he didn't need to talk to Luciano: "I can do this on my own." Later documented in federal court testimony, the meeting makes it clear that New York and Chicago were already working together on national enterprises and that Lepke was almost on the same level as Luciano.

At the Louisville convention, all went as planned. Browne's campaign manager, Frank Maritote of the Chicago outfit, only beat up a few delegates for show. President Browne was congratulated by his mob backers who now announced they were two-thirds partners in the enterprise. Their new partners ordered Browne and Bioff to produce some big money quickly. The only available source was the movie industry—talkies had essentially killed stage shows. The obstacle was a tough Irishman named Tommy Malloy, who headed Local 110 of IATSE, the Chicago motion picture projectionist union. He was no stiff who could be slugged into retirement. Suspected in twenty murders, Tommy had his own guns on the payroll. The Chicago outfit had a department that specialized in these problems. In February 1935, some Capone gang gunmen staked out the Windemere East Hotel, where Malloy kept a nightclub entertainer on the side. When Tommy departed in his car, they tailed him, pulled abreast, and dispatched him with a shotgun and .45-caliber pistol.

The outfit appointed Nick Dean as Malloy's replacement. IATSE's new leadership informed Chicago motion picture theater owners like Barney Balaban that they would have to put two men in every projectionist's booth or face a strike. A sudden doubling of their workforce would have bankrupted them, so they settled for a $100,000 payoff. The New York movie theater owners got stuck for $150,000. The mob had hit Hollywood in its most vulnerable area, the individual box offices. Always a chancy business, the economics of the industry were expressed in the adage, "You're only as good as your last picture." The industry's ruling elite were men who had been furriers or junk dealers. Early in the century, they began investing in "moving pictures" by buying a few nickelodeons as a sideline. When they started making money, the patent-holding Edison combine took legal action to run them out of business. They fled New York for California, where the sunny climate facilitated filming, and built their studios in an orange grove known as Hollywood. By the 1920s, many were fabulously rich and their stars, like Mary Pickford, her husband Douglas Fairbanks, and Charlie Chaplin, were icons who greatly influenced the manners and morals of the American people. Across the country, the studios acquired chains of motion picture houses, like Paramount's Balaban & Katz, to show their movies exclusively. Theaters such as the Roxy in New York and the Oriental in Chicago resembled palaces. The Depression cut deeply into the revenue stream, forcing the studio moguls to scale back drastically on salaries and other expenses. Credit lines dried up and the only source of cash was the ticket windows of thousands of moviehouses, themselves struggling to survive with promotions like dish nights and five acts of vaudeville.

In 1933 the elite Hollywood craft unions, whose wages had been cut 50 percent, went on strike. The studio moguls screamed that it was a communist plot and beat them back after a bitter struggle. In the wreckage,

IATSE was left with just thirty-three members. Economic problems opened the door for the mob to move in.

Los Angeles, Hollywood's giant neighborhood, was a city of contrasts. Its population was made up of transplanted midwestern farmers, and the most influential political figures were the crusading Protestant ministers, who sought to impose small-town morality on a community whose social life was dominated by film stars. Politicians campaigned as reformers and governed as Tammany bosses. When Mayor Frank Shaw was elected in 1933, he installed his brother as "bagman," and with the police department as his enforcers ran an administration notably corrupt even for Los Angeles.

In 1923, seventeen-year-old Filipo Sacco had fled Boston to avoid a larceny charge, settling in Chicago. He got to know mob guys, changed his name to Johnny Roselli, and was sent to Los Angeles to work with Jack Dragna. By the 1930s, the City of Angels was a colony of the eastern mobs. But because it was so different and distant from Chicago or New York, they allowed local chieftains like Dragna to rule under the observation of one of their resident pro-consuls. By 1934 Johnny Roselli was the Chicago mob's man in Hollywood. Twenty-nine, slim, and handsome, he was both tough, as befit his gangster background, and an innate gentleman who dressed well and spoke courteously. In contrast, Dragna looked and talked like a B-movie heavy. Roselli was a regular at the Santa Anita racetrack and the Bel-Air Country Club, dined at places like the Brown Derby and Ciro's, and lived in apartment buildings preferred by movie stars, such as the Garden of Allah or the Wilshire Palms. He dated stars like Lana Turner, and in 1940 he married a beautiful blond actress named June Lang.

When the mob decided to move in on Hollywood, Johnny was their point man. He had already been employed by studio officials as a "labor consultant" to break the 1933 strike. The bosses brought him to Chicago to brief them on the economics of the industry and identify who in Hollywood should be approached. He suggested Pat Casey, an executive he had worked with in 1933. An appointment was made for Bioff, Browne, and Dean to meet Casey in the New York offices of the Hollywood Producers Association. At the scheduled time, Dean was too drunk to leave his room in the

Warwick Hotel, so his two colleagues went to the meeting without him. Bioff proposed to Casey that the IATSE International take over all twenty-seven craft unions, warning that if it didn't happen, he would shut down the box offices. To his surprise, Casey was amenable, partly out of fear of a work stoppage, but also because IATSE promised to provide a less troublesome workforce. Bioff and Browne returned to the Warwick to tell Dean the good news, but doubting that the pimp and the stupe could have done so well on their own, Dean blew up, accusing them of selling out. To get to the bottom of it, he grabbed Bioff and took him to a sanitarium on West 57th Street where Johnny Roselli was being treated for his chronic tuberculosis. There, Dean immediately began to address Roselli in Italian. Johnny, always courteous, turned and apologized to Bioff for excluding him from the conversation, then continued to speak to Dean. When both finished, Johnny confirmed that what Bioff had told Dean was what he too had learned by speaking with Casey.

At first things went smoothly. Many of the studio heads were already on good terms with mob bosses. Longy Zwillman had loaned Harry Cohn the money to start Columbia Pictures. Harry, the most hated man in Hollywood, put Roselli on at the studio as a so-called producer, although according to one observer all Johnny did was "hang around the corner of Hollywood and Vine, talking out of the side of his mouth." Joe Schenck, who bossed 20th Century-Fox, was so friendly with mobsters that when his wife, Norma Talmadge, began running around with fellow star Gilbert Roland, the hoods offered to kill her for free. Schenck, a great womanizer himself, thanked them but opted to proceed with the more conventional option of divorce. Warner Brothers star George Raft was a mob intimate since his New York days, and the brothers themselves were acquainted with some rough characters. The craft unions succumbed to IATSE control, and to sweeten the deal Bioff obtained a 10 percent across-the-board raise for all 10,000 new members.

In 1937 union organizers were again beaten off with the help of mob gunmen, but at a price. Studio heads were informed that they would have to kick in $50,000 annually, though some of the smaller ones were let off with a $25,000 assessment, including Zwillman and Roselli's buddy Cohn at

Columbia.[1] Joe Schenck and an aide delivered the industry contributions to a room in New York's Waldorf Astoria Hotel and hung around until Bioff and Browne counted it, after which the mogul was dismissed as though he were a messenger boy.

The New York mob realized they had better appoint their own resident overseer to keep an eye on the Hollywood gold mine and the job was given to Bugsy Siegel. George Raft introduced Bugsy around town and gave him the notion that he too could be a star. As a result, Siegel spent a lot of time in his bedroom rehearsing love scenes with starlets. Longy Zwillman occasionally dropped in to squire an actress: Jean Harlow was his special favorite, and during his absences he asked Johnny Roselli to keep his eye on her.

Other mob bosses visited frequently at IATSE expense and were received like royalty. Bioff built himself a big mogul-style home complete with the obligatory swimming pool. On one visit Louis "Little New York" Campagna noticed sprinklers watering Willy's lawn. "Order me six hundred of those, Willy," he commanded. Bioff explained that would be enough to water the entire Chicago park system, but Campagna brooked no dissent. Paul Ricca was more reasonable and only asked for three hundred. So IATSE paid for nine hundred sprinklers.

By the late 1930s, the eastern gangsters were a major force in the movie industry. Their hold on unions allowed them to extort tribute from both the theater chains and the studios. As in any industrial racket, the next step was to become part of management. Metro-Goldwyn-Roselli or 20th Century Siegel had a nice ring to it. As Bioff would later put it, "We had about 20 percent of Hollywood and were on the way to getting 50 percent."

Many of the top mob bosses were shrewd businessmen, but they were largely untutored in complex subjects like economic theory. Among the topics the bosses had not studied was the notion of countervailing power, and that concept would lead to a major disaster for the Chicago mob. The movie industry was the fifth largest in the United States, with outlets in every city.

---

[1]Years later, Zwillman and Roselli would use their relationship with Cohn to "persuade" him to cast Frank Sinatra in the movie *From Here to Eternity*. The incident is described in the first *Godfather* movie, though there was never a horse's head put in Cohn's bedroom.

Its health was important to the national welfare; its payrolls carried beloved stars, brilliant writers, and slick publicists. The mob could not strong-arm or silence all of them, and when they began to squawk, people would listen. As long as the gangsters were useful to the moguls in keeping labor quiet, or to the workers in obtaining modest raises, many people were willing to go along. But others were not happy, and it was just a matter of time before powerful forces would be mobilized against the mob.

Already, gangsters in another city were learning about the dangers of defying massive political and economic forces, despite having been invited to the scene by one of the most powerful industrial organizations in the world—the Ford Motor Company. In many ways, the auto industry resembled Hollywood. Its production companies were largely concentrated in a single location, with sales outlets in every small town and city neighborhood in America. Like Hollywood, it had come into being early in the century and quickly revolutionized American life. Its "stars"—the Model T, Olds, and Chevrolet—had fans everywhere. Its fractious moguls also eyed each other suspiciously, only unifying when threatened by hostile outside forces such as organized labor. The best known of its chiefs, Henry Ford, was an American legend—a production genius with a social conscience. He was the man who gave his workforce a $5-a-day wage in 1914, double the industry average. But by the 1930s, the legend had worn thin. During World War I, Ford led a delegation to Europe on a chartered ship to stop the fighting. The derision that accompanied the voyage of the "Peace Ship" made him look ridiculous. While being cross-examined at a 1920s civil trial over anti-Semitic articles that appeared in a newspaper he backed, Ford came over as an ignoramus at best. And while the rest of the automotive industry made money, Ford clung too long to the outmoded Model T and had to shut down production and lay off some employees for a couple of years in the 1920s while he retooled. Just as that process was ending, the Depression hit and thousands more workers had to be laid off.

By the early '30s Ford had made his son Edsel head of the company, at least on paper—the old man still controlled it. The real power in the daily operations of the Ford organization was a man who was essentially head watchman. Harry Bennett had left school after eighth grade and later joined the navy, where he developed a small reputation as a lightweight boxer. In 1916, he was employed by Ford. The big boss took a liking to the neat, cocky young man and put him in charge of the watchmen at one of his plants. By the 1930s, Bennett was head of the Ford service department, a guard and detective force whose ranks at one point swelled to 3,000. Its job was to spy on workers and maintain discipline throughout the Ford empire: the *New York Times* called it the largest private secret service force in America.

Bennett was one of those characters who occasionally manages to insinuate himself into a prominent position for which he has no real qualifications. He lacked a background in police work or law, but he fancied himself a master detective, and with Ford clout was able to carve out a leadership role in Michigan law enforcement and develop useful connections in the field nationally. Though his title and salary were modest compared to many other Ford executives, Bennett became the final arbiter on personnel decisions and other organizational matters, and represented Ford in Detroit and Michigan state politics.

Among Henry Ford's enlightened policies was a willingness to hire ex-convicts. Bennett took the policy a few steps further, showing a preference for violent men who had served time for murder, rape, or robbery. In the 1930s, it was estimated that as much as 20 percent of the 50,000-man Ford workforce had prison records. Some of them were employed in the service department. The servicemen Bennett described as "tough bastards, but gentlemen" were known for ruling the plant with a heavy hand. When a worker would show his ID at the gate, they would shout at him, "Who's your boss?" or "Where did you get that badge?"—tactics designed to discourage workers from lending their credentials to union organizers. The service department maintained regular surveillance over bars and other recreational places throughout the Detroit area, on the lookout for Ford employees who might be meeting with representatives of the United Auto Workers.

Bennett developed connections with many well-known hoodlums. After the old Jewish Purple gang had been taken over by Italians, the principal figure was Chet La Mare, who directed rackets on the West Side of town.

Bennett gave La Mare a Ford dealership and a contract for $100,000 a year providing fruit to the company's River Rouge plant. In 1930, La Mare started a gang war by ordering the murder of a rival gangster. To patch things up, another Ford dealer (and former U.S. Secret Service agent) was brought in from New York, but his efforts were unavailing. Eleven gang murders were recorded in the city that year. One put heat on the mobs all over the country. Radio reporter Jerry Buckley led a successful campaign to recall Detroit mayor Charles Bowles. On the night the citizens voted him out, Buckley was broadcasting from a victory rally at a downtown hotel when a gunman shot him eleven times. It was one of the incidents that eventually caused the national commission to ban the assassination of journalists.

While the mob war raged, Chet La Mare hid out in his home with an arsenal of guns, gas bombs, and 4,000 rounds of ammunition. His enemies still managed to assassinate him. His friends feared that his angry foes might shoot up the funeral, so his wife used hired pallbearers to carry the body. Bennett immediately took up with the successors. More mob figures were given Ford dealerships and the new top boss Pete Licavoli recommended men for jobs with the service department. Bennett's dealings were not confined to the Detroit area. By some mysterious process, Brooklyn's Joe Adonis was given a lucrative contract hauling cars from Ford's Edgewater, New Jersey, plant to showrooms throughout the Northeast. Over eight years, it earned him $3 million. Adonis proved a useful investment. When Bennett refused to raise some of Licavoli's friends' pay rate from $6 a day to $15, the gangster had his henchman run Bennett's car off the road. Bennett called on Adonis to mediate the situation and the disagreement was resolved.

Mob and law enforcement contacts helped the Ford Company to fight off workers' demands. In 1932, a communist-led group of "hunger marchers" attempted to enter the Detroit suburb of Dearborn where the Ford plants were located. The town was completely controlled by the company and the police chief was a former service department employee. The local police tried to turn the marchers back, but they persisted, battling through the streets until they reached the plant gates. As they arrived, Harry Bennett raced out in an automobile to assist the cops and was promptly felled by a brick, whereupon the police and Ford servicemen opened fire, killing four and wounding twenty of the demonstrators.

Spearheaded by Walter Reuther, in the mid-'30s the United Auto Workers (UAW) began to make inroads in the auto industry. Early in 1937, General Motors and Chrysler recognized the union. Henry Ford swore he would not. In May, it was announced the UAW would distribute leaflets outside the Ford plant. Bennett beefed up his service department with recruits from the Detroit underworld. The UAW decided to use women for the job, believing that they were less likely to be slugged. When the ladies alighted from the buses many of them were knocked cold. Reuther and his colleague Dick Frankensteen began talking to workers on the overpass leading into the plant, but Ford servicemen claimed it was private property and ordered them off. When the UAW leaders were slow to comply, they were beaten by Ford servicemen. Pictures of the "Battle of the Overpass" became a symbol of industrial strife in the Depression era.

As in Los Angeles, local law enforcement presented no barrier to the gangsters. In 1939, a grand jury investigation led to the indictment of the mayor, the police superintendent, and the county prosecutor for taking payoffs from gamblers, and in the 1940s all three were sent to prison. Big mob bosses like Pete Licavoli remained untouched. By then it was clear the gangsters had chosen the wrong side in the struggle between management and labor. Until the mid-'30s, government was almost always on the side of the employers—Teddy Roosevelt's forced arbitration of the 1902 Pennsylvania coal strike being a notable exception. It was common practice for corporations to hire sluggers and put them into a guard's uniform or secure deputy sheriff's badges for them to work alongside the police or militia. But when organized labor became an important element in FDR's New Deal coalition, the federal government set up a National Labor Relations Board (NLRB) to assist union organizing efforts. In 1941, the NLRB managed to compel Ford to recognize the UAW and disband the service department. Bennett was dismissed by Edsel Ford two years later.

Bennett was subpoenaed to testify before the U.S. Senate's Kefauver Committee in 1951. When asked about mob operations in Detroit, he first denied knowing Licavoli or Adonis, but then snapped, "Do you want me to get my head blown off?" Committee counsel asked Bennett, "Is it to the credit of the Ford Motor Company that it hands over its agencies to people who have a criminal record, with no legitimate businesses, with no assets and no experience in the automobile business?" Bennett coolly replied, "Yes; if they could cut down on the gangs that way, we would give them all an agency."

While mob goons were slugging UAW organizers in Detroit, back in Hollywood the first challenge to the mob came from the popular actor Robert Montgomery. He talked the Screen Actors Guild (SAG) into putting up $5,000 to hire two ex-FBI men to investigate Willy Bioff. Montgomery was so certain that they would find something rotten he agreed to personally pay the $5,000 if they did not. Their investigation turned up the six months Willy owed to the state of Illinois on his old pimping charge and a $100,000 check from Joe Schenck. When the findings were leaked to the press, columnist Westbrook Pegler began writing about Bioff and Browne in a series that eventually won a Pulitzer Prize. When Willy was extradited from California to Chicago to serve his six months in the city jail (known as the "Bridewell," or by the hoods, the "Bandbox"), he informed his outfit bosses that he wanted to quit the business. Louis Campagna reminded him that the organization's retirement plan could only be invoked feet first, and Willy wisely withdrew his application.

The revelations about the mobsters' infiltration and their suppression of non-mobster unions reverberated to Washington and brought Treasury secretary Morgenthau's intelligence agents in to audit Bioff, Browne, and Schenck. To their surprise, they learned that the $100,000 check was not a bribe. When Bioff decided to buy his 80-acre estate, he did not want to plunk down $100,000 cash lest it arouse suspicion. He got Schenck to write him a check for business services and reimbursed him. Clearly it was a bit of money laundering, but the IRS did not have enough to proceed. A thorough examination of Schenck's books, however, found widespread tax evasion. The transaction with Bioff had occurred in New York City, so the tax problem fell within the jurisdiction of the U.S. attorney for the Southern District of New York who assigned a sharp tax lawyer, Boris Kostelanetz, to the case.

Schenck was a man with powerful connections, and unlike most moguls he was a New Dealer. The industry preferred to cast him as a victim of vicious gangsters, and their happy ending would have been for the Feds to run the mob out of the industry and leave the moguls alone. "Cherry Nose" Gioe introduced Bioff to a thirty-two-year-old Chicago lawyer named Sidney Korshak, telling Willy, "I want you to do what he tells you. He is our man." Korshak would later become a major figure in the movie industry himself, as well as counselor to top corporate and labor leaders. He instructed Bioff and Browne to make Joe Schenck the patsy by claiming he had contacted them about raising slush fund money for obtaining favorable treatment for the movie industry from the California legislature. Neither scenario commended itself to the IRS, nor were Schenck's political connections of any value—under Henry Morgenthau's administration, the Treasury was not a place that welcomed outside "advice." According to Kostelanetz there was no effort to interfere with the prosecution of the case. Joe Schenck was convicted and received a three-year sentence—two more than his lawyers had told him to expect. Used to an opulent life centering around women, gambling, and big homes, Schenck served exactly one month before he contacted Kostelanetz's office and asked to cooperate. His revelations led to a federal anti-racketeering investigation—a crime that fell under FBI jurisdiction. The bulk of the work, though, was still carried on by the Treasury agent who conducted the original investigation, Alf Oftedal, a man so straight that Kostelanetz said, "He was the kind when you first met him you would want him to be the executor of your will." As a result, Bioff, Browne, and Nick Dean were indicted.[2]

At the trial, Nick Dean declined to take the stand, no doubt on mob orders to avoid cross-examination. He was convicted and sentenced to eight years. Bioff and Browne did testify and, as Willy later admitted, "Lied, and lied, and lied." He got ten years and Browne, eight. Kostelanetz and Oftedal

---

[2]Interestingly, J. Edgar Hoover did not take credit for the case at the time, although according to Kostelanetz, FBI agent Tom Wade worked closely with Oftedal. It appears that the FBI, gearing up for a war about to break out, simply deferred to the Treasury agency that had already developed the case and worked cooperatively with them. It would have been easy to draw a conclusion unfavorable to the FBI if Boris Kostelanetz, still practicing law in a prestigious New York firm, had not been available for interview.

were not through. The agent continued to visit the defendants in jail trying to get them to tell the full story, but they hung tough. Aware that the government was still poking around, the Chicago mob sent a message. Nick Dean had a girlfriend named Estelle Carey, a minor mob functionary who served as "Queen of the Dice Girls."[3] In February 1943, Chicago firemen extinguished a blaze at Carey's apartment and found her strangled, beaten, and sexually assaulted with a broken bottle. Such torture wasn't necessary just to send a message; obviously they wanted her to answer some questions, like where Nick's money from the Hollywood shakedown was. At the same time, Browne's wife received a phone call warning her that she and the children would be in danger if "Brownie" talked. Though Dean stayed silent, the tactics were counterproductive. Bioff told Browne, "Here we are doing time in jail for these guys and they're threatening our wives and kids." They asked to see Kostelanetz, and at the meeting Bioff opened with, "What do you want to know, Boris?" Bioff and Browne revealed the whole story of the Hollywood shakedown and a grand jury in New York indicted Frank Nitti, Paul Ricca, "Little New York" Campagna, Frank Maritote, "Cherry Nose" Gioe, Johnny Roselli, Phil D'Andrea, Ralph Pierce, and a minor New Jersey IATSE official. Frankie Rio had died of natural causes in 1934. The previous year, thirty-seven-year-old Johnny Roselli had joined the army despite severe arthritis and chronic TB. He was brought back from training with a tank battalion to be arraigned. If Johnny hoped for sympathy from the jury because he was a serviceman, he was disappointed—the U.S. attorney's office obtained a court order stripping him of his uniform.[4]

The whole top echelon of the Chicago mob had been snagged and they were not happy. An emergency meeting convened at Nitti's mansion. Paul Ricca lashed out at Nitti for the stupid way the affair had been handled.

---

[3]Every nightclub in the Chicago area employed pretty girls who shook dice and smiled and chatted with the customers. It was the practice to leave the girl a nice tip, though of course she had to turn most of it in to the house. If she didn't, her arm would be broken.

[4]If, as some claim, Roselli simply joined the army to avoid the probe rather than for patriotic reasons, he probably could have wangled a softer assignment than an armored division that later ended up in combat in Normandy. Sergeant Albert Anastasia was assigned to teach recruits how to be longshoremen. Lieutenant Moe Dalitz ran the laundry at army headquarters on Governors Island in New York harbor. More likely, Roselli wanted to behave the way he thought a dashing Hollywood swashbuckler should.

Others in the group sided with Ricca and the conversation grew heated. Finally, Frank ordered the whole bunch out of his house—a shocking breach of mob protocol. The claustrophobic Nitti had hated his previous prison stretch and vowed never to go back. After the meeting he got drunk and went staggering off to a nearby railroad yard. A train crew jeered at him until he pointed a pistol their way. They fled into a caboose while Nitti fired the gun into his head. Suicide was rare for a mob boss, but doing it publicly ensured that there would be no rumors that his colleagues had murdered him because he was about to talk.

At the trial, supposed tough guy George Browne was so petrified that he couldn't remember the names of men he had known for twenty-five years. In contrast, Willy Bioff stood up under nine and a half days of examination and cross-examination. Kostelanetz's masterful performance convinced the jury that Bioff, who had admittedly lied in the previous trial, was now telling the truth. When he asked Willy why he had perjured himself before, Willy answered, "I'm just a no-good, uncouth person." Again, none of the defendants dared take the stand and be questioned. The case of Ralph Pierce, who was only peripherally involved, was dismissed before trial. The remaining seven were all found guilty and got ten years in prison (except the IATSE official, who got seven). An appeal was taken, but again Kostelanetz was successful, although he drew a rebuke from the great Judge Learned Hand for referring to "the Chicago outfit."

Three years later, the federal parole board released the defendants on the first day they were eligible with a lightning speed not usually encountered in Washington bureaucracies. This sparked an investigation as to why Chicago defendants had hired Missouri and Texas lawyers with close connections to the Missourian President Truman and the Texan U.S. attorney general Tom Clark to help obtain their release. Even a congressional subpoena could not obtain release of the parole board minutes, and to avoid questioning the board resigned en masse.

All of the Chicago leaders returned to their old haunts except Nick Dean. He went off to Latin America where he lived well on the money Estelle Carey may have died to protect. As the defendants were led out of the courtroom at the conclusion of the trial in the district court, Campagna warned

Bioff and Browne, "We can wait a long time." After his release from prison, Bioff took his wife's name of Nelson and, with $6.5 million he had saved, went off to an undisclosed location—Phoenix, Arizona. There he became friends with a popular young businessman named Barry Goldwater who occasionally took Mr. Nelson along when he flew his plane to Las Vegas. Goldwater's clothing chain opened an outlet in Moe Dalitz's Desert Inn. Bioff tried to insinuate himself into the Las Vegas scene and was spotted by a visiting Chicago mobster. Back in Arizona, a car bomb exploded and killed him in 1955. Goldwater, then a U.S. senator (who by that time no doubt knew who Bioff was), wept at his funeral. It was not a happy Hollywood ending for any of the principals.

13:   The Prime Minister

What cops call "sitting on a wire"—eavesdropping on telephone conversations—can be a tedious assignment. On a July day in 1943 detectives working for Manhattan district attorney Frank Hogan heard a conversation that made them sit up and take notice. The court-authorized tap that they were monitoring was on the home of Frank Costello, prime minister of the New York mob world and rated by many the most important organized crime figure in America. World War II was raging, but things were good for the mobs. The war had diverted attention from organized crime and allowed gangsters to flourish.

The racket busters had essentially suspended operations for the duration. The New York Citizens Crime Commission, formed out of the 1935 runaway grand jury that had led to the appointment of special prosecutor Dewey, closed its doors in 1943. Dewey himself was now governor, but with his eyes on the White House he had little interest in fighting organized crime. Mayor La Guardia, in the midst of his third term and anxious to get into the war, constantly lobbied President Roosevelt to be given a major role such as a general in charge of the Allied military government in Italy. Only district attorney Hogan, Dewey's successor, continued to keep an eye on the mob overlords.

A single phone conversation rarely disclosed any significant information. Men like Costello did not say "Kill Smith," "Bribe Jones," or "Take the two million that I haven't paid taxes on and buy the XYZ Corporation." However, a pattern of messages could reveal the nature of relationships. Phil Kastel's frequent calls from New Orleans involved slot machines. Willie Moretti, who called himself "Mr. Moore," always addressed Costello as "Chief." Other people called to solicit a favor or thank Costello for having done one. Today's caller began by saying, "Good morning, Francesco, how are you and thanks for everything." To which Costello replied, "Congratulations, it went over perfect. When I tell you something is in the bag, you can rest assured." Then, after Frank suggested that they and their wives "have dinner some night real soon," the caller replied, "That would be fine, but right now I want to assure you of my loyalty for all you have done; it's undying."

The caller was Thomas Aurelio, a city magistrate, who had just been slated for a state supreme court judgeship, courtesy of Costello. It was not New York State's highest court, but one of general jurisdiction. Still, it was a big jump up for a little magistrate way down in the judicial ranks. A supreme court justice served a fourteen-year term and was almost always renominated; the annual salary was equivalent to a quarter of a million in today's dollars. There was no shortage of candidates, and obtaining the designation required powerful political backing. The nomination had almost been given to a congressman sponsored by Franklin Delano Roosevelt. FDR's intervention presented a bit of a dilemma for the Tammany county chairman, Congressman Mike Kennedy, who explained to Frank he could not go against his own president. Costello believed a man's word was his bond. He prided himself on never breaking his own, no matter what the cost. He asked Kennedy, "Are you a man or a mouse?" Kennedy owed his own job to Costello and it would have required more courage to defy him than the president. Kennedy's life wasn't at stake—Costello was too smooth a businessman for that. He controlled 10 of the 16 Tammany district leaders, so it would have been simple to have Kennedy voted out as chairman, or even refuse to renominate him for Congress at the next election. The Tammany chief gave the nod to Aurelio.

When D.A. Hogan learned about the recording, he immediately revealed its contents to Kennedy, who pretended to be shocked and indicated he would take some sort of action. When that didn't happen, Hogan made the conversation public. The story caused a furor. Yet despite official investigations and attempts to disbar Aurelio or invalidate his nomination, he stayed on the ticket. A last-minute write-in campaign against him failed and he was elected a supreme court justice. The only one who lost his job was Congressman Kennedy, who had to step down as chairman. Ironically, Aurelio's decisions as a magistrate had been strongly supportive of police-prosecutorial positions. When Mayor La Guardia reappointed him in 1935, he had praised the jurist's record. Costello had not backed him because he wanted to put a crook or a hack on the bench, but because Aurelio was a friend of a friend and an Italian. But the incident demonstrated that organized crime now ruled what had once been the most important political machine in the United States, and also had more influence than the president in certain matters.

Until the Aurelio affair Frank had led a charmed life, teaming up with Big Bill Dwyer to make a fortune in bootlegging and throwing in his lot with Lucky Luciano, the biggest winner in the 1931 mob wars. As a result he was given control of slot machines in New York City. When Mayor La Guardia ran the slots out of the city, Frank found a safe harbor for them in Louisiana, where he also obtained an interest in local gambling clubs. When Lucky was jailed in 1936, Vito Genovese should have succeeded to the leadership of the family. The ruthless Genovese—who had recently acquired a new bride by the simple expedient of having her husband killed—resented Costello's autonomy and might well have tried to rein him in. But a murder investigation began to get too close to him so he took a bundle of money and fled to Italy where he lived under the protection of Mussolini. The leadership role fell to Costello instead, bringing him additional income from such rackets as Harlem policy and the Fulton Fish Market. By the 1940s he owned buildings on Wall Street, oil wells in Texas, and a piece of two scotch whiskey distributorships.

Frank's low profile and smooth ways made him the ideal leader of organized crime in an era when reformers like Mayor La Guardia and district attorney Dewey were in power. Unlike Luciano or Genovese he did not make himself a target of law enforcement. Costello also satisfied the other bosses by following a policy of live and let live. He formed close alliances with Albert Anastasia, the real power in the Mangano family; Joe Adonis, the chief political fixer in Brooklyn; and Willie Moretti, who ran the New Jersey family.

If pressed, Costello would concede that he still owned a few slot machines down in New Orleans, where folks saw them as harmless toys. In 1939 when Morgenthau and Irey's T-men had brought a criminal tax case against Costello and Kastel, a Louisiana judge threw it out, though the two had to pay six-figure civil penalties. A little bit of financial finagling didn't make one a bad person. Costello once told a Wall Street broker that they were both in the same business—"Gambling with other people's money." He frequently complained that men like Joe Kennedy had lived down their bootlegging past and become socially acceptable, but he never could.

Costello had come a long way from his humble origins. Born Francesco Castiglia in Calabria in 1891, he was five when his family moved to 108th Street in East Harlem. He grew up in the shadow of Lupo and Morello's murder stable. In 1915 he served ten months for carrying an illegal gun, getting off easy because he was just a small-time punk. Under the Sullivan Act, he could have received seven years. In 1914 he married a Jewish girl, and many of his friends were Irish. Even his adopted name had a Hibernian ring. A detective who began to take note of Costello in the 1920s remembered that for a long time the cops thought he was Irish. Prohibition gave him the opportunity to advance from a Rothstein hireling to a big shot. His success was not due to muscle work: he was only five-foot-nine, about 165 pounds. His older and bigger brother Eddie was the family slugger; Frank had the brains.

Costello's tastefully furnished seven-room penthouse was atop an elite building on fashionable Central Park West. Visitors to the apartment were given royal treatment. The bar was stocked with premium liquor and behind it two gangsters in blue serge suits stood ready to serve. If a guest was hungry, a chef was on hand to broil a steak. In each corner was a slot machine that was rigged to pay off. He and his wife, Loretta, or "Bobby," had married when he was twenty-three and she was probably fifteen; childless, they doted on their two pet dogs. On weekends, they retreated to their twelve-room home in exclusive Sands Point on the north shore of Long Island.

Costello's daily routine was as regular as clockwork. At 10 A.M., he showed up at the Waldorf Astoria Hotel barbershop for some fancy grooming. Afterward he hung around for a while, making himself available for any mob associates who wanted to see him. He would have lunch in the hotel's Norse Grill, where his generous tips ensured he got star treatment. Then he went to a business office on nearby Lexington Avenue. Three times a week he went to the steam baths at the Biltmore Hotel where he gossiped with prominent New Yorkers like political boss Jim Farley and department store tycoon Bernard Gimbel. At five o'clock he adjourned to the Madison Hotel cocktail lounge in the East 50s, another spot where his cronies knew he could always be found. After a few scotches he headed home. At one stage of his life, cops who trailed him noted that on some evenings along about seven he would slip quietly into a luxury apartment building on Fifth Avenue where he was known to maintain an apartment for a lady friend, remaining until nearly nine. He and his wife might go out to a late dinner with other couples. One of his favorite spots was the city's top nightclub, the Copacabana, or as everyone called it, "the Copa." Costello claimed he had no connection with the place, but Hogan thought otherwise and was hoping to collect wiretap evidence to prove it was his. A generous host, Costello invariably picked up the tab for the whole party.

Costello had decidedly upscale tastes. For two years in the 1940s he consulted a Park Avenue psychiatrist. According to the shrink, Frank sought help to overcome the feelings of resentment he had over still being treated like a gangster rather than the respectable businessman he fancied himself to be. The psychiatrist advised him to try to meet with "the better people." When the doctor later revealed this to a reporter, the angry Costello snorted, "I was the one who introduced him to better people." He struck up a platonic friendship with novelist Santha Rama Rau, daughter of a prominent Indian family. Ms. Rau told people she found him "fascinating." His clothes were well tailored and he was always immaculately turned out. He sought out knowledge and sprinkled his conversation with big words, sometimes using them incorrectly. A heavy smoking habit caused throat problems, and a botched operation on his nodules left him with a permanently raspy voice.

He was not the kind of mob boss who rode around in a chauffeured limo with a retinue. Instead he relied on cabs. Once, after he got out of a taxi, the driver found $27,200 cash in the backseat. He reported it to the police, who traced it back to Costello. Frank was inclined to deny that it was his, but his lawyer persuaded him that would make him look like a gangster. Costello trooped down to the police station to fill out the necessary forms to reclaim his property—too late. Reporters were on to the story and Mayor La Guardia personally called the property clerk and threatened to fire him if he handed the money back. Maintaining his pose as an honest man, Costello sued the city and won, but by the time the IRS took its cut for back taxes and Costello gave the driver 10 percent, only $130 was left.

Frank was first among equals in the mob, although as in the British cabinet, the prime minister was always *more* equal. Even the crude Los Angeles mobster Micky Cohen was in awe of Frank. He said, "Class just leaked out of him—your presidents, your kings, or whatever, nobody compared with Frank Costello." Costello was the voice of moderation. Contemporaries said he could prevent a murder with a phone call. A reporter claimed, "If he hadn't been around, there would have been a lot more killings. He kept the animals in line." Costello's leadership was largely based on his management skills. In meetings he made it a practice to be the best-informed man at the table. He was also exceptionally good at analyzing complex problems—in mob parlance, "figuring all the angles." When his colleagues would stray from the subject, he could always bring them back to the topic without giving insult. Costello never carried a gun and rarely traveled with bodyguards, observing, "If [rivals] want to kill you, the guards are the first ones they will bribe." The more traditional mob bosses did not share his view that bodyguards were simply employees who sold their services to the highest bidder. Men like Bonanno and Profaci regarded theirs as virtual blood relations who were expected to die for their chief.

Important visitors regularly came to the penthouse to seek his counsel. Detectives occasionally dropped by, particularly after a hit had occurred, when they would go through the ritual described in tabloids as "Cops Quiz Mob Boss." Frank would greet them cordially and press a $100 bill into their hands. It was not a bribe, simply an act of respect. Even honest cops shrugged and accepted it—otherwise Costello would grow suspicious and clam up. If that happened, they would not be able to get their paperwork done without having to go through a long rigmarole with a lawyer. His usual response to questions about the latest homicide was that he had no idea who would want to kill such a fine fellow as Mr. So and So. And would the officers like a drink or a meal before they departed?

In December 1942, Frank had been asked to throw a little gathering for U.S. Army Major William O'Dwyer. The previous year O'Dwyer, then Brooklyn district attorney, had almost defeated La Guardia for mayor. Now he was seeking to ensure Costello's Tammany support when he ran again in 1945. Frank invited some of his friends, like Congressman Kennedy, a judge, and others, to meet the candidate. It was just the usual New York political thing, or so both principals thought.

Like Costello, O'Dwyer was another immigrant success story. He was born in County Mayo, Ireland, and studied for the priesthood in Spain. Lacking the vocation, he eventually landed in New York where he worked briefly as a longshoreman. He joined New York City's Finest in 1917 and was assigned to patrol a beat in a tough Brooklyn waterfront district. After years of study on the side, he left the force in 1924 to practice law and dabble in politics. Eventually he became a county judge, one notch below a state supreme court justice. After the 1939 investigation of district attorney Geoghan sparked by the New York Crime Commission, the Brooklyn Democratic machine replaced him with O'Dwyer. Two months after taking office he was handed a prosecutor's dream case, the kind that could carry a minor official to a big-city mayor's office, or governor's mansion.

At the core of what the press would label "Murder, Incorporated" was the Brooklyn waterfront, part of the Port of New York, the richest harbor in the world. A third of America's foreign trade passed through it. The world of the waterfront was as different from Costello's gambling enterprises as a

Brooklyn slum was from Park Avenue. Most gamblers were not innately violent men. A few strong-arm guys and police raids were enough to keep them in line. The dock workers were tough guys who had to be controlled by force. The economic principles the port operated under were made for exploitation by gangsters. The ratio of applicants to jobs was about 2 to 1. This surplus of labor meant wages could be held down and the workers kept docile. Two or three times a day (at 7:55 A.M., 1 P.M., and sometimes in the evening) men "shaped up," hoping to be hired as longshoremen, the foot soldiers of the port who loaded and unloaded ships or hauled cargo on the docks. Hiring was the province of the pier foreman, the lowest rank in the hierarchy of labor contractors or stevedores who provided the officer class of the waterfront. One way to obtain the foreman's nod was for a worker to make it known he would kick back a portion of his day's wages—20 percent was the norm. If a man put a toothpick behind his ear, it was a signal he would play ball. Some were picked because they had friends—a word from a gangster was an especially good endorsement, because the foremen were either hoodlums themselves or under their control. Being known as a bad guy was good for a dock boss, since his job was to keep the workers in line and push them hard.

A second fundamental principle was that ships did not make money sitting in port. Workers had to be quick, and amid the rush to move heavy cargo in all sorts of weather, injuries were frequent and death a regular visitor—murders could easily be disguised as accidents. Just beyond the pier, trucks waited in crowded streets to pick up or drop their cargo. Crews of "public loaders" carried boxes from the trucks to the pier. The loaders were also under mob control, and a trucker who wanted his vehicle unloaded in a timely fashion paid off.

The surrounding neighborhoods were crowded with dingy saloons filled with workers drinking, gambling, and whoring while they waited for the shape-up. Loan sharks were always available to advance money to men whose employment was irregular. Those who were unable to pay the shark or a bookie could sometimes work it out by stealing some valuable cargo, or a drug dealer might pay them to pick up and deliver a certain package. Despite the hardships, it was the kind of work that appealed to many men.

Like coal mining, soldiering, or athletics, loading a ship required strength and skill, and those who could do it well were respected by their peers. In the insular world of the docks, someone who had little status outside of it might rank high because he was "a good man."

During World War I, the Brooklyn docks expanded and business boomed. In the early 1920s, Irish gangs from the nearby slums controlled the area. Then Frankie Yale and his gunmen began murdering the Irish dock bosses. "Dinny" Meehan was in bed with his wife when a mob sniper got him. One of his successors, "Wild Bill" Lovett, was known as the man who had scared Al Capone out of town. Lovett made the mistake of getting drunk and falling asleep in a bar. A stoolie alerted Yale's crew and they caved in Wild Bill's head. By the late 1930s the top figure was Costello's man Umberto "Albert" Anastasia. In 1917, fourteen-year-old Anastasia jumped ship in New York Harbor. After working briefly as a longshoreman, he began a career as a slugger, gunman, murderer, and an official in the Longshoreman's Union. He emerged from the 1931 mob wars a major figure in the New York gang world.

Anastasia approved all 1930s mob murders in Brooklyn and assigned the contracts to hitmen. Informally he was known as the "Lord High Executioner." Among his shooters were a Jewish gang from the Brownsville–East New York area and an Italian gang from the Ocean Hill section of the borough. They were so efficient that mob bosses in other parts of the city and beyond New York sought their services. Between 1930 and 1940 they were responsible for at least a hundred murders. Many were not just simple shootings. When "Happy" Maione and "Dasher" Abbandando of the Ocean Hill crew were assigned to knock off a squealer, they used a meat cleaver to shatter his skull and an ice pick to inflict sixty-three stab wounds on him. In 1934 a longshoreman named Pete Panto began complaining about working conditions, managing to rally 1,200 fellow workers to join him in a protest. The dock bosses spread the word that Panto was a communist agitator. Shortly thereafter Anastasia and two of his men threw Panto into a car, strangled him, and buried his body in a lime pit out in Jersey. Killing a victim in an especially brutal way helped to spread terror among the other workers and maintain mob control.

Murder, Inc. was a long way from Frank Costello's penthouse, and in one sense he could claim he had nothing to do with it. But it was Costello who ultimately maintained the political contacts that ensured men like Anastasia could operate. His political clout was based on his control of Tammany and his alliance with the Brooklyn king maker, Joe Adonis. Together the Manhattan and Brooklyn organizations had a powerful voice in the councils of the New York Democratic Party, one that Bronx boss Ed Flynn, President Roosevelt's and Governor Lehman's top lieutenant in New York City, could not ignore, even if he wished to.[1]

Empowered by the New Deal, organized labor had become a major political force. In New York its most powerful figure was Sidney Hillman, head of the Amalgamated Clothing Workers Union. He employed Lepke Buchalter's sluggers to battle union rivals, sometimes with fatal results. Hillman was high up in President Roosevelt's New Deal coalition and frequently touted for secretary of labor. At the 1944 Democratic convention when the party bosses proposed Harry Truman for vice president, FDR uttered the famous remark, "Clear it with Sidney." Since Lepke had a close alliance with the Italian mobs who also operated in the garment center Costello could rely on the support of organized labor.

In 1939, La Guardia's cops started a drive on Brooklyn hoodlums. A jailhouse stool pigeon fingered Brownsville gangster Abe "Kid Twist" Reles for murder. Reles was named either for a well-known Lower East Side gangster of an earlier generation, or because Reles like to twist his fingers around people's necks (probably both). Only five-foot-two, with a fat ugly body, long gangling arms, piercing eyes, thick lips, and a flat nose, he was often compared to a gorilla. Reles was a man who enjoyed his work, killing for sport as well as profit. When an African-American car washer in a Manhattan garage did not move fast enough to suit him, Reles stabbed him to death. He was acquitted and not long afterward, in the same garage, he became angry with another car washer and beat him to death. Again Costello's Tammany-controlled criminal justice system freed him.

---

[1]And he did not wish to. Despite a pose of respectability, the Bronx organization played ball with the mob. When Flynn had been sheriff of the Bronx, Dutch Schultz had been issued a deputy's badge.

In March 1940, the jailed Reles asked to see O'Dwyer. When he was granted an audience he told the district attorney he would make him "the biggest man in the country" by providing details on eighty-five murders. As a result of Reles's information, eight men, including Maione and Abbandando, went to the electric chair and another fifty to prison. He incriminated Anastasia directly, claiming to have been present during a planning session. Another man Reles blew the whistle on was Lepke Buchalter, who had funneled his contracts through Anastasia. In implicating Buchalter, the "Kid" also fingered Sidney Hillman.

Reles's revelations were not entirely welcome in the district attorney's office. If the waterfront rackets were completely exposed, it would likely bring down the Brooklyn political organization to which O'Dwyer owed his career. The Brooklyn waterfront was also being investigated by special prosecutor John Harlan Amen. In May of 1940, O'Dwyer asserted his own jurisdiction and demanded that Amen turn over the investigation to him. Amen gave O'Dwyer his case files, and a few days later O'Dwyer shut down the waterfront investigation completely, announcing that all his resources were needed to conduct the Murder, Inc. probe, though he knew the two were closely related.

The Murder, Inc. investigation began to bring "Bill O," as the press nicknamed O'Dwyer, the same kind of publicity that Dewey had gotten as a racket buster. Unlike the distant and stiff Dewey, O'Dwyer was a charmer with "a smile that could melt a skyscraper." Democratic Party bosses saw him as the man who could take back City Hall from La Guardia and gave him the party's nomination for mayor. Four years earlier La Guardia had won reelection handily. In November 1941, he polled only 53 percent of the vote. Without Roosevelt's strong support for La Guardia, O'Dwyer probably would have been elected.

During the investigation Reles and other witnesses were kept in isolated quarters on the sixth floor of the Half Moon Hotel along the Coney Island waterfront, guarded by a detail of eighteen cops working out of O'Dwyer's office. Shortly after the mayoral election, Reles went out the window of room 623 and was killed, even though five police officers were on guard duty that night. One of them reported that while making a routine check at

7:10 he discovered Reles missing, looked out the open window, and saw him sprawled on a hotel extension roof five stories below. Curiously, a draft board official reported that he was the one who had first noted the body when he looked out his office window at 7:30 and called a hotel employee, who notified the police. Two bedsheets were knotted together around Reles's feet and attached to them were four feet of insulated wire from piping on the radiator in Reles's room. O'Dwyer theorized that Reles was attempting to drop down and escape through an empty room on the fifth floor when the wire broke. The commanding officer of the Brooklyn D.A.'s detective squad and intimate of O'Dwyer's, Captain Frank Bals, later offered the novel idea that Reles had actually been attempting to play a practical joke, in which he would enter the fifth floor and then come back to the sixth to surprise his guards. Some writers have alleged that the police detail was bribed to throw him out the window, noting that the spot where the body landed was too far from the main building for Reles to have fallen straight down as he attempted to lower himself to the fifth floor. Underworld rumor had it that in an effort to protect his friend Anastasia, Frank Costello had put up $100,000 to have Reles killed. The guards were put on departmental trial by Police Commissioner Valentine. After O'Dwyer unexpectedly testified on their behalf they were acquitted, though they were demoted from plainclothes assignments and sent out to walk beats.

Various investigations failed to produce conclusive evidence on the circumstances of Reles's death. It is not likely that five cops would have agreed to murder a prisoner they were guarding. They would have been obvious suspects, and in such a large group it's likely one of them would have broken down.[2] The hotel where the prisoners were held was a public place, with workmen and employees constantly coming and going on the sixth floor. One of the workers had left the wiring that Reles had wrapped around him. It would have been easy for paid assassins to have obtained a key to the area and slipped past the obviously dozing guards into Reles's bedroom. There they could have blackjacked him, tied him with the wire, thrown him out the

---

[2]Though it may be surprising to laymen, skilled interrogators know that cops (because of their internal commitment to law enforcement) are among the easiest subjects from whom to extract a confession.

window, and departed. This scenario might lie behind the cryptic explanation offered a decade later by Burton Turkus, the Brooklyn assistant district attorney who prosecuted the Murder, Inc. cases, that one or two persons murdered Reles. In any event, Kid Twist, whom the mob labeled "the canary who could sing but not fly," was dead. According to O'Dwyer, the case against Anastasia had gone out the window with him.

O'Dwyer's assertion is doubtful. If Reles was the key to convicting Anastasia, why was he never brought before a grand jury during the twenty months he was in custody? In the later stages of the investigation Anastasia dropped out of sight and a wanted order was issued by the district attorney's office. Early in 1942, the order was removed from the files by chief clerk James Moran, who had been O'Dwyer's personal court officer when he was a judge and who exercised considerable authority in the D.A.'s office. After O'Dwyer took a leave of absence to enter the army in June 1942, he left Moran behind to keep an eye on things. As mayor he would name him deputy fire commissioner. There Moran ran an extortion scheme for which he would receive a sentence of twenty-five years imprisonment. Moran's long and intimate association with O'Dwyer, and his proven corruption, caused many people to question O'Dwyer's own integrity.

In 1945, Mayor La Guardia announced he would not run for a fourth term. Polls indicated that he would have been defeated. Surprisingly, the candidate most favored by respondents was Jimmy Walker, who had resigned the mayoralty thirteen years earlier and fled to Europe to avoid criminal charges. The electorate had no doubt about whether Jimmy was on the take as mayor—they knew he was—or about his attitude toward working hard at his job: he was against it. The poll results could only mean that people were tired of economic depression, war, and a reform mayor. They wanted to go back to the happy days of the 1920s with a mayor who smiled a lot and dished the blarney. Walker's health was too precarious to allow him to make the run (he died the following year) and the nomination went to the personable O'Dwyer. During the campaign there was some discussion about the Reles case and O'Dwyer's visit to Costello. But the charges did not stick. O'Dwyer's opposition was split between two candidates, and in November he was elected the 100th mayor of New York.

For the first time in twelve years the mob had a man they liked in City Hall, one known among them as "Frank's man." Throughout his administration, O'Dwyer would go through the charade of denouncing the various Tammany leaders who came and went with great frequency, but whoever was chairman, he was always approved by Costello.

Everything seemed to be breaking just right for the mobs. Turned over to the state of New York for trial in one of the Murder, Inc. cases, Lepke Buchalter had been convicted and sentenced to death. Rumors had abounded that he would save his life by singing about Sidney Hillman's role in mob murders. If he talked he might also have sent Anastasia to the electric chair. To many people's surprise, Lepke went to his death without revealing anything. It was generally believed that he had been warned that if he talked, his beloved wife and child would be murdered.

Another hangover from the past was Vito Genovese. When the Allies overran southern Italy in 1944, Genovese was taken into custody. He quickly made arrangements with American army officers to begin running a large black market operation and was released. Orange Dickey, a lowly sergeant in the army criminal investigation division and former campus cop at Pennsylvania State University, began to probe the operation despite receiving no cooperation from the military brass. With the assistance of British troops, he arrested Genovese and found on his person letters of recommendation from U.S. Army officers describing him as "trustworthy, loyal, and dependable." A background check disclosed that Genovese was wanted for murder in New York. When Dickey sought advice from Colonel (and former New York governor) Charles Poletti and Brigadier General William O'Dwyer he was essentially ignored. Spurning bribe offers as high as $250,000 from Genovese and his intermediaries, Dickey arranged to transport Genovese back to New York, where he turned him over to the Brooklyn district attorney's office. Shortly after Genovese's return, the main witness against him died in a Brooklyn jail from what the medical examiner described as "enough poison to kill eight horses." Because the Brooklyn criminal justice system once again lost a key informant against a mob big shot, the charges against Genovese were dropped.

Costello allowed Genovese considerable autonomy, even permitting him to engage in the drug business, though he had warned all his other followers to stay out of it. Costello's admirers claim his stance on narcotics was due to moral scruples. There were more practical reasons for Costello's drug ban. Twenty-year sentences for dealers were common, which meant plenty of motivation for them to turn informer on their bosses. Frank also knew that were he to become identified as a drug lord, many of the politicians who were his friends would turn away from him. When a Federal Bureau of Narcotics supervisor named him as a top drug dealer, Costello stated publicly that he was willing to appear in front of a grand jury, waive immunity, and deny the charges. District attorney Hogan declined to take him up on the offer.

Costello stumbled into bad publicity during one of his efforts to enhance his image. A New York society figure sent out a form letter to businessmen requesting that they sponsor fund-raisers for the Salvation Army. When Frank got one at his Wall Street office he was delighted. He arranged to pick up the tab for a dinner at the Copacabana, ensured that the place was packed, and added a generous personal contribution to the money raised. He even attached a statement to each menu: "For the generous contributions of my many dear friends to this great cause and for their assistance in making this affair possible, thanks from the bottom of my heart." Socialite Igor Cassini, then the gossip columnist of the local Hearst paper, disguised himself as a waiter and managed to gain entrance to the Copa. When he wrote a story identifying the sponsor and naming the guests who attended, including a congressman and eight judges (one of them Justice Aurelio), there were many red faces around town. The embarrassed Salvation Army returned the money, though why it did so was not clear. Even criminals were allowed to contribute to the needy, and no one suggested Frank was planning to take over the Salvation Army. Cassini's bold incursion prompted internal mob discussions about his future health, but finally the no-kill rule for journalists was invoked and he was spared.

While the mayor managed to escape the fallout from the Brooklyn waterfront probe, he became engulfed in another one on the Manhattan waterfront, an area that Costello and his friends did not control. There the West Side Irish gangs still ruled. At the top of the hierarchy was William

McCormack, who represented the harbor's businessmen, and president of the International Longshoremen's Association (ILA), Joe Ryan. McCormack had started as a teamster on the Jersey side of the river. By the time he was twenty-three, his drive and ability to use his fists had earned him fifteen wagons and thirty horses. When the port boomed during the World War I era, so did his business, and he grew close to Jersey City mayor Frank Hague, political boss of the state. After the war, McCormack formed the U.S. Trucking Corporation and installed as president (or front man) Al Smith, who had just been defeated for reelection as governor of New York. When Smith was reelected in 1922 he made McCormack chairman of the New York State Boxing Commission's license committee, where he had a hand in arranging many of the great prizefights of the era at Madison Square Garden. Eventually he obtained the contract to handle all the stevedoring business of the Pennsylvania Railroad, the largest shipper in the metropolitan area.

Joe Ryan, about five years older than McCormack, switched from being a trolley conductor to a longshoreman. After only a year of work he was injured and given a job as a minor union official. Assigned to organizing, he demonstrated ability at public speaking and as liaison man with Tammany politicians. In 1927 he became president of the international union and was named president for life in 1943.

Employers and unions had a cozy relationship in New York. There were no dock strikes between 1919 and 1945. Then in 1945 some New York longshoremen rebelled against Ryan and walked off the job. To get them back, he had to obtain concessions from the employers, like eliminating the third daily shape-up. In retaliation for the walkout, Ryan began to purge dissident ·leaders from the union. When one asked if he could still work on the docks, an ILA official said he could, but "if he fell and hurt himself, it'll be no one's fault." The day after the man returned to work, he fell and hurt himself. Only after the dissident recanted, claiming he had been "duped by the communists," did he cease being accident-prone.

Whenever Ryan was asked about mob influence on the waterfront he would vigorously deny it. McCormack, on the other hand, usually refused to answer any questions. Ryan's lieutenants included the leaders of ILA Local

824, known as "the pistol local" because of frequent outbursts of gunfire and occasional murders on its piers. Following one homicide, district attorney Hogan brought union leaders into his office for questioning. Within an hour, longshoremen on several piers walked off their jobs and Ryan called Hogan to complain, blaming the prosecutor for causing a shipping tie-up. Another of Ryan's followers was Johnny "Cockeye" Dunn, who controlled sixty piers on the Lower West Side. One of Dunn's enforcers was Andy "Squint" Sheridan. When one longshoreman began complaining about working conditions, Sheridan stopped by the pier to ask him to step into the toilet for a conference. There he pumped three shots into the man's brain, stuffed his body down a drain, and walked away. When another dockworker had some unflattering things to say about the union, Sheridan drove up in a car, walked to the platform, and said, "Who's Moran?" When Moran stood up, Sheridan pulled a gun, fired two shots, and killed him.

In 1947, one of Hogan's assistant district attorneys, Bill Keating, managed to make a case against Dunn, Sheridan, and another accomplice for the murder of a hiring stevedore. After the accomplice turned informer, the other two were sentenced to death. In the summer of 1949, Dunn offered to expose corruption on the waterfront, including payoffs to politicians, in return for a commutation of his death sentence. Upon hearing the news Mayor O'Dwyer stated he would not run for reelection that year. Dunn did not go through with his threat and was executed in July. The next day Joe Ryan visited the mayor. Shortly afterward O'Dwyer announced that he would be a candidate, and in November was reelected by a large margin.

Ironically, it was not the mob but an obscure headquarters vice detective, Jim Reardon, in partnership with low-level gambler Harry Gross, who ruined the O'Dwyer administration. Reardon's connections enabled him to make deals with police brass and soon he was doing so well that he quit the force to devote all his energies to gambling. He and Gross were bold and drew a lot of attention to themselves. A reporter began writing about the pair and the Brooklyn district attorney, Miles McDonald, no friend of O'Dwyer's, launched a probe. Instead of playing it smart by firing the police commissioner and announcing that he was "shocked, shocked to find gambling," O'Dwyer denounced McDonald and the whole investigation.

When indictments were handed down against eighteen cops—some high-ranking—he and his police commissioner quit. His friends persuaded President Truman to appoint him ambassador to Mexico. A smoothie to the end, O'Dwyer tearfully announced that he was resigning because "My country needs me," while his aides spread the word that he was going south of the border to foil a communist plot. City Council president Vincent Impellitteri was named acting mayor until a special election could be held in November.

"Impy," as he came to be known, was a cipher. In 1945, under the rules of New York City's tribal politics, it had been necessary for the Democrats to geographically and ethnically balance the ticket by finding a Manhattan Italian to run with the Brooklyn Irish O'Dwyer and a Jewish comptroller candidate from the Bronx. There were no Italians in high office at the time. Impellitteri was an obscure law secretary to a state supreme court justice—Tammany claimed it hit on his name in the city's *Green Book,* which listed thousands of officials, but actually he was slated on the recommendation of East Harlem congressman Vito Marcantonio, acting on behalf of mob boss Tommy Lucchese. His selection was the equivalent of picking a clerk for a federal district judge to run for vice president of the United States. Because the job had few duties and Impy kept a low profile, he was reelected along with O'Dwyer in 1949. No one considered him a serious mayoral prospect and it was assumed that he would only hold the job until the election, then three months off.

The Tammany candidate was state supreme court justice Ferdinand Pecora, well-known from his days as an assistant district attorney, as counsel to a congressional probe of Wall Street, and as the judge who had declared a mistrial in the Jimmy Hines case. Pecora was the favorite, but to everybody's surprise Impy announced that he was running. As acting mayor, Impellitteri had immediately named Tom Murphy as his police commissioner. Murphy was an assistant U.S. attorney who had just finished successfully prosecuting accused communist spy Alger Hiss for perjury and would later be revealed to be a personal friend of Lucchese.

The ascent of Three Finger Brown's friends to City Hall and police headquarters was not a pleasing prospect to Frank Costello, because it might upset the delicate balance of power in the New York mob world. Lucchese might want to move up to prime minister, supported by bosses like Profaci and Bonanno. If Frank were removed or diminished in stature, it would also open the way for Genovese to make his own move to replace him as head of their family. In a power struggle, Anastasia and Moretti would support Costello, but Moretti was so ill from paresis that Frank had sent him on a long vacation. In the worst-case scenario, the results of the mayoral election could prompt a mob war of the type not seen since 1931. Frank had to make sure Tammany won. He departed from his respectable pose and dispatched gunmen to hold some wavering district leaders in line for the regular ticket. During the campaign Impellitteri's press secretary claimed that the mayor had turned down a $400,000 bribe to give up the race. The charge was based on the fact that he had been offered a state supreme court judgeship, the salary of which, over a fourteen-year term, was equal to the supposed bribe amount. Running as the "unbossed and unbought" candidate, Impellitteri was elected to serve out the remaining three years of O'Dwyer's term. The voters may not have realized it, but they had chosen Tommy Lucchese's candidate over Frank Costello's.

14:

New Worlds to Conquer: Postwar Expansion

At the end of World War II, the American economy went into high-growth mode. Like other business leaders, mob bosses looked to expand to the South and to the West as well as into new enterprises within their own domains. As a result, the late 1940s would be the apogee of the American Mafia.

The twin pillars of the national syndicate, the New York and Chicago mobs, had already established beachheads in three key areas—Florida, Louisiana, and California—and were well positioned for postwar expansion. To be successful they had to adapt their methods to the local situation. In New York and Chicago they had political bases, guns, and money for bribery. In the South and the West they had no political base, outside guns offended local sensibilities, and even money had to be used in a discreet fashion. It was like gaining admission to an exclusive club where wealth was not sufficient without the right sponsors. Those who failed to understand the subtleties risked the embarrassment that often comes to parvenus.

After the Hollywood extortion trial Bugsy Siegel became the syndicate's number one man on the West Coast. Siegel owed his career to Meyer Lansky, his mentor since the two were teenagers on the Lower East Side. When the young punks appeared then before magistrate William McAdoo, he told them, "You guys are bugs," and Benny became Bugsy. In the 1920s they had risen from running dice games and stealing cars to become major bootleggers. After the 1931 mob reorganization, they ranked only a half a step down from Luciano himself. Sending Siegel to Hollywood in the late 1930s seemed logical because, as the New York bosses said, while they pursued money, "Benny always went for the girls." In Hollywood, looks, charm, and brains helped in getting ahead and Siegel was well endowed with all of those qualities. But he lacked one essential that his mentor Lansky possessed—the ability to control his temper. With local boss Jack Dragna as his partner and Michael "Mickey" Cohen his lieutenant, Siegel began taking over gambling in Southern California.

Cohen, who did not have looks, charm, or brains, was born in Brooklyn, but had lived in Los Angeles since the age of two. In 1928, when he was fifteen, he ran away to join relatives in Cleveland and began boxing. He didn't get very far and settled in as a slugger for the Cleveland Jewish mob. In 1939, he drifted back to Los Angeles, where he cut a conspicuous figure in his usual costume of a long, heavily padded sports jacket, topped off by an excessively wide brimmed hat. And he was reckless. No sooner had he arrived in Los Angeles than he assembled a crew and held up one of Jack Dragna's racing wire rooms, a big one with thirty phones. It even rated two deputy sheriffs as guards, though when Mickey's troops waved a shotgun, the lawmen chose discretion over valor and Cohen departed with $30,000. Dragna screamed to Ben Siegel, but even after Siegel called him on the carpet, Mickey refused to give up the money. Cohen had come to California with the blessing of Moe Dalitz's Cleveland outfit. Cleveland was an imperial city, Los Angeles was just a colony. Killing Cohen without the approval of the eastern bosses would have been an act of lèse-majesté. Instead, Bugsy played Dutch uncle, arranging a second meeting with Johnny Roselli as a silent, but not unnoticed observer. Finally, even Cohen realized that the New York and Chicago overseers of Hollywood had the power to have him declared persona non grata—mob style. Mickey consented to be generous and returned a treasured diamond stickpin that had belonged to the wire room boss. He also agreed to be a good boy and take orders from Ben Siegel—but not from a colonial like Jack Dragna.

California politics were beginning to become respectable. In 1938, Los Angeles's Shaw machine had been ousted by a reform administration, and law-and-order zealot Earl Warren was elected attorney general of the state. As a result, the Los Angeles cops became markedly less friendly to the mob—though not totally unfriendly. Warren zeroed in on the gambling ships that operated just outside the three-mile limit. One of them was owned by the hot-tempered Tony Cornero, whom the cops had allowed back in town after Mayor Shaw took office. The shipowners operated Hollywood style, with full-page newspaper ads, billboards, and skywriters. Tony Cornero's ad boasted that his ship, the *Rex*, offered a wider range of slots, roulette wheels, and blackjack tables than the others. In those days, Warren didn't worry too much about the niceties of due process. Even though the ships were in international waters, he sent raiding parties to board them. All surrendered peacefully except Cornero. For ten days he held off the lawmen with fire hoses while newsreel cameras recorded the scenes. Delighted with the attention, Cornero threw bottles of imported brandy to the photographers' boats. Finally he was starved out and agreed to forfeit his ship after legal proceedings.

Neighboring Nevada was a huge, thinly populated desert. After its silver mines played out early in the century, it became a rest stop for cross-country travelers in the automobile era. To boost its Depression-ravaged economy, the state legalized gambling in 1931. Siegel, Dragna, and Cohen's ascension caused some Los Angeles gamblers to migrate to Nevada. Billed as "The Biggest Little City in the World," Reno had always been the gambling center of the state—as well as the place where rich folks got divorced—but it was much closer to San Francisco than to Los Angeles. So the L.A. exiles set up shop in downtown Vegas. Their dingy saloons in the shabby downtown district did reasonably well. Before the postwar aviation boom, Vegas was too far away from the population centers of the East and Midwest and still too reminiscent of a frontier town to become anything more than the gambling capital of Nevada. If California had legalized betting, Nevada would have dried up and blown away. There was no chance of that: California's population of transplanted Iowa and Oklahoma farmers was too upright to ever legalize sin, instead, they just enjoyed it.

Siegel began to imagine Nevada studded with ornate casinos, his own gambling ships out in the desert. There, oil millionaires and Hollywood celebrities could engage in high-stakes action away from the uninspiring downtown and the cheap tourists, and no cops could bother them. The end of the war freed up construction workers, building materials, and planes to haul in customers, and Siegel began constructing his dream palace, the Flamingo Hotel and Casino. The business was new to him, and he was too eager to take time to assemble a top staff to advise him on subjects like construction, the tourist industry, and casino management. Building materials were still in short supply and Siegel had to pay prohibitive black-market prices for them. The plans for the hotel were hastily drawn and some of the work had to be redone. Siegel wanted everything top of the line, ordering solid concrete walls that were unnecessary in a desert climate, and importing wood and marble as though he were putting up a museum. The original cost estimate was $1.5 million. By the time he had burned through $1 million of his own money, the estimate had quadrupled. In order to continue, he sought financing from the bosses back east. Meyer Lansky persuaded men like Frank Costello to advance Benny $3 million. It still was not enough. To raise $2 million more he offered to sell the syndicate his West Coast wire service. The problem was, the Chicago mob already thought they owned it.

Mob empire builders were not only colonizing the South and West, but acquiring neglected assets in their own territories. This was especially true of the Chicago gambling scene. Frank Nitti's suicide and the imprisonment of Paul Ricca and other leaders left Tony Accardo, a.k.a. "Joe Batters," as the number one figure in what Chicagoans still referred to as "the Capone mob." When the bosses went to jail in 1943 he was only thirty-seven years old. His career had followed the typical pattern. Born of Sicilian parents in a tough neighborhood northwest of Chicago's Loop, as a teenager he joined a gang that hung out at the Circus Café. Among the leaders of the "Circus gang" was Jack McGurn. "Machine Gun Jack" became Accardo's mentor and the younger man followed him into Capone's service. His duties at the time involved simple muscle work, and he got his nickname from Capone in recognition of the skillful way he swung a baseball bat on some recalcitrant's head. By the 1930s he was a crew chief and at the end of the decade, a member of the inner circle. After Accardo's ascension, Jake Guzik remained the mob's minister of finance, and Murray "The Camel" Humphreys secretary of commerce and labor.

One area for local expansion was the policy game, where African-Americans still played a leading role. The Chicago version of policy was played by inserting pellets into a "wheel" and turning it to produce the winning combination, just like present-day state lotteries. Some days the wheel managers just picked the winning numbers, displaying a preference for ones that had received light play. The standard story of the 1946 takeover assigns the brainstorm to Mooney "Sam" Giancana, a minor figure at the time. Serving a stretch in a federal prison, he noticed an African-American named Ed Jones was being treated like he was Emperor Jones. A few inquiries disclosed that the favored con was the policy king of Chicago's South Side. Giancana struck up a friendship with Jones who proceeded to tell him about how the nickels and dimes mounted up—Jones's Maine-Idaho-Ohio wheel, Chicago's largest, was turning a profit of $1 million a year. When Giancana was released he reported all this to Accardo, who eventually authorized him to move in. The Chicago outfit might tip its hat to some red-necked Dixie sheriff, but on the South Side they played rough. Jones was waylaid at a busy intersection with his wife and secretary. Giancana's crew dragged him out of his car, hit him over the head, and threw him into their vehicle. When a police patrol car spotted the kidnapping and gave chase, the gangsters opened fire and wounded one of the officers in the shoulder. Jones's family had to come up with $100,000 to obtain his release. The shaken Jones and his brother turned over their organization to their third partner, Teddy Roe, and moved to Mexico City where each of the brothers continued to receive 20 percent of the profits from the wheel.

The expansion upset what had been a stable, long-term arrangement, both within the Chicago outfit and between it and the black independents. Until 1946, three of the top policy wheels in Chicago were run by lower-level white mob figures, in some cases for nearly twenty years. In 1942, Irey's T-men had charged black and white policy operators for tax evasion. The gangsters' reluctance to consolidate the game by moving in on the African

Americans can be attributed to politics and a bit of sociology. The African-American policy operators had the backing of the South Side's most important political boss. Congressman William Dawson had led his people out of the Republican Party into the Democratic fold, a boon that earned him considerable clout at City Hall. (The conversion had been spurred by the police raids on policy wheels ordered by the Democratic machine after it took power in 1931.) On the West Side, one of party boss Pat Nash's top lieutenants was an African American, "Big Jim" Martin, overlord of policy in that part of town.

Then there was the race question. Black policy bosses were men of substance who contributed significantly to the economy of their depressed community. Not only did they pay off cops and politicians, but they kicked in heavily to local churches and charities and provided several thousand jobs in their industry. They were widely known and admired by other blacks. If they were forcibly displaced, there was always the possibility that the customers just might stop playing policy.

Boss Nash died in 1943. In the postwar era Mayor Kelly's power began to wane. Housing shortages and school board scandals had eroded his popularity. The timing was right for the Capone gang to move in, hence the 1946 attack on Ed Jones. Some lesser black policy operators gave way to the outfit, but Teddy Roe and Jim Martin both refused to step aside. Roe was hailed as a hero by his community for not giving in to the white gangsters. Martin cut a deal with another West Side white political leader and continued to operate. A complete takeover was delayed for a few years. In 1950 Martin was shot and badly wounded, and his white protector was threatened by mobsters. Both men left town. Roe was murdered two years later.

Another Chicago expansion that began locally ended up with major national implications, because it involved the racing wire service, the lifeblood of gambling. Originally it had belonged to Mont Tennes who later took on a partner named Jack Lynch. When Tennes retired in 1927, Moses Annenberg bought into the operation and became Lynch's new partner. Annenberg and his brother Max had been top circulation managers for several Chicago newspapers from the pre–World War I era into the '20s. A circulation manager's job was not to run promotional contests but to ensure that newsstands carried their employers' papers and not their competitors'. Rival armies of sluggers roamed the streets of Chicago beating and killing newsboys and one another. The Annenbergs gave employment to a number of street toughs like Dion O'Bannion, providing them with valuable training for the bootlegging wars. Annenberg's general manager was a former associate from the news wars, James Ragen. In 1934 Lynch got into a dispute with Annenberg and Ragen and sued them. Eventually the matter was settled by giving Lynch $750,000 for his share of the business. Ragen also gave $100,000 to Frank Nitti for using his "good offices" to help resolve the matter.

Attracted by the public dispute, in 1939 Irey's T-men brought a case against Annenberg and Ragen for income tax fraud. Annenberg pled guilty, was sentenced to a year in jail, and was made to pay $8 million to the federal government. He also sold his business, then known as Nationwide News, to Ragen and Arthur "Mickey" McBride, another alum of the news wars. McBride remained in Cleveland where he owned a taxicab fleet and later the Cleveland Browns football team.

The wire service, now under the name Continental Press, was a strange entity: a legal business set up to provide information to individuals engaged in illegal bookmaking. Its operations were hardly a secret. In most downtown districts of American cities, race results blared forth from loudspeakers in little cigar stores and giant betting parlors. The stentorian tones of the announcer, "They're off and running in the sixth at Rockingham," or "Results from the eighth race at Hialeah are" were as much a part of the urban scene as traffic noises.

Annenberg had paid tribute to the Chicago mob, but it had not moved in on him because his connections were too powerful. Ragen was not on the same level, so he hoped McBride's charm and contacts would keep the Capone gang at bay. In Cleveland McBride was on amicable terms with Moe Dalitz's group, Al Polizzi's Mayfield Road mob, and the reform city administration. The bosses of Continental were also well connected to legitimate communications businesses like Western Union and AT&T. When a 1942 plane crash in California knocked out some wires, Continental had its service restored in fifteen minutes. The U.S. Army Western Defense Command, with responsibility for preventing a Japanese invasion, had to wait three hours for its line to a vital airbase to be repaired.

For a while things went smoothly for Continental, then trouble developed. Accardo, Guzik, and Humphreys tried to become Ragen's "partners." Ragen had no intention of playing along with the outfit. Such an arrangement, he felt, was sure to end with him being "found some morning dead in an alley." The Chicago gang decided to open a rival racing service, Trans-American, to steal customers and pirate information from Continental. When a Trans-American bookie switched back to Continental he was murdered as a warning to others. McBride remained neutral during this time, possibly because he thought Ragen was too hot-headed, or perhaps simply to protect his own interests.

Ragen, always a generous contributor to the local Democratic Party, arranged a meeting with high city and party officials to ask for their help. As noted, 1946 was a period when the organization was at a low ebb and was not about to go up against the "West Side Bloc," a group of elected city and state legislators.[1] The machine had learned long ago that fighting organized crime was a bad idea. After Mayor Harrison closed down the Levee in 1914, the Democrats were cast out of City Hall for eight years. In 1927, Mayor Dever, who defied the Torrio-Capone outfit, was defeated for reelection. Forced to choose between the $100,000 or $200,000 that a gambler might kick in and the 100,000 plus votes the bloc controlled, the organization's choice was obvious.

In his anger, Ragen forgot the gambler's maxim, "Only a sucker beefs." When one of his managers jumped ship for Trans-American, Ragen revealed that thirty years earlier the man had escaped from a Chicago courtroom while he was being tried for robbery. The case had been conveniently forgotten in true Chicago style, but Ragen kicked up so much fuss that the man was jailed on the old charge. After an incident when two men in a car pursued Ragen until he managed to drive to a police station and run inside, he hired two ex-cops as bodyguards. Next he went to the Cook County state's

---

[1] Despite its name, the West Side Bloc included the old First Ward, which was actually on the South Side, and a couple of North Side wards in the vice areas.

attorney and gave him a 98-page statement describing how he was being muscled. In it Ragen predicted that he might be murdered and named Accardo, Guzik, and Humphrey as the probable culprits. Ragen also detailed accounts of murders and payoffs to politicians. He let it be known that the same information was in a safe-deposit box to be opened upon his death. Since Ragen understood how Chicago worked, he was not really seeking an investigation, just making it clear to the outfit how much trouble his murder would bring them.

It was a dangerous game and he knew it. Three years earlier Spike O'Donnell, a frequent target of gangland guns over the years, had gone to City Hall and battered the Chicago street commissioner so badly that he had to be hospitalized for several months. When O'Donnell was arrested, he claimed he was angry because he had not been paid off for arranging some paving contracts, and told the press he would "blow the lid off" of Chicago politics by revealing payoffs to top figures. Shortly afterward, he was machine-gunned to death outside his home. Ragen went one step further. A man who had been "mobbed up" all his life, he contacted the local office of the FBI and laid out a case of attempted extortion from a business that was conducted in interstate commerce, a clear violation of federal law. J. Edgar Hoover could not refuse to handle a matter squarely within his jurisdiction. He ordered a squad of agents assigned to the case, which the bureau code-named "Reassembly of the Capone Gang" or Capone gang, for short (abbreviated in bureau communications as CAPGA). As one FBI agent commented, it was as if Hoover believed that the mobsters had been on sabbatical since Al went away in 1931. The FBI set up a wiretap in the Loop hotel barbershop that was known as a mob message center (the hotel was also the headquarters of the Cook County Democratic organization). For a while it appeared as though the Feds were going to make another Hollywood-sized case. Then, in June 1946, as Ragen was driving along during the height of the evening rush hour with his two guards following in a car behind him, a tarpaulin-covered truck pulled alongside and the occupants began shooting. Ragen's guards returned the fire, but the gunmen escaped. Though badly wounded, Ragen was still alive and it looked as if he would pull through; six weeks later he died in the hospital. According to the

FBI he was poisoned. Hoover withdrew his agents from the case and went back to his pattern of noninvolvement.

The principal suspects in the killing were some West Side heavies, supposedly acting on orders from the top bosses. Two Chicago police commanders, Captain Tom Connolly and acting Captain Bill Drury, picked up the suspected shooters and Jake Guzik for questioning. Drury had tried to make a case against Tony Accardo for dice queen Estelle Carey's murder and was known for being hard on mob guys. The state's attorney's office declined to prosecute Guzik and eventually dropped the charges against the suspected shooters. It also ruled that the information contained in Ragen's statement and the papers in his safe-deposit box were of no legal value. Instead, it hauled the two captains in front of a grand jury, and when they both refused to sign an immunity waiver (as was required by department regulation), they were put on trial by the city Civil Service Commission and fired from the police force.[2]

After Ragen's death Mickey McBride resurfaced as the official owner of the Continental wire service and reached an accord with rival Trans-American. He even made his son head of the business. Chicagoans just shrugged. The wire service seemed immortal. From the time of Tennes in the 1920s, through all the various changes at the top, it remained headquartered at 431 South Dearborn, on the edge of the Loop, and throughout the period the loudspeakers on the adjoining blocks continued to blare forth race results. The race wire was regarded as such a normal business that when McBride was asked why he made his son the replacement for a man who was assassinated, he replied, "That business has been in existence for over sixty years and one man got killed in it. I know a hundred lawyers that got killed in the last forty years."

In the same year the wire service war ended, the Chicago outfit attempted to move in to new territory in the Southwest. A Texas drug dealer named Paul Jones took advantage of an acquaintanceship with Guzik and Humphreys (who were not involved in drugs) to pitch them a lucrative gambling

---

[2]A confidential investigation undertaken at the time by the Chicago Crime Commission did cast doubt on the validity of the charges against the West Side heavies accused in the Ragen murder.

operation in Dallas. At the time, local independent Dallas gamblers had become involved in a murderous feud, and a new county sheriff was about to take office. Given the opening, Guzik and Humpheys authorized Jones to start negotiations. First he got in contact with Lieutenant George Butler of the Dallas municipal police, who introduced him to county sheriff-elect Steve Guthrie. A payoff of $150,000 a year was broached with Guthrie. After preliminary negotiations with the two, Jones brought down a Chicago mob lieutenant, Pat Manno, to close the deal. Pat's presentation was straight out of the Johnny Torrio school of business. "Once you get organized," he said, "you don't have to worry about money. Everything will roll in a nice quiet manner, in a businesslike way." He told them he did not believe in having a half a dozen joints scattered throughout the city, just one big place hidden out in the county. In addition, he pledged mob support in going after any ordinary criminals who might commit robberies or burglaries. Unbeknownst to Jones and Manno, their meeting was being recorded and photos snapped of them entering and leaving. Shortly after Manno flew back to Chicago, Jones was arrested, eventually convicted, and given three years in jail for attempted bribery. Efforts to extradite Manno to Texas failed. They were probably lucky the deal fell through. Local Dallas gamblers were in the process of hitching up their shooting irons to give the Chicago boys a good old Texas welcome.[3]

The New York mob also ran into some difficulty in the South. In 1946 New Orleans's new mayor, deLesseps "Chep" Morrison, began cracking down on Frank Costello and Phil Kastel's gambling operations in the city. While posing as a reformer, Morrison was on friendly terms with local gambling interests opposed to Costello. Ten years in the area had given the New Yorkers a good acquaintanceship with officialdom. When they lost out in the city, Sheriff Frank "King" Clancy of adjoining Jefferson County allowed them to open up the plush Beverly Club, which catered to high-stakes gamblers.

---

[3]During the preparatory stage for the Capone gang's entrance, a small-time Chicago hoodlum named Jacob Rubenstein was sent to Dallas. After the deal collapsed, he remained and was allowed to operate strip joints. He made friends with the police and, in 1963, by which time he was known as Jack Ruby, he was able to enter Dallas police headquarters and kill Lee Harvey Oswald.

Costello and Kastel also formed a partnership with Carlos Marcello, a Sicilian from Tunis, who headed the local Italian faction.

Florida was open to both New York and Chicago. Broward County, north of Miami, was an ideal area for casinos and racetracks and Sheriff Walter Clark, a gambler himself, posed no obstacle. With his chief deputy, who was also his brother, he operated the local Cuban *bolita* (lottery) and slot machines. The most lucrative gambling area was Miami Beach, where the great hotels attracted winter vacationers. Some hotels were owned by mob bosses like Al Polizzi of Cleveland, but gambling on the beach was run by locals who aimed to keep it that way. In 1944, in anticipation of a postwar invasion by out-of-towners, five big Miami gamblers formed two hundred local bookies into the S&G Syndicate, which grossed $30 to $40 million annually, most of it during the winter tourist season. When Costello's partner Frank Erickson paid $45,000 for the three-month season gambling rights at one of the hotels, he was warned by the Miami Beach cops that he would not be allowed to operate. He went ahead anyway, the place was raided, and Erickson's operation was shut down, costing him a bundle. In the North this would have led to serious consequences for the principals of S&G, but in the South (particularly Miami) the rule was no guns. Instead, the Chicago mob proposed a partnership with S&G, claiming the infusion of their capital would make everyone more money. The locals were not hicks and they turned it down.

A transplanted Chicagoan named William Johnston operated horse and dog racing tracks in the Miami area. In 1948 he contributed $100,000 to the campaign of Fuller Warren, who was elected governor of Florida. After Warren took office, he appointed William "Bing" Crosby (no relation to the crooner) as a state crime investigator. Crosby immediately began making raids on the S&G gambling places. The Chicago outfit, now in control of the Continental Press, shut off racing information to the S&G bookies. For a while the locals managed to get bootlegged information from a friendly Continental customer in New Orleans. Chicagoans warned the New Orleans subscriber that, southern courtesy or no, another such flagrant breach of business ethics would not be tolerated and the pirating ceased. S&G reevaluated their situation and decided a partnership with Chicago was sound

business. They sold one-sixth of their interest in their $30 million-plus oper-
ation to Chicago for $20,000.

Back in California, Bugsy Siegel had set up a branch of Trans-American
on the West Coast during the wire service wars. With peace restored it was
expected that it would be turned over to Continental. Despite entreaties
from his eastern partners, and needing the cash for his money pit Vegas
casino, Bugsy refused to release it without payment of $2 million. At about
the same time he had taken up with Virginia Hill, the favorite bed partner of
mobsters from coast to coast. As a teenager, the green-eyed, auburn-haired
beauty had left her impoverished family in Alabama to come to Chicago
during the 1933 World's Fair to work as a waitress and turn tricks. Soon she
became the girlfriend of a small-time hoodlum. According to mob lore, Virginia was tops in her profession and caught the fancy of many big shots. Virginia was also useful to the mob as a courier of money and messages, though
frequent public displays of her ability to curse like a sailor and use her fists
could make her unfortunately conspicuous. Siegel became so smitten with
Virginia that he announced he was going to marry her, which made him look
foolish in the eyes of his mob peers.

With funds beginning to run out, Siegel decided to generate cash flow by
opening the casino before construction work was finished. He chose the
night after Christmas in 1946, a very bad time for a travel-related business.
Siegel relied on his Hollywood friends to turn out en masse. He donned a
white tie and swallowtail coat and waited in the casino to welcome guests,
accompanied by Virginia in a flamingo-colored gown. Jimmy Durante was
headlining the show and Siegel's old pals like George Raft showed up. Other
invited guests such as Cary Grant and Clark Gable did not. Business was
poor, and after two weeks Siegel closed the place and sought to raise more
money to finish construction, necessitating another trip to the East. In the
meantime, the mob bosses had gotten word that Virginia Hill was making
frequent trips to Switzerland to deposit cash. Some of them wanted to cut
their losses and cut down Benny. Meyer Lansky managed to talk them into
putting up more money and giving Siegel a little more time, but he warned
him that he had to succeed.

Finally the hotel was completed and business did pick up, but it was not bringing in big money. In addition, Siegel had sold shares in the Flamingo several times over, so that people who thought they owned 10 percent found out they only owned a half of 1 percent. Siegel made one more trip to the East where the commission warned him that he should give up the wire service at once and straighten out financial matters in the desert. Siegel was defiant and talked about going off to live in Europe with Virginia. A lesser figure would have been killed long before. But Benny had been an integral part of the New York mob structure and the national syndicate since they were formed. He and Lansky were virtually members of the national commission. Killing a man of his stature would set a precedent and could not be undertaken lightly.

In legal businesses the usual way of dealing with an associate who misappropriates funds and won't make restitution is to file criminal or civil charges. CEOs can be voted out by the board of directors or, in theory, by the stockholders. Even in the mob's legitimate businesses, running to the law is unwise—the Chicago wire service lawsuits had brought unwelcome IRS inquiries about whether the principals had paid their proper taxes. Organized crime had its own, unwritten rules. Jim Colosimo had been "removed" because his associates believed he was no longer up to his job. Dion O'Bannion was killed because he cheated on a business deal. Salvatore Maranzano paid the price for being too dictatorial. Al Capone and Owney Madden were sent into exile because their irresponsible behavior and the bad publicity it generated hurt all the mobs. Dutch Schultz should have left New York City after his acquittal upstate. Instead he came back and resumed his reckless ways, thereby sealing his fate. Lepke Buchalter might have survived if he had gone abroad, but by remaining in New York and trying to eliminate witnesses, he generated so much heat that he was delivered to the authorities for execution.

Lansky managed to buy a bit of time for Benny to redeem himself. When he didn't, there was only one recourse. Bugsy had cheated his partners, proven unfit for his job, and attracted unwelcome attention. Even Lansky could not continue to champion him without raising serious doubts about his own fitness for office.

Siegel had acquired a Moorish-style mansion in Beverly Hills, formerly occupied by screen and opera star Lawrence Tibbett. In June 1947, Bugsy was sitting on a couch with a male business associate when he was cut down by a shotgun blast fired through the window. Virginia was in Europe. It was widely known that her boyfriend was marked for murder, and she may have decided to remove herself from the line of fire. It is generally believed that the shooter was working for Jack Dragna, who assigned him on orders from New York and Chicago. The night of Siegel's murder, a crew of mobsters representing the eastern interests walked into the Flamingo and took over.

While never as vast or as illicitly organized as some people made it out to be, the national syndicate was at its height in 1950. In New York City, Costello and his key cabinet members Lansky and Adonis consulted with the other family heads to run things smoothly. As long as they were reasonably discreet they had little to fear from law enforcement. Outside New York, Costello and his inner circle were able to exert influence from the Atlantic to the Pacific, and from the Canadian border to the Gulf Coast, mostly through business and personal ties rather than by direct control. Across the Hudson in New Jersey, Costello's ally Willie Moretti and Longy Zwillman ran things. In the late '30s Joe Adonis had also set up shop in the Garden State. In the South, the New Orleans suburbs were a New York playground, though the Crescent City itself was closed to Costello until a new Huey Long could arise and put the locals in their place. Hot Springs and Miami were shared with the Chicago outfit.

Missouri was within the Chicago orbit. The head of the gambling interests in Kansas City was Charles Binaggio, and his enforcer was a vicious murderer named Charles Gargotta. They were opposed by both the reformers who had taken over the city in 1939 and the remnants of the Pendergast machine. Some cynics even believed that Pendergast's fall had been partially engineered by organized crime rivals. One result of the change of government was return of control over local police to a four-member board of commissioners appointed by the governor. As Moe Dalitz had proved in Cleveland, there were ways to work around a reform administration. The first requisite for a Kansas City mob boss was to ensure a friendly governor was in office, or, as Binaggio once put it, "I gotta have a governor." Since Missouri elected its governor every two years, there was plenty of opportunity for influence to be brought to bear in the appointment of police commissioners, and often the board was divided 2–2 between those who wanted restraint and those who wished at least a partial return to the wide-open-town days in order to stimulate business. As one of them put it, "People don't come to Kansas City to sleep."

Philadelphia, Detroit, and New England had their own mobs, but they worked in conjunction with the New York–Chicago axis, and by the 1940s were represented on the national commission.

After Ben Siegel's murder, open warfare broke out in Los Angeles between Jack Dragna and Mickey Cohen. Mickey was able to survive five murder attempts, but the headlines generated were devastating. Attorney general Fred Howser sought to organize gambling statewide and even assigned one of his detectives to guard Cohen. In 1948, when Dragna's gunmen opened up on Mickey outside a Sunset Strip nightclub, the guard was badly wounded and the attorney general highly embarrassed. Earl Warren, who was then the governor, looked askance at Howser's activities and appointed a private statewide crime commission to investigate organized crime and corruption. The LAPD had moved away from its worst corruption days, and in 1950 William H. Parker was appointed chief. Among his high priorities was making life miserable for Mickey Cohen.

The Los Angeles County Sheriff's Office was not infected with the reform bug. Hollywood's Sunset Strip was on a piece of land just outside the boundaries of the City of Los Angeles in county territory. An organization known as the Guarantee Finance Company, posing as a legitimate loan corporation, ran a $200 million gambling operation there. When an LAPD lieutenant descended through the skylight and seized records, a sheriff's captain wrote the lieutenant an official letter warning him not to operate in the county. The absence of a boss such as Siegel maintaining firm control over local mobsters and the struggles among Los Angeles city and county lawmen, the governor, and the attorney general spelled trouble for California organized crime.

Bugsy had been right; the future of the region was in Las Vegas. There would be no problems with Nevada politicians. The lieutenant governor was a Vegas lawyer who owned pieces of three gambling joints. His law partner was the local district attorney. Meyer Lansky brought his talents to bear and made the Flamingo a success. A few years later he opened the Thunderbird. Moe Dalitz followed up with the Desert Inn, and Longy Zwillman, the Sands. Eventually the Chicago outfit built the Riviera and acquired the Stardust; the New England mob, the Dunes; and Frank Costello and Carlos Marcello, the Tropicana. For a long time everyone existed in peace and prosperity. They even had their own generous banker—the Central States Teamster Pension Fund, courtesy of Jimmy Hoffa. If anything demonstrated that there was a national syndicate, it was Las Vegas.

Ironically, as Vegas blossomed, the old Hollywood studio system began to collapse. In the 1950s, the place to recapture the glamour and excitement of prewar Hollywood was the Vegas Strip. When their crude ways got them blackballed at the stars' country club, the mobsters had decided to create their own, a wonderland of opulence where the only membership prerequisites were money and muscle.

15:   TV's Greatest Hits: Senator Kefauver
                        Presents the Mafia

Despite J. Edgar Hoover's views to the contrary, by the beginning of 1947 many reporters and cops believed in the existence of a national crime syndicate. The problem was they could not agree on its precise composition and scope. Was it run from Italy with drugs as its lifeblood, or was it dominated by American mobsters who owned racing wires and gambling joints from coast to coast? Was it controlled by a "Mr. Big" or a committee? With the war over and the Soviet menace not fully emergent—Joe McCarthy and the Korean War were still a few years off—the menace of the mobs was an ideal story to fill news columns. But it was too vague to be grasped by the average reader.

In April 1947 Herbert Asbury, who had been writing bestselling chronicles of big-city gangs since the 1920s, set out to fill in the picture with a two-part series in *Collier's*. Asbury put a face to the story by identifying "Mr. Big" as Frank Costello, and he did not let inconvenient facts get in the way of a colorful yarn. The title he chose, "America's Number One Mystery Man," was a clever ploy. At one stroke he made Costello America's problem—not just New York's—and by tagging him as a mystery man he could present various assertions as the best available information, even if it might not be correct.

In the opening paragraph, Asbury pulled off the journalistic coup of describing Costello's innermost thoughts:

His dreams if any have been against a soothing background—the profitable clanking of his slot machines, the remunerative rattling of the dice in his gambling houses, and the soft and lovely rustle of folding money harvested by front men and collectors in such golden fields as bookkeeping, policy, Italian lottery, and nightclubs.

Only occasionally are these delightful sounds intruded upon by the ugly thud of the blackjack with which his laws are enforced. While he slept, the high-fliers and unfortunates of a score of states were pouring money into his multifarious enterprises. Eventually most of it will come to him. In cash.

A somewhat fanciful version of Costello's career followed. According to Asbury, after the 1931 murder of Joe Masseria Costello became boss of the Unione Siciliana, with Lucky Luciano as his lieutenant and Dutch Schultz as one of his employees. Names and places were repeatedly dropped to illustrate Costello's national reach. The Federal Bureau of Narcotics supervisor's claim that Frank was behind large-scale drug dealing in New York was accepted as bona fide.

In the second part Asbury made an interesting observation. "It is likely that only a full-scale congressional investigation could trace the ramifications of America's underworld empire and its relations with politicians and elected officials." The allusion to a congressional investigation was significant. Capone had been brought down on direct orders from President Hoover. The Kansas City, New Orleans, and Atlantic City machines were smashed by Morgenthau's T-men. But like other crime reporters, Asbury realized that with Harry Truman in the White House, the IRS shot through with corruption, and Hoover at the FBI, the executive branch of the United States government was not going to take action against the mobs. In 1948, when it appeared that Tom Dewey (with Earl Warren as his running mate) was going to become president, the prospects for a federal drive against organized crime brightened. A Republican win would not only remove President Truman but, given Dewey's background, might spark interest in a war on the rackets. But Truman's surprise victory guaranteed four more years of inaction against the syndicate.

A handful of people were not willing to accept this policy of benign neglect. One was Virgil Peterson, operating director of the Chicago Crime Commission. Peterson was a product of the heartland, born and raised in the Swedish Lutheran community of Olds, Iowa (population 250). In 1930, he received a law degree from Northwestern University just as the Depression hit. Jobs were scarce and he signed on as a special agent with Hoover's Bureau of Investigation. He rose rapidly, becoming chief assistant to the legendary Melvin Purvis, whose roving anti-gangster squad mowed down John Dillinger, "Baby Face" Nelson, and "Pretty Boy" Floyd. While the fiery Purvis was a swashbuckler, racing around with a machine gun in pursuit of public enemies, the quiet, unassuming Peterson spent most of his time in the office doing administrative work. Never too busy to give an interview or be photographed, Purvis received so much publicity that a resentful Hoover forced him out of the Bureau. Peterson remained in the FBI and rose to be a special agent in charge, serving as head of three different field offices. He was hardworking and loyal, though not blindly so: some things about Hoover's organization disturbed him, such as the excessive preoccupation with bureaucratic ritual and the emphasis on risk avoidance.

While serving as head of the Boston office in 1942, Peterson was recruited for the job of operating director of the Chicago Crime Commission, replacing Henry Barrett Chamberlain. As head of the commission he eschewed quick, flashy crusades against the target du jour in favor of more comprehensive efforts. Essentially he operated as an intelligence officer, collecting, evaluating, and disseminating information, always with his eye on the big picture. He began by compiling dossiers on organized crime with information from the existent commission files, his law enforcement contacts, and reports from a handful of investigators he employed. In a short time he built up a database he shared with journalists, other private anti-crime groups, and selected law enforcement officers. By the late 1940s, he had established a reputation as the leading expert on organized crime in America.

• • •

Peterson wanted to get the federal government to take on the national crime syndicate. One of his principal allies was ex-FBI agent Dan Sullivan, executive director of the Miami Crime Commission, which had been formed by local businessman after Chicago mobsters began buying up property in the area. Another ally was Warren Olney, leader of the California Crime Study Commission. Olney had led the raids on offshore gambling ships as chief of the criminal division under California attorney general Earl Warren. Later, when Governor Warren provided state funds for a body of citizens to investigate organized crime, he named Olney, then in private practice, to run it. Its first target was the corrupt relationship between Los Angeles mob boss Mickey Cohen and California attorney general Fred Howser.

In September 1949, speaking on behalf of the American Municipal Association, an organization that represented 10,000 local governments, Peterson called on U.S. attorney general J. Howard McGrath to bring the federal government into the fight against organized crime. According to the *New York Times,* Peterson cited the activities of Frank Costello as proof "that crime and gambling syndicates operated on a country-wide basis." When the November 21, 1949, edition of *Newsweek* hit the stands, Costello's picture was on the cover. A week later, he was on the cover of *Time.* The *Time* article noted that Costello was "fast becoming a figure of U.S. legend . . . a kind of master criminal, shadowy as a ghost and cunning as Satan, who ruled a vast mysterious and malevolent underworld and laughed lazily at the law." And while it concluded that some of this was "politicians' talk or crime reporters' romance, a gritty residue of the charges were probably perfectly true." Addressing the municipal association's annual conference in Cleveland on December 2, Peterson again called for federal assistance in the fight against organized crime. With the organizational wheels already greased and the press alerted, the society adopted a resolution supporting his proposal and the story was carried nationally. The timing was perfect. Main Street had formally requested that the U.S. government help them fight mobsters, like that fellow whose *Time* and *Newsweek* cover photos were still lying around every barbershop and doctor's office in America. In January 1950,

Estes Kefauver, a Democratic freshman senator from Tennessee, introduced a resolution to authorize a nationwide investigation of organized crime's impact on interstate commerce. Peterson and his allies' outflanking of Truman and Hoover had begun.

The forty-six-year-old Kefauver was a minor player on the Washington scene. Born to eastern Tennessee gentry, the grandson of a Baptist preacher, he was raised in a strict religious background. He graduated from the University of Tennessee where he was a substitute lineman on the football team (as his star rose, some profiles would promote him to All-American). He went on to Yale Law School and practiced in Chattanooga after graduation. In 1939, he entered Congress as a New Dealer. In 1948, he sought the Democratic nomination for the Senate. The liberal Kefauver was anathema to the old guard, so Memphis boss Ed Crump played the Red card, deriding Kefauver as a "fellow traveler" and "pet coon for the Soviets." Kefauver fought back in a folksy manner. Pointing out that the coon was a peculiarly American animal, he declared, "I may be a coon, but I'm not Mr. Crump's coon," and began wearing a coonskin cap, a potent symbol in the birthplace of Davy Crockett. The voters loved it and sent him to the Senate. It is not clear what motivated Kefauver to get involved in the fight against organized crime. It may have been no more than the usual hopes of a back-bench legislator to get noticed by heading a high-profile investigation.

Kefauver's resolution had been introduced without the approval of the Democratic Senate leadership and its adoption was unlikely. Some Republicans did favor an inquiry into organized crime. When Dewey lost, the stunned GOP had to cast about for an explanation. One was the relationship between big-city political machines and their gangster allies. The city votes of the industrial states were crucial to the 1948 election. Mob money and muscle kept the machines strong. In places like Chicago, New York, and Kansas City, a Democratic presidential candidate often received thousands of fraudulent or purchased ballots while Republican votes mysteriously disappeared. In a close election, such shenanigans could tilt the outcome. An attack on organized crime might weaken the gangster–Democratic Party alliance.

Within his own party, Kefauver's resolution was not backed by Senate majority leader Scott Lucas of Illinois, who owed his election to the Cook County Democratic machine, or by the powerful chairman of the Judiciary Committee, Senator Pat McCarran, the political boss of gambling-fueled Nevada. U.S. attorney general McGrath, a former Democratic National Committee chairman and senator from Rhode Island, unexpectedly invited some local officials and heads of anti-crime groups, like Peterson and his cohorts, to attend the annual conference of U.S. attorneys to be held in Washington in February. President Truman agreed to address the session. There he advised federal, state, and local prosecutors to "cooperate" in stamping out organized crime. Peterson characterized the event as "window dressing" to sidetrack demands for a thorough investigation of organized crime. With Kefauver's resolution languishing in the Senate, it appeared as though the flanking attack had been beaten back. Then came a mini-Valentine's Day Massacre in Harry Truman's backyard.

In April, Kansas City mob boss Charles Binaggio and his enforcer Charles Gargotta were gunned down in the First Ward Democratic clubhouse. It was the ward that had boosted Jim Pendergast to power and created the political machine that made Truman's career possible. Photos of the murdered men's bodies lying under a portrait of the president appeared on the front page of newspapers across the country. Even though Binaggio had been part of an anti-Pendergast faction that Truman loathed, explanations of this would only have opened a discussion of the president's own history. A midterm congressional election was due in November and the Republicans were threatening to regain control of Congress. Truman had to give way, and in May the Senate approved the appointment of a special committee to investigate organized crime. Kefauver was named chairman and was joined on the committee by two other Democrats, Lester Hunt of Wyoming and Herbert O'Conor of Maryland, neither one likely to upset party bosses. The Democratic leadership was able to sidetrack the appointment of Republican senator Homer Ferguson of Michigan, who before his Senate career had led the probe that brought down the mayor, district attorney, and police superintendent of Detroit. An ambitious Republican junior senator from

Wisconsin named Joe McCarthy pushed hard to be appointed, but he was shunted off to another investigating committee where he began his probes of alleged communist influence in government.[1] The Republican members chosen instead were the other senator from Wisconsin, Alexander Wiley, and Charles Tobey of New Hampshire.

Most observers thought the committee would hold a few hearings, issue a report with some tepid recommendations, and disappear. That was probably the desire of the majority, but Kefauver had begun to harbor presidential ambitions. Seventy-year-old Senator Tobey, a strict Baptist teetotaler, was a strong moralist. He also faced a reelection contest in November and some good publicity would not hurt him. With the congressional election pending, Tobey and Wiley's fellow Republicans were expecting them to strike some hard blows against the Democrats.

The real work of an investigating committee usually falls on its chief counsel. In 1933, Ferdinand Pecora had so blistered Wall Street that major reforms such as the creation of the Securities and Exchange Commission and the separation of commercial and investment banking had followed. A few years back, when Kefauver had chaired a congressional committee looking into charges against a Pennsylvania federal judge, he had worked with Boris Kostelanetz, the prosecutor who had sent the Chicago mob bosses to jail in the Hollywood case. Kefauver wanted him for chief counsel, but Kostelanetz was not available. The post was given to a tough, smart, thirty-seven-year-old New York lawyer named Rudolph Halley. After graduating from Columbia Law School at nineteen, he had become a protégé of Pecora. During the war Halley served as a counsel to the Senate committee chaired by Harry Truman that probed fraud in wartime contracts. The publicity given to the Truman Committee helped propel its chairman to the vice presidential nomination. Halley hoped that service with the Kefauver Committee would lead to his becoming mayor of New York. Pecora counseled him

---

[1]One might speculate that if McCarthy had been put on the Kefauver Committee, he would have tried to build his career by attacking organized crime. If so, there would never have been a "McCarthy Era" and the history of the 1950s might have been very different. Later, one of McCarthy's Committee's counsels, Robert Kennedy, made the switch from fighting Reds to fighting the Mafia.

that public success lay in bringing down a Mr. Big. When Pecora had probed Wall Street, his target was J. P. Morgan.

The committee knew little of organized crime and it had to rely on Peterson, Sullivan, and Olney. Another key adviser was Federal Bureau of Narcotics commissioner Harry Anslinger. While all were vigorous mob fighters, Anslinger and the Crime Commission leaders did not share the same view on the origins of the problem. Anslinger was convinced that the Sicilian Mafia was the major directing force of organized crime in the United States. Peterson and his allies were skeptical. Their experience persuaded them that organized crime, though national in scope, was not as tightly organized or ethnically exclusive as Anslinger believed, and that its roots were in American politics, not foreign conspiracies. Peterson saw gambling as the lifeblood of the syndicate, not narcotics. Like a criminal prosecution, the investigation needed a theory of the case. The FBN–Crime Commission split meant the committee would have to choose between competing notions.

The Kefauver Committee began its hearings in Washington with testimony by witnesses like Anslinger and Peterson. The latter spent two days on the stand outlining the operations of the national syndicate. If organized crime was a problem worthy of federal intervention, it was necessary for the committee to document it by conducting investigations in a number of widely scattered cities. The road show began in Miami in July 1950. It was a safe choice. Dan Sullivan was able to provide volumes of material in advance, so the committee was well prepared. It could also rely on assistance from some local investigations that were in progress. Two metropolitan Miami sheriffs, Walter Clark of Broward County and Dade County's "Smiling Jimmy" Sullivan (no relation to Dan), were brought before the committee and questioned about their inability to suppress gambling. Using Dan Sullivan's information, the committee was able to get Clark to admit that over the previous three years his income had been in excess of $1 million. Smiling Jimmy acknowledged that in his five years in office he had been able to parlay his net worth from $2,500 to $70,000. By the time Sullivan was finished he was no longer smiling and was soon suspended from office. The committee also probed the incursion of the Chicago mob into the local S&G

gambling setup and the activities of Governor Warren's criminal investigator "Bing" Crosby. When Warren restored Sheriff Sullivan and some other officials to office, his actions created a firestorm in the state. The *Miami Daily Herald* ran an editorial with a black border around it saying, "How lousy, stinking—and obvious—can a governor of Florida be before the people rise up and strike him down?"

In the first few cities visited, the committee garnered only local attention. Nobody outside of Florida had ever heard of Sheriff Clark or Governor Warren. To merit national coverage, the committee would require stars or sensations. It had scheduled hearings in Chicago for October, but even before it arrived, it was caught up in two murders. When the committee was formed, some crime reporters urged that former Chicago police captain Bill Drury be given a starring role in the upcoming hearings or even made a staff investigator. Counsel Halley was reluctant to place too much credibility in a man who had been fired from the police department and whose career even Virgil Peterson characterized as "stormy."[2] Halley did agree to call Drury as a witness. In September, as he was parking his car in his garage, Drury was assassinated mob-style with a shotgun and a pistol, and three hours later a Chicago attorney he had spoken to the day before was also murdered. Immediately reporters raised the cry that Drury had been killed to silence him and blamed the Kefauver Committee for not giving him adequate protection.

It was a harbinger of the difficulty the committee would encounter in the Windy City. Illinois was Senate majority leader Scott Lucas's state, so Kefauver had to tread carefully lest he spend the rest of his career in the Senate as a pariah. Chicago was also the bailiwick of Captain Dan "Tubbo" Gilbert, formerly chief investigator for the state's attorney office and widely known as "America's richest cop." In an incredible instance of bad judgment, the Cook County Democratic organization had slated Gilbert as their candidate for sheriff in the November elections. The party was not eager for Gilbert to testify on the public record, particularly since Senator Lucas was heading

---

[2]For example, in 1944 Drury was one of seven police captains suspended en masse for allowing gambling in their districts.

the ticket in a tough fight against a congressman named Everett Dirksen. For reasons not fully understood until much later, the committee decided to examine Gilbert in a private executive session. When questioned, Tubbo admitted to a net worth in excess of $300,000, explaining that he made a great deal of money betting—illegally—on sporting events. He also detailed his successful speculation in the grain market and other business deals, causing Rudy Halley to ask Gilbert when he found time to carry out his law enforcement responsibilities. Just before the election, a *Sun Times* reporter tricked the manager of a court reporting service into giving him the transcript of Gilbert's testimony. Its publication was widely credited for defeating Gilbert and Senator Lucas (incidentally clearing the way for the eventual ascension of Lyndon Johnson to leader of the Senate and sparking the revolt that later brought Richard Daley to the head of the Cook County Democrats). The furious Lucas berated Kefauver in the Senate cloakroom and refused to accept his apology.

The November hearings in Los Angeles resulted in another murder and more national headlines. Crime investigator Warren Olney prepped the committee, and the new chief of the Los Angeles Police Department, William H. Parker, was eager to cooperate. Parker testified that an attorney named Sam Rummel was the brains behind Mickey Cohen. After the hearings the committee announced it would return in February for another round. It was rumored that Rummel would be called to testify. In the interval the officer who had objected to the L.A. police lieutenant entering the Sunset Strip, Sheriff's Captain Al Guasti, set up meetings between Rummel and some other high-ranking Sheriff's Department officers. Shortly afterward Rummel was murdered. By the time the committee returned to California, Guasti was under indictment on corruption charges. When he took the stand, his mouth trembled as he sought to explain why he and his fellow cops were holding secret meetings with Cohen's lawyer.

In Philadelphia, the committee heard from the local chief of detectives, who denied that he knew about payoffs from policy gamblers to cops. According to committee investigators, in some districts the numbers operators were paying $100 a week to patrolmen and $1,000 to captains. When the inspector in charge of the vice squad was summoned to testify, he shot himself. Stories of murder and police corruption in the number two, three, and four cities of America were, if nothing else, educating the public about organized crime.

Most of the Kefauver Committee's other hearings were not as dramatic. In Detroit, it spent time on the Ford Motor Company's history of kindness to gangsters, bringing Harry Bennett back from retirement to testify. Ford management could not satisfactorily explain why Joe Adonis continued to have a hauling contract, but since there was no local crime commission or friendly police chief to dig up information, little attention was paid to the Detroit mobs.

Sometimes the committee pulled its punches. In Louisiana, Mayor deLesseps Morrison was allowed to testify that he had driven organized crime out of New Orleans and was complimented by the senators for doing so, even though according to historian Stephen Fox they had evidence that Morrison had received payoffs from local gamblers. Kansas City presented a problem for Kefauver because of President Truman's long association with its politics. The committee did not apply its Detroit tactic of historical inquiry, which would have meant discussing the Pendergast machine and its relationship to men like Johnny Lazia and Charles Carolla. Instead, they focused on the efforts of various factions to gain control of the police board by influencing the governor, though after the Binaggio-Gargotta murders the entire four-member board had resigned.

After a few months the committee settled down into a regular format. The leading figure was its chairman, Kefauver, who came over as an honest fair-minded seeker of truth, courteous to all without being soft. His colleague Tobey was the avenging angel, browbeating witnesses he deemed morally deficient. In New Orleans he blasted Sheriff King Clancy, saying, "Why don't you resign . . . ? It seems to me that a man like you . . . is not worth a damn. . . . Do you feel guilty as hell about these things? . . . I simply cannot sit and listen to this type of what I call political vermin." The other three senators were bit players. In March 1951, Kefauver appeared on the cover of *Time* magazine, which declared him a hot prospect for the presidential nomination.

The workhorse of the committee was Counsel Halley, routinely putting in eighteen-hour days and undergoing twenty hours of nonstop briefings from committee investigators, friendly cops, journalists, and local crime commissions before cross-examining a witness. In his interrogations he fired questions in a high nagging voice, pitched just below whining and bullying, but by no means folksy. Few witnesses were prepared for the volume of names, dates, and places that Halley threw at them, sometimes involving episodes many years in the past. When they hesitated to answer—sometimes genuinely unable to recall details—they came across as crooks.

Some mob chieftains like Moe Dalitz of Cleveland and Tony Accardo of Chicago managed to dodge the committee by leaving town. Dalitz testified in Los Angeles and Accardo in Washington, but the impact was lessened by the distance from their home bases. Dalitz at least answered questions (without giving any information), but Accardo took the Fifth.

At the end of its road show the committee was ready for the big town. In the later stages of its investigation, the committee had allowed local news cameras into the hearing rooms without attracting much notice, at least not nationally. Even New Orleans residents were not riveted when Carlos Marcello invoked the Fifth Amendment 152 times. In New York, the committee had some big names willing to testify: mob star Frank Costello and former mayor William O'Dwyer. Costello was anxious to do so, believing he could convince the committee and the public that he was just an ex-gambler turned legitimate businessman. O'Dwyer was reluctant to appear for fear that criminal charges would be brought against him while he was in New York; not until he was granted legal immunity for the duration of the hearings did he consent to return. In the previous year Costello had testified before another Senate committee which included Senator Tobey, and it had not gone badly. In November he testified at one of the Kefauver Committee's executive sessions. It took a soft line, and Costello seemed to get by without too much difficulty. His lawyers should have warned him that interrogators sometimes behaved differently at public and private hearings. Another factor Costello did not count on was the impact of a new element in American life—television.

Television had just become a staple of urban households. Its fare was largely light entertainment, delivered in prime time. Daytime programs were mostly boring and usually fewer than 2 percent of the TV sets were in use then; airtime could be purchased at bargain rates. The local New York TV station, owned by the *Daily News,* had already arranged to carry the hearings. *Time* magazine, then in the middle of a subscription drive, decided to sponsor it on the national networks. When Frank Costello sat down in a Foley Square courthouse to begin his testimony on the morning of March 13, 1950, he had no idea he would become an instant television star. In New York, seventeen times the normal daytime audience tuned in, and the national ratings were twice as high as those for the World Series. In Chicago people stood in 15-degree weather staring at the television screens through store windows. In many cities schools dismissed students to watch the hearings. Housewives did their chores with one eye on the TV set.

Halley had cleverly held back on Costello in the earlier executive sessions. Now he went after him hammer and tong. Most of the questions were meant to demonstrate that Costello was a national leader of organized crime by showing that he had relationships with mobsters all over the country. Costello complained that the TV lights bothered him, and his lawyers asked that the camera be shut off. As a compromise the cameras showed only his hands. This was a huge mistake—it told the audience that Costello had something to hide. Hour after hour, for two days, the camera focused on his hands nervously toying with a water glass, a wad of paper, or his spectacles—gestures that suggested he was lying. His voice became more gravelly and hoarser than usual; he sounded like a movie heavy. In modern times, a high-priced consultant would have coached him on how to avoid all this. His lawyers had neglected to ensure that the restrictions on the TV cameras also applied to the newsreel photographers in the room, and their shots of a stunned Costello wiping his brow were fed to the evening news shows.

On the third day of his testimony, Costello claimed he was too ill to go on. Kefauver was not about to let him slip away, and he ordered Halley to continue the questioning. Costello responded, "I am in no condition to testify." Kefauver asked, "You refuse to testify further?" "Absolutely," Costello said, asking, "Am I a defendant in this courtroom?" Halley replied, "No." "Am I under arrest?" Costello asked. Again Halley replied in the negative. "Then I am walking out," Costello said. As he did, bedlam broke out in the courtroom as newspapermen rushed to their phones. It was another mistake, though later Costello would claim he had to take a break until he could find out what O'Dwyer was going to say in his testimony.

Costello came back after a weekend of rest, but it was more of the same, with Tobey spelling Halley as grand inquisitor. In one exchange, Tobey asked Costello, "What have you ever done for your country as a good citizen?" "Paid my tax," Costello meekly replied. The answer brought down the house, because everyone knew the government had evidence that he had not paid them in full. It was the highlight of evening news shows and was replayed for the next fifty years in programs about gangsters. At the end, under Kefauver's gentle hand, Costello consented to let the television audience see him full face and even agreed to smile for the camera like a schoolboy at graduation. It did not save him from a contempt citation for refusing to reveal his finances. Frank's peers were appalled that their prime minister had done so badly. Joe Adonis, who had already taken the Fifth at both his private and public appearances, watched the television muttering, "What a sucker, what a sucker."

The dapper, well-groomed O'Dwyer was a witness with the potential to turn the tables on his inquisitors. "Bill O" had once been very popular in New York. When he smiled and turned on the charm he could be as smooth and winning as Jimmy Walker, who a generation back had been loudly cheered when he appeared at the Seabury Hearings, despite his well-founded reputation as a crook. O'Dwyer began his testimony with a long rambling statement describing his early years and his wartime services. It was meant to remind people of his Horatio Alger life story, but it was also designed to waste time and bore the audience. Viewers flooded the TV stations with demands that his monologue be cut off. Finally, Halley interrupted with a blistering cross-examination about O'Dwyer's failure to prosecute mobsters when he was D.A. of Brooklyn, the death of "Kid Twist" Reles, and the mayor's relationship with Costello. O'Dwyer's smile faded from his face and his hair became ruffled from wiping his brow.

Finally he lost his composure completely, accusing Senator Tobey of accepting a campaign contribution from New York gamblers. When it was quickly revealed that the ex-mayor was wrong, he had to publicly apologize. The Horatio Alger beat-cop-to-mayor image vanished and he seemed like nothing more than a gangster's stooge. It was a sad spectacle, and his testimony did a lot to convince people that municipal government was hopelessly corrupt.[3]

Willie Moretti and Virginia Hill provided the comic relief at the hearings. Moretti, deteriorating rapidly from venereal disease and prone to blab mob secrets, tried to be friendly. He invited Kefauver to drop by his home in New Jersey for a good dinner and, when asked about rackets, quipped, "Everything is a racket." First questioned in executive session, Hill provided little information and quickly lost her temper. In a voice described by Kefauver as a mixture of "southern poor white and Chicago gangsterese," she began using words that would have shocked a longshoreman. When asked why she was able to acquire so many mob boyfriends, she attributed it to being outstanding at oral sex (though she used a more graphic term). Some staffers believed that she was too unpredictable to be called to the public session, but her publicity value outweighed any other considerations. Garbed in a silver mink stole and huge broad-brimmed hat, she stormed into the March hearings as flash bulbs popped, threatening to slug photographers. In her testimony, Hill claimed she knew nothing of mob affairs—she was just social friends with a few gentlemen who were accused of being members of organized crime. She reverted to type in her exit, punching a woman reporter and telling the press that she hoped an atom bomb landed on them. Her testimony contributed little to knowledge about organized crime but a lot to the TV ratings.

---

[3]Since, unlike Costello, O'Dwyer was never formally charged with a crime (though had he remained in New York he might have been), some defense of his career should be placed on the historical record. O'Dwyer, like most New York politicians of his time, had to go along to get along. Al Smith's distinguished career had been made by Tom Foley, and La Guardia himself accepted support from Joe Adonis. Some people who lived through that period believe that O'Dwyer was genuinely devoted to the city he loved. O'Dwyer's tragedy may have been that he tried to be an honest man and thought he, like Smith, could achieve mastery over the forces that had produced him. Instead, they mastered him.

• • •

In its final report the Kefauver Committee concluded that there was a nationwide crime syndicate controlled by the Italian Mafia, synonymous with the Black Hand and the Unione Siciliana. In effect, the Mafia became the real "Mr. Big" of the hearings. But the proof or even the probable cause was missing. During hearings in California, two outstanding San Francisco detectives, Frank Ahern and Tom Cahill—later successive police chiefs of their city—claimed that they had developed evidence of the existence of the Mafia. In 1947 they had been assigned to investigate the strangling of a drug dealer turned informer named Nick DeJohn, who had fled to the West Coast from Chicago. Their probing revealed the victim had ties to other murdered drug dealers, like Caramussa of Missouri. A Federal Bureau of Narcotics agent testified that the Mafia was run by an overall superior in Palermo, who appointed the head of the organization in the United States and district heads in each part of the country. When asked to identify the American chief, he named Joe Profaci, though the committee had already cast Costello as Mr. Big. The FBN's own secret list identified (Neapolitan) Vito Genovese as the number one figure in the American branch and Lucky Luciano as the top man internationally. Costello was not involved with drugs so he only ended up in twelfth place. Since opium and coca leaves were not grown in the United States, it was hardly a revelation that drugs were smuggled into the country. Nor was it a secret that dealers were a murderous lot. Neither fact was sufficient to conclude that the Italian Mafia ruled American organized crime.

The committee did find intercity ties between organized crime figures, and that many of the principal mob bosses were of Italian descent and shared certain ties of kinship and heritage. Its own evidence, however, strongly suggested their gangs were products of American society, particularly corrupt local politics. Building on that basis, the committee might have forsworn the use of terms like Mafia, Unione Siciliana, and Black Hand, or replaced them with "American Mafia." Instead, by buying into Anslinger's theories, the committee disappointed supporters like Virgil Peterson, who felt the search for international conspiracy shifted the focus away from American mobsters and their corrupt alliance with politicians.

Perhaps a direct attack on the relationship between politics and organized crime was too much to ask a group of politicians to undertake. Already their investigations had cost Senator Lucas his seat and injured governors, mayors, and other public officials around the country. When proposals were made to extend the life of the committee, even Senator Kefauver opposed them. Nor did the senators do more than express mild disappointment at J. Edgar Hoover's lack of involvement in the fight against organized crime.

The Kefauver revelations triggered a changing of the guard in the New York organized crime world. A month after the investigation concluded, Vince Mangano was murdered in Brooklyn and his brother Phil disappeared and was presumed dead. Albert Anastasia, the real power in the family for years, became the formal head. Willie Moretti was murdered in October 1951. The illness that had loosened his tongue made him a menace, and the mob commission declared it a "mercy killing." In 1951, Joe Adonis was jailed in New Jersey on gambling charges and voluntarily left for Italy to avoid deportation when he was released two years later. He constantly plotted to return to America, but never did, dying in his homeland as Luciano did. Like Capone and Luciano before him, Frank Costello paid the price of fame. In 1952 he was convicted of contempt of Congress and sentenced to eighteen months imprisonment. Two years later, he received three years for tax evasion. In 1957, one of Vito Genovese's gunmen wounded Costello in the head, and a few months later a Genovese crew killed Anastasia while he was sitting in a Midtown barber's chair. Costello was allowed to live, but after 1957 he was not permitted any say in mob affairs. He died of natural causes in 1973. Genovese became the number one figure in New York, but within a couple of years he would be sent to the Atlanta penitentiary for drug dealing, where he would remain until his death.

The Kefauver investigation did not lead any of its principals to glory. Under the television lights, Senator Kefauver had looked like a hot prospect for the presidency. But when he resigned the committee chairmanship on the grounds of exhaustion shortly before the hearings ended, many rumors were floated about him. A few months before the New York television hearings, Kefauver, a man of modest means, suddenly deposited $25,000—a significant sum in 1951—in his bank account. For years it was rumored that Sid Korshak blackmailed Kefauver into taking it easy on the Chicago mob. In 1976, *New York Times* investigative reporter Seymour Hersh described how Korshak arranged to have Kefauver photographed in a compromising position with a young lady in a room at the Drake Hotel. After the senator was shown the photo he decided not to hold public hearings and to keep Captain Gilbert's testimony secret.[4]

In 1952, Kefauver won a number of Democratic presidential primaries and arrived at the Chicago convention with the most delegates, though not a majority. A coalition of party bosses and President Truman united to throw the nomination to Illinois governor Adlai Stevenson, who had not run in a single primary. In 1956 Kefauver beat Senator Jack Kennedy to win the nomination to be Stevenson's running mate, but again the ticket was unsuccessful. In 1963 Kefauver died at the age of sixty, still a senator. In 1953, Rudy Halley finished third in a race for New York mayor and a few years later he died of natural causes.

The real accomplishment of the Kefauver Committee was that it brought men like Adonis, Accardo, Dalitz, Costello, and the rest before them and spread their histories on the public record. No longer were they simply names in the newspaper, but living human beings. On TV they looked mighty menacing to the average citizen. Their shadowy relationships with politicians were out in the open. At first there was little official follow-through, but the hearings marked a sea change in the way organized crime was portrayed. No longer were mobsters presented as Damon Runyon characters. The existence of a vast secret empire of crime, controlled by a cabal of evil men, became the common belief of most Americans. Ultimately the

---

[4]Sid Korshak became counsel to large corporations and an associate of important political figures. He had a major say in Jimmy Hoffa's Teamsters Union and according to the Justice Department functioned as a senior adviser to organized crime groups in California, Nevada, Chicago, and New York. He was so powerful on the Hollywood movie scene that according to *Los Angeles Times* gossip columnist Joyce Haber, "If you're not invited to his annual Christmas party it's a disaster." Still, he was always subordinate to the mob. Once, when he failed to return a phone call as quickly as Murray Humphreys thought he should, the "Camel" told Korshak, "We brought you up. You're our guy. Any time we yell, you come running."

Kefauver investigation laid the groundwork for the federal government's assault on the American Mafia in the second half of the century. Because of that, Peterson and his allies could be said to have succeeded in their goal.

The story of the American Mafia's rise had not been a long one. In 1920 it was a collection of local gangs confined to operating in Italian colonies. By the 1940s its scope was national, its leaders not only powerful mob bosses but successful businessmen with significant economic and political power. Despite assertions of the anti-immigrant lobby, they had not created organized crime in America, they found it here when they arrived. Their contribution was to make it even more powerful by being tougher, smarter, and more daring than their rivals or law enforcement. The period of its rise was so short it could be summed up in the life of a single individual. If anyone could claim to be the architect of modern organized crime, it was Johnny Torrio. Early in 1957 he died quietly in Brooklyn at the age of seventy-five. Johnny always knew the right time to make his exit. Six months later Anastasia's murder led to the convening of the Apalachin conference and the arrest of sixty-three mobsters (all of Italian descent) from cities across the country. Almost as many managed to flee the scene. While no charges against the participants could ever be made to stick, it convinced most people that there was a national syndicate. After Apalachin, even J. Edgar Hoover could no longer remain aloof from the fight against organized crime. The Kefauver hearings had created the climate of public opinion and Apalachin forced the federal government to move. It would take a generation for the Feds to prevail, but from then on it was mostly downhill for the American Mafia.

Epilogue: The Decline of the American Mafia

If the story of organized crime in the first half of the twentieth century was the rise of the American Mafia, the story of the second half would be its decline, if not quite fall. After the Kefauver hearings, the federal government began a series of assaults on the mobs that steadily intensified until the 1980s, when Uncle Sam found the formula for virtually destroying what had come to be known as "traditional" organized crime.

There was no change in the basic structure and operations of the American Mafia in Kefauver's immediate aftermath, even in New York where the hearings had led to Costello's and Adonis's incarceration as well as sparking a number of killings. The five families continued to dominate rackets like the Fulton Fish Market, numbers, and the garment center. To these were added the construction industry and waste hauling. When the Port of New York declined in importance, the mobs found a new source of income by taking control of cargo handling at Kennedy International Airport. But the kind of leadership that had existed before Kefauver was missing. After 1951 the country's strongest mob city lacked a Rothstein, Luciano, or Costello, the kind of magisterial figure who could lead the gangsters and influence the politicians. Vito Genovese became head of the old Luciano-Costello group, which was duly renamed the Genovese family, but he did not assume the mantle of prime minister. Costello's wounding and Anastasia's murder should have strengthened his hand, but instead they triggered the Apalachin meeting. The resulting raid brought so much heat on the mobs that within a couple of years Genovese was sentenced to Atlanta on drug charges. Even behind bars he retained control of his family until his death.

Genovese was replaced by Vincent "The Chin" Gigante, whom law enforcement officials had always fingered as the man who shot Frank Costello. Perhaps noting the fate of previous high-profile leaders, Gigante not only shunned the prime minister role but feigned mental illness. Joe Profaci's family was rent by an internal rebellion led by the Gallo brothers, and eventually leadership descended to Joe Colombo. In the 1960s he organized an Italian-American civil rights league, which picketed New York City FBI headquarters and held huge rallies. Such activities were frowned upon by other mob families, and in 1971 Colombo was shot at a rally in Columbus Circle. He remained comatose until his death seven years later. The family that Albert Anastasia had headed eventually came under the control of Carlo Gambino, taking his name. In the 1980s Gambino's successor, Paul Castellano, was murdered on the orders of an ambitious capo, John Gotti.

Always out of step with his peers, Joe Bonanno allegedly plotted to kill the other family heads and was brought up on charges before the mob commission. He disappeared from a New York street in 1964, and when he reappeared two years later he claimed that he had been kidnapped. In 1983 he published a gangland tell-all, including secrets such as the existence of a national commission.

Chicago saw no significant changes as a result of Kefauver. Until 1957 Tony Accardo provided strong leadership, had no opposition, and managed not to attract too much attention. In the post-Apalachin period Accardo voluntarily turned over leadership to Sam Giancana and settled into a behind-the-scenes role as grand vizier.[1] Unlike Torrio, Nitti, and Accardo,

---

[1]In 1959 Accardo slipped up by going off with Mrs. Accardo and a Chicago police lieutenant and his wife on a European vacation. When pictures of the happy tourists were sent back to Chicago newspapers, a storm arose and the lieutenant was fired.

Giancana adopted a high profile, cavorting openly in nightspots with singer Phyllis McGuire. After serving a short jail sentence in the late '60s, he went off to Mexico and Accardo resumed leadership of the mob. But from then on, everyone he tapped to be his successor failed. The management decline in the American Mafia was typical of a pattern often seen in legitimate enterprises. After the generation of empire builders and skilled managers leaves the scene, the successors are often mediocre men unfit for their responsibilities and unable to adjust to a changing business environment.

Kefauver's public exposure of the mobs caused them to lose political influence, with a marked loss of clout in cities such as New York and Chicago. Some lesser politicians continued to play ball, but the more important ones kept their distance. Costello's old ally Carmine DeSapio was the boss of Tammany Hall for a time in the 1950s, but he presented a more modest and progressive face than traditional Tammany chiefs and was widely credited with engineering the election of quality candidates such as Robert Wagner as mayor in 1953 and Averell Harriman as governor in 1954. Eventually Senator Herbert Lehman led a drive that ousted DeSapio. After DeSapio's fall no similar figure arose on the New York scene. Chicago's Daley machine, which ran City Hall from 1955 until 1979, did not maintain the kind of mob liaison that mayors like Thompson and Kelly had, and was too powerful to be pushed around by gangsters, though it did not attempt to purge political leaders in the river wards. The inability to name mayors, governors, and senators in key localities meant the mobs lacked influential protectors when law enforcement began to crack down.

After the Apalachin conference, FBI director Hoover established a top hoodlum program (THP), ordering field offices in mob-infested cities to compile a list of the most important local gang leaders: 25 in New York, 10 in Chicago, 6 or 8 in other cities. Each had a single FBI case agent assigned to him, which was about ten or twenty too few per target. It was in effect a bargain-basement version of the old "Get Capone" drive. In Chicago, the Bureau did not even know who the top hoodlums were. Nonetheless agents began to gather information and even managed to plant an electronic eavesdropping device known as "Little Al" in a mob headquarters on the Near North Side.

Hoover's modest efforts were soon eclipsed by Robert Kennedy's. As chief counsel for a Senate committee he unearthed a number of mob ties to labor, especially Jimmy Hoffa's Teamsters Union. In 1957, he and Hoffa clashed during nationwide televised hearings, commencing a long and bitter personal feud. As attorney general in his brother Jack's administration, Bobby was in a position to force federal law enforcement agencies to devote significant resources to organized crime investigations. In 1967, he had the satisfaction of seeing Jimmy Hoffa jailed. The following year Robert Kennedy was assassinated. In retrospect, the Kennedy-Hoffa feud was a diversion from more comprehensive anti-Mafia efforts. Hoffa had been a good union leader at securing benefits for his membership. He was never a member of the national syndicate, though he did make the mistake of doing business with them. Later he came to regret that decision and vowed that when he got out of jail he would break with the mob. In 1975, on parole and fighting to regain control of his union, Hoffa disappeared—presumably he was murdered by mob figures who preferred to continue their relationship with his more pliant successors.

Robert Kennedy's actions have caused many people to believe that mobsters were behind President Kennedy's assassination. Some researchers have cited patriarch Joseph Kennedy's longtime ties with certain organized crime figures, and the assistance men like Sam Giancana furnished to the Kennedys in the 1960 presidential campaign. According to these accounts Frank Sinatra led the mob bosses to believe that with John Kennedy's election the federal government would cease its activities against them. When instead Robert Kennedy vastly increased the pressure, the leaders felt double-crossed. As yet, however, it has not been proven that the mob was behind the assassination.[2] At any rate, after Robert Kennedy left the Justice Department during

---

[2]From a logical standpoint it is easier to argue that no well-organized group had any connection to the Kennedy assassination. If the Mafia, Cuban intelligence, or rogue American government agents had plotted to murder the president, why would they have planned such a hit-or-miss operation in an unfamiliar city like Dallas? Instead of chancing a shot at a motorcade—which for any number of reasons might have changed its route, timing, or been canceled—it would have been more sensible to pick a site, such as one of the Kennedy compounds or the routes thereto, where they could become familiar with the president's movements and even conduct dry runs. This is the pattern that most organized attempts against heads of state have followed.

the Johnson administration, the steam went out of federal efforts. In Chicago, the number of agents assigned to the top ten hoodlums was cut in half and "Little Al" was removed.

Some organized crime operations actually expanded in the period after Kefauver. When Batista returned to power in Cuba in 1952, Meyer Lansky, Moe Dalitz, and others turned Havana into an international gambling center, which it remained until Castro ousted the mobsters in 1959. The crown jewel of organized crime, Las Vegas, continued to flourish. It was a cash cow for the mobs until the late '70s, when internal dissension and law enforcement pressure caused them to sell out to the big corporations.[3]

In a strange way, the Mafia wasn't finished with Cuba. Following the theory that your enemy's enemy is your friend, the Kennedy administration used mobsters in plots to remove Castro. In the 1970s, Sam Giancana and Johnny Roselli were identified as having been involved in CIA efforts to kill Castro. After the story broke, they were both murdered. Like the Hoffa feud, Cuba proved to be a negative in the fight against organized crime.

Drugs made a big comeback after World War II. Narcotics were both a threat and an opportunity for the mob. Some families recognized that drug dealing was a sure source of trouble with the Feds and bad for their image, and they ordered their members not to get involved. Those who disregarded the prohibition were murdered. Others, like the Luccheses, were heavily into the traffic. The drug involvement of some elements of the American Mafia did indeed generate more bad publicity and undermined their remaining political ties. By the 1980s, drug cartels based in Asia and Latin America were at least as powerful as the Mafia.

Drugs remain a largely intractable problem. Many strategies have been tried to deal with it—education, interdiction, enforcement, treatment, etc. In light of this some people have urged legalization, citing the Prohibition

---

[3]Facing federal indictment on charges of skimming money from Las Vegas casinos and not paying income tax on it, Meyer Lansky fled to Israel and sought asylum under a law that permitted Jews to return to their homeland. The Supreme Court of Israel turned down his petition in 1972 and he was returned to the United States and arrested. He was too ill to stand trial and retired to a secluded life in the Miami area.

experience while ignoring certain major differences between the two. Legalization might reduce the price of drugs, and thereby make the trade unattractive to mobsters, but it would also make it much easier for ordinary citizens to obtain access to deleterious substances that most Americans think are harmful. In any event, it is unlikely to reduce the power of organized crime. As the end of Prohibition demonstrated, the mobs can easily find new fields in which to operate. In 1933, the distinguished criminologist Harry Elmer Barnes, testifying before a U.S. Senate committee, observed, "The idea that when Prohibition is ended the racketeers and criminals who have made millions in illicit selling of booze will meekly and contritely now turn to blacking shoes and slinging hash is downright silly. They will apply the techniques they have mastered to the dope ring, kidnapping, bank robberies, hijacking of legitimate liquor supplies, and the like." If big-city drug gangs of today are suddenly put out of business, their most likely recourse will be to try to take over small and midsize businesses using the industrial racketeering tactics of the 1930s.

After many false starts, the enactment of new laws put federal enforcement efforts on the right track. In 1968 Congress passed an Omnibus Crime Control Act, which among other provisions authorized electronic eavesdropping, providing a continuous source of valuable intelligence. In 1970, it followed up by enacting the Racketeering Influenced and Corrupt Organizations (RICO) statute, which made it possible to go after organizations, not just individual bosses.[4] It took ten years to learn how to use it, but by the 1980s, federal prosecutors were jailing mobsters wholesale. After Joe Bonanno published his book in 1983, U.S. attorney for the Southern District of New York Rudy Giuliani observed, "If he can write a book about the commission I can prosecute them." And he did just that, jailing the five family heads in New York and many of their subordinates. Today, the old mobs are but a shadow of what they once were.

---

[4]Among other provisions, the RICO Act makes it illegal for persons to conduct the affairs of a criminal organization (or a legitimate enterprise) through the commission of a series of already defined crimes. Thus, RICO places the focus of the illegal conduct on the organization or enterprise.

At present, the greatest opportunity for racketeering lies in the development of telecommunications, which enhances the ability of slick operators to perpetrate frauds and to move vast amounts of money virtually instantaneously. As early as 1961 a high official of the Securities and Exchange Commission warned that the underworld was "invading the financial community." At the time counterfeiting traveler's checks and bank drafts was on the rise and criminal syndicates engaged in narcotics traffic, prostitution, gambling, and extortion were entering the securities business. In practice, though, mob efforts have been overshadowed by those of ostensibly respectable figures. One of the most blatant examples of financial crime— and the U.S. government's failure to deal with it—occurred in the 1980s case involving the Bank of Credit and Commerce International (BCCI). Organized by Middle Eastern potentates, it successfully infiltrated the U.S. banking system by using many respectable Americans as fronts. Though federal prosecutors in Florida brought an indictment against BCCI for laundering drug money, a report by a U.S. Senate committee charged willful obstruction of further investigation by U.S. officials. Eventually New York County D.A. Robert Morgenthau, son of FDR's Treasury secretary, took up the case, indicting individuals as prominent as former Secretary of Defense Clark Clifford.[5]

A 2001 report by a U.S. Senate investigating committee identified private banks, particularly those offshore, as being heavily associated with drug trafficking, financial fraud, Internet gambling, and other misconduct. It noted that thousands of U.S. securities firms do not have even basic controls against money laundering in place.

Some law enforcement experts believe traditional organized crime will move even further into the area of financial crime, or, as it is sometimes expressed, "The mob will marry Wall Street." More likely, a variety of players from many backgrounds will co-opt the methods of the American

---

[5]The criminal charges brought against Clifford were dismissed on the grounds that he was too infirm to stand trial, but as a result of Morgenthau's efforts the bank was liquidated in 1991. Twelve years later creditors who lost $7 billion are still involved in lawsuits against such pillars of the financial community as the Bank of England.

Mafia—muscle, bribery, and political influence—to achieve economic gain. Wherever there are opportunities for significant financial rewards, organized crime in some form will always be present, and the most that can be hoped is that government will learn from previous efforts to combat it. Attacks on "Mr. Bigs" and preoccupations with foreign conspiracies are not as productive as facing squarely our own shortcomings.

Notes

Much of what is written about organized crime is by necessity somewhat speculative. Though leaders like Meyer Lansky might claim that the national syndicate was bigger than General Electric, records were not kept nor were its business dealings well reported. In addition, many popular accounts tend to follow the rule of "Never let the facts get in the way of a good story." As Robert Lacey, in his extensively researched biography of Meyer Lansky, has observed, "The vast corpus of secondary literature on organized crime is shot through with inaccuracy and exaggeration. The challenge is to separate the truth from the tissue of hearsay and folklore woven around it."

In my own research it has become obvious that highly respected law enforcement officials have frequently enhanced their own roles and marginalized or excluded those of other key players. In the notes that follow I identify examples of this.

A few works, however, are notable for their accuracy, including Humbert Nelli's (*The Business of Crime, From Immigrants to Ethnics*, and *Italians in Chicago*) and Virgil Peterson's 1952 book on organized crime in Chicago (*Barbarians in Our Midst*), which was based on Chicago Crime Commission files, then a more authoritative source than the records of the Chicago Police Department or the local FBI.

In his book on New York organized crime (*The Mob*, 1983), Peterson did not have the same personal knowledge of that city as he did of Chicago. However, he used his extensive law enforcement contacts to obtain reliable data and was careful to stick to the facts.

A book I was not acquainted with until I began research for this one is Thomas M. Pitkin and Francesco Cordasco's *The Black Hand*, a useful work of history on the period before 1920, especially since most accounts of organized crime commence with the Prohibition era.

From chapter 6 on, my personal knowledge, experience, and family history helped to inform the narrative, especially in the sections dealing with Chicago and New York. Some time in the 1860s, the Reppetto family of Genoa, along with a number of their relatives, emigrated to New Orleans. There my grandfather and grandmother were born, met, and married. Around 1890, they and their relatives moved to Chicago. Whether this was in reaction to the anti-Italian riots that occurred after the murder of the New Orleans police chief that year, I do not know. During my childhood, such things were never discussed, at least not in my presence.

Perhaps they simply relocated for economic reasons. Dynamic Chicago, the second largest city in the United States, offered more opportunities than the slower and smaller New Orleans. A number of them were able to enter into the professions or to become established in business. The notable exception was my father. Attracted to the excitement of the streets in ragtime-era Chicago, he departed early from high school. After serving overseas during World War I, he returned to a "dry" America and soon entered the bootlegging industry. Some of my father's associates later rose to prominence in the world of organized crime. One pulled off a spectacular train robbery and from that beginning pursued a career that by the 1950s earned him the distinction of being the first man to be placed on the FBI's "Ten Most Wanted" list.

In time, Dad settled down as a professional gambler, an occupation in which he displayed considerable talent. By the late 1930s he had acquired several bookie joints. Never a member of what Chicagoans called the "syndicate," or the "outfit," my father was nevertheless required to do business with them.

After my mother and father divorced, I saw him infrequently. Our "quality" time was often spent listening to conversations in saloons, and on a few occasions attending gangsters' wakes. Normally secretive around strangers, men of my father's background tended to drop their guards when children were present (even though young kids are keen observers once their interest is aroused).

My mother had been raised in the Irish section of the stockyards district and had many friends in the police department. For a time she herself was a civilian employee of the park district police.

When I joined the Chicago city police department in the 1950s, most of the ranking officers, veteran detectives, and sergeants had begun their careers back in Prohibition days. Stories of incidents that had occurred over the previous thirty years, funny, sad, or dramatic, were a major part of the lore passed on from veteran to rookie. In my progress from patrolman to commander of detectives I was able to observe organized crime close up.

My familiarity with New York came later. I did not arrive in the city until the early 1970s. There, my duties as professor and dean at the City University College of Criminal Justice

(John Jay) and then as head of the New York Crime Commission for over twenty years, plus research I conducted as coauthor of a history of the NYPD, have enabled me to gather considerable information (including some not in the public domain) about organized crime in its capital city.

1: "We Must Teach These People a Lesson": A Murder and Lynching in New Orleans
The Italian Background

On the background of the Mafia and Camorra, and conditions in nineteenth-century Italy, I have primarily relied on Barzini, *The Italians*; Nelli, *The Business of Crime*; and Mack Smith, *Modern Italy*. Nelli, p. 11, contains murder figures for the island of Sicily. Other works I have used include Pitkin and Cordasco, *The Black Hand*, and Train, *Courts, Criminals, and the Camorra*.

Events in New Orleans

Accounts of the career of Giuseppe Esposito, the Hennessy murder, the events leading up to it, and the lynchings that followed tend to differ considerably in detail. I have followed Nelli, *The Business of Crime*, and Persico, "Vendetta in New Orleans." Nelli is especially useful for information on Italian life in New Orleans in the late nineteenth century. The account of the Rose kidnapping in the *New York Times* of December 2, 1876, makes it clear that the victim was not, as is usually claimed, a simple clergyman.

The Pinkerton Investigation

On Dimaio's role see Horan, *Pinkertons*, chapter 34. Agency files are found in the Pinkerton files, container 114, at the Library of Congress. These were written in 1938 as background for magazine articles on the case. It is clear from them that several operatives were involved in the investigation, though Dimaio had the principal role. By 1938 he was past seventy and retired from the agency but he was able to provide detailed recollections.

On lynchings of Italians in other parts of America see Higham, *Strangers in the Land*.

2: A Place in the Sun: Italian Gangs of New York
Italian Life in New York City

The condition of Italians in turn-of-the-century New York is described in Nelli, *Immigrants*; Amfitheatrof, *Children of Columbus*; Riis, *How the Other Half Lives*. Figures on immigration are contained in Nelli, *Immigrants*, pp. 41, 62. Fiaschetti, *You Gotta Be Rough,* is the source of the Italian detective's comments.

Crime and Criminals

The Flaccomio murder is described in Pitkin and Cordasco, *Black Hand*. A good summary of the activities of the Lupo and Morello gang is found in Bowen and Neal, *Secret*

Service, chapter 5. Other information on them is contained in Selvaggi, *Rise of the Mafia*, and the confession of Anthony Comito, in the Lawrence Richey files of the Herbert Hoover Library. On Paul Kelly, Asbury's *Gangs of New York*; Nelli, *Business of Crime* and *Immigrants*. Italian crime in New York City generally is described in McAdoo, *Guarding a Great City*.

An account of the barrel murder from the Secret Service point of view is presented by Chief William Flynn, in *The Barrel Murder*. The NYPD version is contained in Inspector Carey's *Murder Man*. The two diverge in important details. Detective Petrosino's role is discussed in detail in Petacco, *Joe Petrosino*, though the New York sections of the book are not always accurate. See also the *New York Times,* April 15, 16, 17, 26, and May 2, 1903.

Chief Flynn's description of the Mafia as the most secret and terrible organization is quoted in Pitkin and Cordasco, *Black Hand*, p. 38.

Material on Larry Richey is contained in the National Archives, and in the Lawrence Richey files of the Herbert Hoover Library.

New York Politics
On the workings of Tammany see Werner, *Tammany Hall*. Kelly's role in the 1901 election in the 2nd Assembly District is described in Stoddard, *Master of Manhattan*, pp. 241–46, and *New York Times*, September 18, 1901.

3: Italian Squads and American Carabinieri: Law Enforcement Wars on the Mafia
Black Hand Activities
On the 1906 bombing at Mott and Mulberry, see *New York Times*, December 17, 1906, p. 1. The activities of the Black Hand in the United States and the background of La Mano Nero in Europe are contained in Pitkin and Cordasco, *Black Hand*.

The Pennsylvania Anti-Mafia Drive
The Pennsylvania State Police role is described in Katherine Mayo's *Justice to All* and Conti, *Pennsylvania State Police*. Accounts of Dimaio and the Pinkertons are contained in Horan, *Pinkertons*, chapter 35, and Nelli, *Business of Crime*. The original reports on the Black Hand investigation in Lawrence County and the Seely Houk murder are in the Pinkerton file, container 117, in the Library of Congress. As with the New Orleans case (see references for chapter 1), much of the material was assembled in 1939 and 1940 to assist in the preparation of magazine stories. It does, however, contain the contemporary agent reports. Stories of the Pennsylvania roundup appeared in the *New York Times*, July 27, August 4, 5, 11, 27, 1907, and *Cleveland Plain Dealer Magazine*, March 28, 1909.

On Rocco Racco's trial see *Commonwealth of Pennsylvania v Racco*, 113 Penn 225 (1909).

The Petrosino Mission

On Commissioner Bingham's views of Italians, see Bingham, "Foreign Criminals." The creation of the NYPD secret service is mentioned in *New York Times*, January 30 and February 20, 1909.

Petrosino's activities in Italy are described in Petacco, *Joe Petrosino*. Other accounts are Pitkin and Cordasco, *Black Hand*. See also *New York Times*, especially March 14, 15, 16, and 18, 1909. On the supposed plot to murder other detectives, *New York Times*, May 2, 31, 1909. On Petrosino's physical appearance and the Mafia-Camorra knife duel see Train, *Courts, Criminals and Camorra*.

Mack Smith, *Modern Italy*, describes Prime Minister Giolitti. Barzini, *Italians*, claims Don Vito Cascio Ferro was the murderer. An account of the Gaynor administration's law enforcement policies is found in Smith, *William Gaynor*.

The Breakup of the Lupo-Morello Gang

The roundup and trial of the Lupo and Morello gang is described in Bowen and O'Neal, chapter 5. Comito's confession is available in the Lawrence Richey file at the Hoover Library. See also *New York Times*, Jan. 11, Feb. 2, Apr. 3 (part 5), 1909.

4: Diamond Jim: Overlord of the Underworld
Italians in Chicago

On the Italians in turn-of-the-century Chicago, see Nelli, *Italians in Chicago*. This also contains information on Jim Colosimo and his relationship with the First Ward, including his early street-sweeping jobs and his political work, and the career of Anthony DeAndrea.

Characters and Events in the Levee

Additional information on Colosimo and the Levee is found in Jack McPhaul, *Torrio*, in which the author draws on his personal familiarity with many of the Levee characters. Kogan and Wendt's biography of Kenna and Coughlin, *Lords of the Levee*, is exceptionally well informed. Charles Washburn's *Come into My Parlor*, based on his interviews with the Everleigh sisters in their mature years, is helpful in recalling many details of the time. Lyle's *Dry and Lawless Years* contains the assertion that he and others believed that Capone murdered Colosimo. For a concurring (though unconvincing) view see Roemer, *Accardo*.

The Levee shootout of July 1914 is described in *Torrio* and *Lords of the Levee*; *New York Times*, July 17, 1914; and *Chicago Tribune*, July 17 and 18, 1914.

On prostitution in the Levee, see Reckless, *Vice in Chicago*.

Captain Max Nootbar is described in Peattie, "Most Unforgettable Character," *Reader's Digest*, and *Chicago Tribune*, July 21, 1914.

General Organized Crime

See Landesco, *Organized Crime*, and Peterson, *Barbarians in Our Midst*. Both contain information on gambling czar Mont Tennes.

5: In the Footsteps of Petrosino: Big Mike
On Detective Fiaschetti and the NYPD

Mike Fiaschetti's *You Gotta Be Rough* is his own story. Fiaschetti, like his mentor Petrosino, was sometimes wont to engage in hyperbole. On his Italian adventure see *New York Times*, December 16 and 21, 1920. Accounts of the 1921 investigation are cited in *New York Times*, August 17, 18, 21 and September 11, 1921 . On his fall from grace in the NYPD and his later career, see *New York Times*, February 5, 1922, February 3, 1923, January 7 and 9, 1934.

Crimes and Criminals

The best account of the scandal involving Lieutenant Becker is Logan, *Against the Evidence*.

The Gallucci case is discussed in Nelli, *Business of Crime*, and *New York Times*, May 22, 1915. On Costabile see *New York Times*, September 6, 7, 1911, and Train, *Court, Criminals and the Camorra*.

Accounts of the Mafia-Camorra war of 1916 are contained in *New York Times*, September 8, 1916; arrest of perpetrators, December 1, 1917; trial and the bribe to detectives, February 15, 16, 1918. See also Reid, *Mafia*. The trial of the principal defendants is reported in *People v Morano*, 183 NYS 483 (1919). The Manhattan aspects of the struggle are described in Peterson, *The Mob*.

On the career of Arnold Rothstein see Katcher, *The Big Bankroll*. The 1919 World Series fix is covered in Asinoff, *Eight Men Out*.

Italians and New York City Politics

On Mayor Mitchel's administration, see Lewinson, *John Purroy Mitchel*. Biographies of La Guardia include Garrett, *The La Guardia Years*; Kessner, *Fiorello H. La Guardia*; Hecksher, *When La Guardia Was Mayor*. Figures on Italian casualties in World War I, Nelli, *Italians in Chicago*.

The Anti-Mafia Drive in Italy

See Mori, *Last Struggle with the Mafia*, and Nelli, *Immigrants*. On Don Vito, see Barzini, *Italians*.

6: Prohibition: The Mobs Strike a Bonanza
Prohibition

On Prohibition generally, see Asbury, *Great Illusion*; Kobler, *Ardent Spirits*; Sinclair, *Age of Excess*; Walker, *Nightclub Era*.

On Chicago

See Kogan and Wendt, *Big Bill*; Landesco, *Organized Crime in Chicago*; McPhaul, *Torrio*; and Peterson's *Barbarians in Our Midst*. See also various Capone biographies listed in references for chapter 7.

On New York

Thompson and Raymond, *Gang Rule in New York*, benefits from the authors' firsthand observations. Katcher's *Big Bankroll* is a biography of Arnold Rothstein. On Herbert Bayard Swope see Kahn, *Swope*. Biographies of Mayor Walker are Fowler, *Beau James*, and Walsh, *Jimmy Walker*. Nown, *English Godfather*, and O'Connor, *Hell's Kitchen*, describe Owney Madden and other West Side Irish gangsters such as Vince Coll. On Damon Runyon's world see Mosedale, *Men Who Invented Broadway*.

Other Cities

Accounts of Los Angeles are contained in Wood's "The Progressives and the Police"; the role of McDonough in San Francisco is cited in Ehrlich, *Life in My Hands*, and of Olmstead in Seattle in Kobler, *Ardent Spirits*. See also *Olmstead v US*, 277 US 438 (1928). On Cleveland see Messick, *Silent Syndicate*. A survey of other cities is contained in Fox, *Blood and Power*.

7: The "Get Capone" Drive: Print the Legend

On Capone

Biographies include Bergreen, *Capone: The Man and the Era*; Kobler, *Capone*; Schoenberg, *Mr. Capone*.

The Law Enforcers

See Heimel, *Eliot Ness*; Irey, *Tax Dodgers*; and Wilson, *Special Agent*. The basis of the Ness legend is contained in Ness and Fraley, *The Untouchables*. The book is not as grossly distorted as the movie and television versions. Ness's career in Cleveland is also discussed in Nickel, *Torso*, and Messick, *Silent Syndicate*. Lyle's *Dry and Lawless Years* (with McPhaul's uncredited assistance) is an account by the judge who issued the public enemy warrants. A useful scholarly study of the "Get Capone" drive is Hoffman, *Scarface Al and the Crime Crusaders*. Accounts of Henry Barrett Chamberlain and Frank Loesch are contained in Hoffman, and Doherty, "History of the Chicago Crime Commission."

General Accounts of Chicago

Kogan and Wendt, *Big Bill*, includes information on Mayor Thompson's third term (1927–31). Peterson's *Barbarians in Our Midst* is an overview based on the records of the Chicago Crime Commission.

8: Lucky: The Rise and Rise of Charlie Luciano

Luciano

Gosch and Hammer, *Last Testament*, is useful for details of Luciano's personality, but it is not considered a reliable account of his life. An account of his kidnapping is found in *New York Times*, October 18, 1929. The article makes clear he was known as Lucky even before the incident.

New York in the '30s

General overview is contained in Peterson, *The Mob*, and Thompson and Raymond, *Gang Rule in New York*. Accounts of other mobsters are Lacey, *Little Man* (Lansky); Messick, *Lansky*; Katz, *Uncle Frank*; and Wolf, *The Prime Minister* (the last two biographies of Frank Costello). On Jewish gangsters see Fried, *The Rise and Fall of the Jewish Gangster*; Joselit, *Our Gang*.

Bonanno, *Man of Honor*, presents the views of the more traditional style mob boss and the Maranzano side of the 1931 struggle. Maas, *Valachi Papers*, recaps the subject's Senate testimony. A devastating attack on Valachi's story is contained in Messick, *John Edgar Hoover*.

The "Sicilian Vespers"

Analyses that debunk the so-called Sicilian Vespers are contained in Block, *East Side–West Side*; Nelli, *Business of Crime*; and Peterson, *The Mob*. Based on their findings, it appears that three additional murders in the New York metropolitan area can be attributed to the events of September 10. On that day James Lepore was killed in the Bronx and Louis Russo and Sam Monaco were found in a river in nearby New Jersey. Other possible victims included Joe Siragusa, killed in Pittsburgh on September 13, and Pete Carlino, in Denver, also on the thirteenth. While Siragusa's death may have been related to the New York war, Carlino's probably was part of an ongoing struggle between some Calabrians in the Colorado area. For the genesis of the legend see Davis, "Things I Couldn't Tell Till Now," *Collier's*, August 5, 1939.

Even official and semiofficial sources have repeated the Vespers legend. The 1967 *Report of the Task Force on Organized Crime* of President Johnson's Commission on Law Enforcement and Administration of Justice placed the number of victims at forty. This was repeated by Johnson's attorney general, Ramsey Clark, in his book *Crime in America*, and by the consultant to the President's Commission, Donald Cressey, in his book, *Theft of a Nation*. The fact that Clark and Cressey, as well as many others, cite the date of Marranzano's murder as September 11, when it was actually on September 10, suggests an overreliance on a single source, such as Turkus's 1951 account which also gives the date as the eleventh, though in Clark's case he also got the year wrong, citing it as 1930.

The Seabury Investigation

See Mitgang, *Man Who Rode the Tiger*, also the Mayor Walker biographies listed in chapter 6 references. On La Guardia, see references for chapter 5.

9: The Commission: The Mobs Go National
The Development of the National Syndicate

The most reliable accounts are Fox, *Blood and Power*, and Nelli, *The Business of Crime*.

On Individual Cities and States

Boston: Whyte, *Street Corner Society*. Chicago: Biles, *Mayor Kelly*; and Peterson, *Barbarians in Our Midst*. Cleveland: Messick, *Silent Syndicate*. Detroit: Kavioff, *Purple Gang*. Florida: Lacey, *Little Man*; Messick, *Lansky*. Hot Springs: Nown, *English Godfather*. Kansas City: Dorsett, *Pendergast Machine*. New Jersey: Stuart, *Zwillman*. New Orleans: Williams, *Huey Long*.

For an account of the mob meeting at the Times Square office building in 1933, see Mooney, *Crime Incorporated*.

10: Racket-Busting: The Dewey Days
On Dewey

See Dewey, *Twenty against the Underworld*; Smith, *Dewey and His Times*; Peterson, *The Mob*; and Irey, *The Tax Dodgers*.

The Luciano Case

On the Luciano investigation, especially the role of "Dan O'Brien," see Horan and Danforth, *The D.A.'s Man*. Accounts of Luciano's parole found in Campbell's pro-Dewey *The Luciano Project* and Gosch and Hammer's anti-Dewey *Luciano* are both unconvincing. Adler's *House Is Not a Home,* a (well-scrubbed) picture of New York City prostitution at the time, is typical of the many accounts that question Luciano's involvement in prostitution.

On Dutch Schultz and Dixie Davis

See Davis, "Things I Couldn't Tell Till Now," 6-part series, *Collier's*, July 22 to August 26, 1939.

On Schultz's assassination see Thompson and Raymond, *Gang Rule*, and *New York Times*, October 26, 30, 1935.

On Bumpy Johnson

See Klienecht, *New Ethnic Mobs*, and Tyler, *Organized Crime*, pp. 242–44.

11: The Feds: Assessing the Menace of the Mafia
Hoover and the FBI

There are numerous books on both subjects, but they tend to be mostly polemical. Don Whitehead, *FBI Story* (the authorized history), and the Overstreets, *The FBI in an Open Society*, provide accounts of the pre-Hoover days at the Bureau. See also *Caminetti v U.S.*, 242 US 470 (1917). Among accounts that deal with Hoover's reluctance to combat organized crime are Powers, *Secrecy and Power*, and Messick, *Hoover*. On the surveillance of Hoover by the NYPD, see McDonald, *My Father's Gun*.

On Walter Winchell, see Mosedale, *Men Who Invented Broadway*.

Treasury Enforcement

Tully, *Treasury Agent*, is the authorized history (written in response to Whitehead's *FBI Story*). It also contains an account of the search for Lepke. On Secretary of Treasury Morgenthau, see *Morgenthau Diaries*.

On the Intelligence Unit, see Irey, *Tax Dodgers*, and Messick, *Secret File*. On the U.S. Secret Service, see Bowen and O'Neal, *The U.S. Secret Service*. On the demotion of the Secret Service agents, see *New York Times*, August 7, 1936.

Anslinger's books, *The Protectors* and *The Murderers*, as well as Siragusa's *The Trail of the Poppy,* recount cases rather than analyze the big picture. A balanced analytical account of the drug problem is Musto, *The American Disease*.

For a comparative analysis of the effectiveness of various federal law enforcement agencies in the 1930s, see Millspaugh, *Crime Control*.

12: Overreaching: Hollywood and Detroit
Chicago Mob Shakedown of Hollywood

Irey's *Tax Dodgers* is the account by the chief of Treasury intelligence. It does not entirely square with the testimony of Willy Bioff, given in federal court in 1943. Since Bioff spent nine and a half days on the stand and was examined and cross-examined by some of the ablest lawyers in New York (and the verdict ultimately upheld by the Second Circuit) I have followed his account. See *U.S. v Campagna et al.*, 146F.2D524(1944). I also benefited greatly from the assistance of Boris Kostelanetz, the U.S. assistant attorney who prosecuted the case. Gabler, *An Empire of Their Own,* is an account of the leading Hollywood moguls of the time. Bruck, *When Hollywood Had a King,* recounts the mob shakedown and the role of Sidney Korshak. Rappleye and Becker, *All-American Mafioso,* is a biography of Johnny Roselli.

On Detroit

Morris, *Not So Long Ago*, and Sward, *The Legend of Henry Ford,* contain information on Harry Bennett and the Ford organization during the period studied. A recent history of the Ford organization is Brinkley, *Wheels of the World*. On the Ford Service Department, see

New York Times, June 20, 1937. Kavioff, *Purple Gang,* describes the rise and fall of that group.

13: The Prime Minister
On Costello
See Asbury, "Mystery Man," *Collier's*, April 12–19, 1947; Katz, *Uncle Frank*; Wolf, *Prime Minister*; "I Never Sold Bibles," *Time* cover story, November 28, 1949.

On O'Dwyer
O'Dwyer, *Beyond the Golden Door*, presents the former mayor's version of his career. Walsh, *Public Enemies*, explores the relationship between Costello and O'Dwyer.

Murder, Inc. Case
Turkus and Feder's *Murder Incorporated* is a work that is much relied upon for an account of the case and of organized crime in America generally. Turkus was the lead prosecutor of Murder, Inc., and the sections dealing with the case are generally accurate. However, the book was written a decade later as an answer to the Kefauver Committee findings. It also accepts Dixie Davis's account of the Sicilian Vespers.

Genovese's Arrest and Return to the United States
Gallagher, *All the Right Enemies*, and Reid, *Mafia*.

Waterfront Rackets
Described in "Pattern of Power," in *Organized Crime in America*, ed. Tyler; Keating and Carter, *Man Who Rocked the Boat*.

General Background
Peterson, *The Mob*.

14: New Worlds to Conquer: Postwar Expansion
Bugsy Siegel and Las Vegas
Reid and Demaris, *Green Felt Jungle*; Roemer, *War of the Godfathers*.

California Politics
White, *Earl Warren*.

The Chicago Mob's Expansion Efforts
Described in Peterson, *Barbarians*, and Biles, *Big City Boss*. On the FBI CAPGA investigation, see Roemer, *Accardo*.

The Wire Services and the Murder of Ragen

New York Times, June 25 and August 15, 1946; Peterson, *Barbarians in Our Midst*; Ogden, *Legacy* (biography of Moses Annenberg).

On Florida Expansion

Lacey, *Little Man* (biography of Lansky) and Messick, *Lansky*. The two authors diverge sharply on the assessment of their subject.

15: TV's Greatest Hits: Senator Kefauver Presents the Mafia

On Virgil Peterson

Fox, *Blood and Power*, and *New York Times*, September 22 and December 3, 1949.

On President Truman

McCullough, *Truman*.

The Kefauver Committee

Bell, *End of Ideology*; Moore, *Kefauver Committee*; Kefauver, *Crime in America*; and U.S. Senate, *Kefauver Committee Report on Organized Crime*.

Impact of the Hearings

Halberstam, *The Fifties*.

Kennedy Assassination

For the mob ties to the Kennedy assassination, see Blakey and Billings, *Plot to Kill the President*; Fox, *Blood and Power*; and Ragano and Raab, *Mob Lawyer*.

Epilogue: The Decline of the American Mafia

On the Prosecution of the New York Commission

Jacobs et al., *Busting the Mob*.

On Statement of Harry Elmer Barnes

Tyler, ed., *Organized Crime in America*, p. 179.

On BCCI Case

U.S. Senate Committee on Foreign Relations, report of Senator John Kerry et al., December 1992.

On Money Laundering

U.S. Senate Permanent Subcommittee on Investigations, Hearings on Private Banking and Senator Carl Levin Staff Reports, 2001. See also U.S. General Accounting Office, *Anti-Money Laundering Efforts in the Securities Industry*, October 2001.

Bibliography

Abadinsky, Howard. *Organized Crime*. 6th ed. Belmont, Calif.: Wadsworth, 2000.

Adler, Polly. *A House Is Not a Home*. New York: Rinehart and Co., 1953.

Albini, Joseph L. *The American Mafia: Genesis of a Legend*. New York: Appleton Crofts, 1971.

Amfitheatrof, Erik. *The Children of Columbus: An Informal History of Italians in the New World*. Boston: Little, Brown, 1973.

Anslinger, Harry, and Will Oursler. *The Murderers: The Story of the Narcotics Gangs*. New York: Farrar, Straus & Giroux, 1961.

Anslinger, Harry, with Dennis J. Gregory. *The Protectors*. New York: Farrar, Straus & Giroux, 1964.

Asbury, Herbert. "America's Number One Mystery Man." *Collier's*, April 12 and 19, 1947.

———. *The French Quarter: An Informal History of the New Orleans Underworld*. New York: Knopf, 1936.

———. *Gangs of New York: An Informal History of the Underworld*. New York: Paragon House, 1990; originally Knopf, 1928.

———. *Gem of the Prairie: An Informal History of the Chicago Underworld*. New York: Knopf, 1940.

———. *The Great Illusion: An Informal History of Prohibition*. Garden City, N.Y.: Doubleday, 1950.

Asinoff, Eliot. *Eight Men Out: The Black Sox and the 1919 World Series*. New York: Henry Holt, 1963.

Balsamo, William, and George Carpozi. *Under the Clock: The Inside Story of the Mafia's First Hundred Years*. Far Hills, N.J.: Horizon Press, 1988.

Barzini, Luigi. *The Italians*. New York: Atheneum, 1964.

Bell, Daniel. *The End of Ideology*. Cambridge: Harvard Univ. Press, 1988.

Bergreen, Lawrence. *Capone: The Man and the Era*. New York: Simon & Schuster, 1994.

Biles, Roger. *Big City Boss in Depression and War: Mayor Edward J. Kelly of Chicago*. Dekalb, Ill.: Northern Illinois Univ. Press, 1984.

Bingham, Theodore A. "Foreign Criminals in New York." *North American Review* 188 (September 1908).

Blakey, G. Robert, and Richard N. Billings. *The Plot to Kill the President*. New York: Times Books, 1981.

Block, Alan. *East Side–West Side: Organizing Crime in New York, 1930–1950*. New Brunswick, N.J.: Transaction, 1985.

Blumenthal, Ralph. *The Last Days of the Sicilians: At War with the Mafia: The FBI Assault on the Pizza Connection*. New York: Times Books, 1988.

———. *Stork Club: America's Most Famous Nightspot and the Lost World of Café Society*. Boston: Little, Brown, 2000.

Bonanno, Joseph. *A Man of Honor: The Autobiography of Joseph Bonanno*. New York: Simon & Schuster, 1983.

Bowen, Walter S., and Harry Edward Neal. *The United States Secret Service*. Philadelphia: Chilton, 1960.

Brinkley, Douglas. *Wheels for the World: Henry Ford, His Company, and a Century of Progress*. New York: Viking, 2003.

Brown, Dorothy M. *Mabel Walker Willebrandt: A Study of Power, Loyalty and Law*. Knoxville, Tenn.: Univ. of Tennessee Press, 1984.

Bruck, Connie. *When Hollywood Had a King: The Reign of Lew Wasserman who Leveraged Talent into Power and Influence*. New York: Random House, 2003.

Campbell, Rodney. *The Luciano Project*. New York: McGraw Hill, 1977.

Carey, Arthur. *Murder Man*. Garden City, N.Y.: Doubleday, Doran, 1930.

Chandler, David Leon. *Brothers in Blood: The Rise of the Criminal Brotherhood*. New York: E. P. Dutton, 1975.

Clark, Ramsey. *Crime in America: Observations on Its Nature, Causes, Prevention, and Control*. New York: Simon & Schuster, 1970.

Conti, Phillip. *The Pennsylvania State Police: A History of Service to the Commonwealth, 1905 to the Present*. Harrisburg, Pa.: Stackpole Books, 1977.

Cressey, Donald A. *Theft of a Nation: The Structure and Operations of Organized Crime*. New York: Harper & Row, 1969.

Davis, Richard J. "Dixie." "Things I Couldn't Tell Till Now." *Collier's*, 6 parts (July 22–August 26, 1939).

Dewey, Thomas. *Twenty against the Underworld*. Edited by Rodney Campbell. Garden City, N.Y.: Doubleday, 1974.

Doherty, James. "History of the Chicago Crime Commission." *Police Digest* (December 1960).

Domanick, Joe. *To Protect and Serve: The LAPD's Century of War in the City of Angels*. New York: Pocket Books, 1994.

Dorsett, Lyle. *The Pendergast Machine*. Lincoln, Neb.: Univ. of Nebraska Press, 1968.

Ehrlich, J. W. *A Life in My Hands*. New York: Crown, 1954.

Eisenberg, Dennis, Uri Dan, and Eli Landau. *Meyer Lansky: Mogul of the Mob*. New York: Paddington Press, 1979.

Fiaschetti, Michael L. *You Gotta Be Rough: The Adventures of Detective Fiaschetti of the Italian Squad as Told to Prosper Buranelli*. Garden City, N.Y.: Doubleday Doran, 1930.

Fowler, Gene. *Beau James: The Life and Times of Jimmy Walker*. New York: Viking, 1949.

Fox, Stephen. *Blood and Power: Organized Crime in 20th Century America*. New York: Morrow, 1989.

Fried, Albert. *The Rise and Fall of the Jewish Gangster in America*. New York: Holt, Rinehart and Winston, 1980.

Gabler, Neal. *An Empire of Their Own: How the Jews Invented Hollywood*. New York: Crown, 1988.

Gage, Nicholas. *Mafia USA*. Chicago: Playboy Press, 1972.

Gallagher, Dorothy. *All the Right Enemies: The Life and Murder of Carlo Tresca*. New York: Penguin Books, 1988.

Garrett, Charles. *The La Guardia Years: Machine and Reform Politics in New York City*. New Brunswick, N.J.: Rutgers Univ. Press, 1961.

Gosch, Martin A., and Richard Hammer. *The Last Testament of Lucky Luciano*. New York: Dell Publishing, 1974.

Griffiths, Arthur. *Mysteries of Police and Crime*. London: Cassell & Co., 1901.

Halberstam, David. *The Fifties*. New York: Villard, 1993.

Haller, Mark. "Organized Crime in Urban Society: Chicago in the 20th Century." *Journal of Social History* (Winter 1971–72).

Harrison, Carter. *Stormy Years*. Indianapolis: Bobbs Merrill, 1935.

Hecksher, August, with Phyllis Robinson. *When La Guardia Was Mayor: New York's Legendary Years*. New York: W. W. Norton, 1978.

Heimel, Paul. *Eliot Ness: The Real Story*. 2d ed. Nashville, Tenn.: Cumberland House, 2000.

Higham, John. *Strangers in the Land: Patterns of American Nativism, 1860–1925*. Boston: Little, Brown, 1973.

Hoffman, Dennis E. *Scarface Al and the Crime Crusaders: Chicago's Private War against Capone*. Carbondale, Ill.: Southern Illinois Univ. Press, 1993.

Horan, James. *The Pinkertons: The Detective Dynasty That Made History*. New York: Crown, 1967.

Horan, James, and Harold Danforth. *The D.A.'s Man*. New York: Crown, 1957.

Irey, Elmer L., and William Slocum. *The Tax Dodgers: The Inside Story of the T-Men's War with America's Political and Underworld Hoodlums*. New York: Greenberg, 1948.

"Italian Life in New York." In *New York: A Collection from Harper's Magazine*. New York: Gallery Books, 1991.

Jacobs, James B., with Christopher Panarella and Jay Worthington. *Busting the Mob: U.S. v. Cosa Nostra*. New York: New York Univ. Press, 1994.

Joselit, Jenna Weisman. *Our Gang: Jewish Crime and the New York Jewish Community, 1900–1940*. Bloomington, Ind.: Univ. of Indiana Press, 1983.

Josephson, Matthew. *Al Smith: Hero of the Cities*. Boston: Houghton Mifflin, 1969.

Kahn, E. J. *The World of Swope*. New York: Simon & Schuster, 1965.

Katcher, Leo. *The Big Bankroll: The Life and Times of Arnold Rothstein*. New Rochelle, N.Y.: Arlington House, 1958.

Katz, Leonard. *Uncle Frank: The Biography of Frank Costello*. New York: Drake Publishers, 1971.

Kavioff, Paul. *The Purple Gang: Organized Crime in Detroit, 1910–1945*. New York: Barracuda Books, 2000.

Keating, William J., and Richard Carter. *The Man Who Rocked the Boat*. New York: Random House, 1956.

Kefauver, Estes. *Crime in America*. Garden City, N.Y.: Doubleday, 1951.

Kessner, Thomas. *Fiorello H. La Guardia and the Making of Modern New York*. New York: McGraw Hill, 1986.

Klienecht, William. *The New Ethnic Mobs: The Changing Face of Organized Crime in America*. New York: The Free Press, 1996.

Kobler, John. *Ardent Spirits: The Rise and Fall of Prohibition*. New York: Putnam, 1973.

———. *The Life & World of Al Capone*. New York: Putnam, 1971.

Kogan, Herman, and Lloyd Wendt. *Big Bill*. Indianapolis: Bobbs Merrill, 1953.

———. *Lords of the Levee*. Indianapolis: Bobbs Merrill, 1943.

Lacey, Robert. *Little Man: Meyer Lansky and the Gangster Life*. Boston: Little, Brown, 1991.

Lait, Jack, with Lee Mortimer. *Chicago Confidential*. New York: Crown, 1950.

Landesco, John. *Organized Crime in Chicago: Part III of the Illinois Crime Survey, 1929*. Chicago: Univ. of Chicago Press, 1968.

Lewinson, Edwin. *John Purroy Mitchel: The Boy Mayor of New York*. New York: Astra Books, 1969.

Lindberg, Richard. *Chicago by Gaslight: A History of Chicago's Underworld, 1880–1920*. Chicago: Academy Press, 1996.

Logan, Andy. *Against the Evidence: The Becker-Rosenthal Affair.* New York: McCall Publishing, 1970.

Lyle, John H. *The Dry and Lawless Years.* Englewood Cliffs, N.J.: Prentice Hall, 1960.

Maas, Peter. *The Valachi Papers.* New York: G. P. Putnam's Sons, 1968.

Mack Smith, Dennis. *Modern Italy: A Political History.* Ann Arbor: Univ. of Michigan Press, 1997.

Maeder, Jay, ed. *Big Town, Big Time: A New York Epic.* New York: Daily News Books, 1999.

Mayo, Katherine. *Justice to All: The Story of the Pennsylvania State Police.* Boston: Houghton Mifflin, 1920.

McAdoo, William. *Guarding a Great City.* New York: Harper and Bros., 1906.

McCullough, David. *Truman.* New York: Simon & Schuster, 1992.

McDonald, Brian. *My Father's Gun: 3 Badges, 100 Years in the NYPD.* New York: E. P. Dutton, 1999.

McPhaul, Jack. *Johnny Torrio: First of the Gang Lords.* New Rochelle, N.Y.: Arlington House, 1970.

Messick, Hank. *John Edgar Hoover.* New York: David McKay, 1972.

———. *Lansky.* G. P. Putnam's Sons, 1971.

———. *Secret File.* G. P. Putnam's Sons, 1969.

———. *Silent Syndicate.* New York: Macmillan, 1967.

Millspaugh, Arthur C. *Crime Control by the National Government.* Washington, D.C.: Brookings Institution, 1937.

Mitgang, Herbert. *The Man Who Rode the Tiger: The Life and Times of Judge Samuel Seabury.* Philadelphia: Lippincott, 1963.

Mooney, Martin. *Crime Incorporated.* New York: Whittlesey House, 1935.

Moore, William Howard. *The Kefauver Committee and the Politics of Crime.* Columbia, Mo.: Univ. of Missouri Press, 1974.

Morgenthau, Henry Jr. *From the Morgenthau Diaries.* Edited by John Morton Blum. Boston: Houghton Mifflin, 1959–1967.

Mori, Cesare. *The Last Struggle with the Mafia.* Trans. Orlo Williams. New York: Putnam, 1933.

Morris, Lloyd. *Not So Long Ago.* New York: Random House, 1949.

Mosedale, John. *The Men Who Invented Broadway: Damon Runyon, Walter Winchell, and Their World.* New York: Richard Marek Publishers, 1981.

Musto, David. *The American Disease: Origins of Narcotics Control.* New York: Oxford Univ. Press, 1987.

Nelli, Humbert S. *The Business of Crime: Italians and Syndicate Crime in the United States.* New York: Oxford Univ. Press, 1976.

———. *From Immigrants to Ethnics: The Italian Americans.* New York: Oxford Univ. Press, 1983.

———. *Italians in Chicago: A Study of Ethnic Mobility*. New York: Oxford Univ. Press, 1970.

Ness, Eliot, with Oscar Fraley. *The Untouchables*. New York: Pocket Books, 1957.

Nickel, Steven. *Torso! Eliot Ness and the Hunt for the Mad Butcher of Willow Run*. New York: Avon Press, 1990.

Nown, Graham. *The English Godfather*. London: Ward Lock, 1987.

O'Connor, Richard. *Hell's Kitchen: The Roaring Days of New York's Wild West Side*. Philadelphia: J. B. Lippincott, 1958.

O'Dwyer, William. *Beyond the Golden Door*. Edited by Paul O'Dwyer. Jamaica, N.Y.: St. John's Univ. Press, 1987.

Ogden, Christopher. *Legacy: A Biography of Moses and Walter Annenberg*. Boston: Little, Brown, 1999.

Overstreet, Harry and Bonaro. *The FBI in Our Open Society*. New York: W. W. Norton, 1969.

Peattie, Donald Culross. "The Most Unforgettable Character I've Met (Max Nootbar)." *Reader's Digest* (January 1944).

Persico, Joseph. "Vendetta in New Orleans." *American Heritage* 24 (June 1973).

Petacco, Arrigo. *Joe Petrosino*. Translated by Charles Lam Markman. New York: Macmillan, 1974.

Peterson, Virgil. *Barbarians in Our Midst: A History of Chicago Crime and Politics*. Boston: Little, Brown, 1952.

———. *The Mob: 200 Years of Organized Crime in New York*. Ottawa, Ill.: Greenhill Press, 1983.

Pinkerton National Detective Agency Files, Library of Congress, Washington, D.C.

Dimaio, Francis P., Container #28.

Hennessy, David, murder, Container #114.

Houk, Seely, murder and "Black Hand" investigation, Container #117.

Pitkin, Thomas M., with Francesco Cordasco. *The Black Hand: A Chapter in Ethnic Crime*. Totowa, N.J.: Littlefield Adams, 1977.

Powers, Richard Gid. *Secrecy and Power: The Life of J. Edgar Hoover*. New York: Free Press; London: Collier Macmillan, 1987.

President's Commission on Law Enforcement and Administration of Justice. *Task Force Report: Organized Crime*. Washington, D.C.: GPO, 1967.

Ragano, Frank, and Selwyn Raab. *Mob Lawyer*. New York: Scribners, 1994.

Rappleye, Charles, and Ed Becker. *All-American Mafioso: The Johnny Roselli Story*. New York: Doubleday, 1991.

Reckless, Walter. *Vice in Chicago*. Chicago: Univ. of Chicago Press, 1933.

Reid, Ed. *Mafia*. New York: Random House, 1952.

Reid, Ed, and Ovid Demaris. *The Green Felt Jungle*. New York: Trident Press, 1963.

Richey, Lawrence. File. Herbert Hoover Library. West Branch, Iowa.

———. File. U.S. Secret Service, National Archives. Washington, D.C.

Riis, Jacob. *How the Other Half Lives.* New York: Hill & Wang, 1957 (orig. 1890).

Roemer, William F. *Accardo: The Genuine Godfather.* New York: Donald I. Fine, 1995.

———. *The War of the Godfathers: The Bloody Confrontation between the Chicago and New York Crime Families for Control of Las Vegas.* New York: Donald I. Fine, 1990.

Russo, Gus. *The Outfit: The Role of Chicago's Underworld in the Shaping of Modern America.* New York: Bloomsbury, 2001.

Salerno, Ralph, and John S. Tompkins. *The Crime Confederation.* Garden City, N.Y.: Doubleday, 1969.

Schoenberg, Robert J. *Mr. Capone.* New York: Morrow, 1992.

Selvaggi, Mario. *The Rise of the Mafia in New York City: From 1896 to World War I.* Indianapolis: Bobbs Merrill, 1978.

Sinclair, Andrew. *Prohibition: The Age of Excess.* Boston: Little, Brown, 1962.

Siragusa, Charles, as told to Robert Wiedrich. *The Trail of the Poppy: Behind the Mask of the Mafia.* Englewood Cliffs, N.J.: Prentice-Hall, 1966.

Smith, Dwight. *The Mafia Mystique.* New York: Basic Books, 1975.

Smith, Mortimer Brewster. *William V. Gaynor, Mayor of New York.* Chicago: Regnery, 1951.

Smith, Richard Norton. *Thomas E. Dewey and His Times.* New York: Simon & Schuster, 1982.

Sondern, Frederic, Jr. *Brotherhood of Evil: The Mafia.* New York: Farrar, Straus & Cudahy, 1959.

Stoddard, Lothrop. *Master of Manhattan: The Life of Richard Croker.* New York: Longmans Green, 1931.

Stuart, Mark A. *Gangster #2: Longy Zwillman, The Man Who Invented Organized Crime.* Secaucus, N.J.: Lyle Stuart, 1985.

Sward, Keith. *The Legend of Henry Ford.* New York: Rinehart and Co., 1948.

Thompson, Craig, and Allan Raymond. *Gang Rule in New York.* New York: Dial Press, 1940.

Time. "I Never Sold Bibles." (Cover story, November 28, 1949).

Touhy, Roger, with Ray Brennan. *The Stolen Years.* Cleveland, Ohio: Pennington Press, 1959.

Train, Arthur. *Courts, Criminals and the Camorra.* New York: Charles Scribner's Sons, 1912.

Tully, Andrew. *Treasury Agent: The Inside Story.* New York: Simon & Schuster, 1958.

Turkus, Burton, and Sid Feder. *Murder Incorporated: The Story of the Syndicate.* New York: Farrar, Straus & Young, 1953.

Tyler, Gus, ed. *Organized Crime in America.* Ann Arbor: Univ. of Michigan Press, 1962.

U.S. General Accounting Office. *Anti-Money Laundering Efforts in the Securities Industry,* October 2001.

U.S. Senate. Committee on Foreign Relations, Report of Senator John Kerry et al., December 1992.

U.S. Senate. Permanent Subcommittee on Investigations, Hearings on Private Banking and Senator Carl Levin Staff Reports, 2001.

U.S. Senate. Special Committee to Investigate Organized Crime in Interstate Commerce (Kefauver Committee). Hearings, 1951.

Walker, Stanley. *The Nightclub Era*. New York: Frederick A. Stokes, 1933.

Walsh, George. *Gentleman Jimmy Walker*. New York: Praeger, 1974.

———. *Public Enemies: The Mayor, the Mob, and the Crime That Was*. New York: W. W. Norton, 1980.

Washburn, Charles. *Come into My Parlor: A Biography of the Aristocratic Everleigh Sisters of Chicago*. New York: Arno Press, 1974.

Werner, M. R. *Tammany Hall*. New York: Doubleday Doran, 1928.

White, G. Edward. *Earl Warren: A Public Life*. New York: Oxford Univ. Press, 1982.

Whitehead, Don. *The FBI Story*. New York: Random House, 1956.

Whyte, William F. *Street Corner Society*. 2d ed. Chicago: Univ. of Chicago Press, 1955.

Williams, T. Harry. *Huey Long*. New York: Knopf, 1969.

Wilson, Frank, with Beth Day. *Special Agent: A Quarter-Century with the Treasury Department and the Secret Service*. New York: Holt, Rinehart & Winston, 1965.

Wolf, George, with Joseph DiMona. *Frank Costello: Prime Minister of the Underworld*. New York: Bantam Books, 1975.

Wood, Joseph. "The Progressives and the Police: Urban Reform and Professionalization of the Police." Doctoral dissertation. Univ. of California, Los Angeles, 1973.

Acknowledgments

This book was made possible through the efforts of my agent Andrew Wylie and his staff, including Tracy Bohan, Sarah Chalfant, and Zoe Pagnamenta. Throughout its preparation, I have received wise guidance from my editor at Henry Holt, Jack Macrae, and his assistant, Supurna Banerjee. I have also received considerable editorial advice and assistance from my former writing colleague, James Lardner, and from Katy Hope.

I would like to thank my researchers, Christa Carnegie, Bindu Methikalam, and Theresa Wang. Among those who shared their knowledge of the history of organized crime and law enforcement, Ronald Goldstock, former director of the New York State Organized Crime Task Force; Boris Kostelanetz, of Kostelanetz & Fink, who, as an assistant U.S. attorney, prosecuted the Hollywood extortion case; and New York County district attorney Robert Morgenthau were particularly helpful.

As with any book on organized crime, there were law enforcement officers, journalists, and others who provided useful information and who would prefer not to be acknowledged. Over the years, various individuals no longer alive also shared a great deal of information and insights that have proved invaluable in the writing of the present work. I have considered acknowledging them by name, but since I am not certain how some of them would feel about that, let me simply record my thanks.

During my research, I drew upon the services of a number of individuals and research institutions, including Lee Lyons, director of research at the Chicago Crime Commission; Lynn Smith, archivist of the Herbert Hoover Library, West Branch, Iowa; Larry Sullivan and the staff of the Lloyd G. Sealey Library at the John Jay College of Criminal Justice in New York City; Ken Cobb of the New York City Municipal Archives; Sara Robinson of the Library of Congress; Mike Sampson, historian of the U.S. Secret Service; the National Archives in Washington, D.C.; the New York Public Library; the Westchester County Library system; and the Columbia University Library.

I also wish to thank Paul S. Miller, chairman of the Board of Directors of the Citizens Crime Commission of New York City, and the members of the board's executive committee for granting me release time to work on the book. (All statements in it, however, reflect the views of the author and not necessarily those of the commission.)

Index

Luciano, Charlie (*cont'd*)
legend of, 132–33
protection of, 164
released and deported, 179–80
rise of, 177
and Schultz murder, 170, 171, 172
success of, 158
as top man in Mafia, 266
Lupo-Morello gang, 30, 31, 52–53
Lyle, John, 61, 126, 129
Lynch, Jack, 239, 240
lynching, 14–16, 17

McBride, Arthur "Mickey," 240, 241, 243
McCarran, Pat, 256
McCarthy, Joe, 251, 257
McClellan, George B., 11
McClellan, George B., Jr., 45
McClusky, "Chesty George," 30–31, 32
McCook, Philip, 176, 179
McCormack, William, 229–30
McDonald, Mike, xi, 61
McDonough, Pete, 102
McErlane clan, 95–96, 98, 99, 126
McGinty, Tommy, 148
McGrath, J. Howard, 254, 256
McGurn, Jack ("Machine Gun Jack") (a.k.a.
Vince Gebardi and DeAmore), 119, 120,
126, 237
Macheca, Joseph, 13, 15
McManus, George, 110
"Mad Butcher of Willow Run," 130
Madden, Owen "Owney," 104–5, 107, 145, 156,
175
gambling, 155, 156
leader in national syndicate, 161
nickname "The Killer," 104
sent into exile, 247
Madonia, Benditto, 32, 33
Mafia, the, ix–x, 3, 4–5, 23, 24, 28, 140, 251–69
American branch of, 26
assessing menace of, 181–97
evidence of existence of, 266
and Italian-American criminals, 80
in Italy, 47
law enforcement wars on, 36–53
murder plot, 88–89
myth of, 4
in New Orleans, 8, 15
portrayal of, 31
power of, 17
in press, 33
rise of, in America, x–xiii
rites and procedures of, 5–6

Secret Service blow against, 51–52
in Sicily, 86–87, 88
term, x, xi, 4
see also American Mafia
Mafia-Camorra War, 79–80
Mafioso, 3, 4, 7, 9, 26, 49, 50, 180
Dimaio as, 43
fleeing Mussolini's crackdown, 135
roundups of, in Sicily, 87–88
Magaddino, Stefano, 88–89, 151
Maione, "Happy," 223, 225
Malloy, Tommy, 201–2
Malone, Mike, 123–24, 127
Mangano, Vince, 141, 267
Mangano family, 218
Manhattan, 27, 142–43, 177
district attorney, 164
Lower Manhattan, 134
Manhattan orgainzation, 224
Manhattan waterfront, 229–31
Mann Act, 60, 61, 183–84, 186, 187
Manton, Martin ("Preying Manton"), 157, 182
Maranzano, Salvatore, 135, 136, 137, 247
killed, 138–39, 141, 145
showdown with Masseria, 136–38, 139, 140
Marcantonio, Vito, 146, 232
Marcello, Carlos, 245, 250, 262
marijuana, 189–90
Marinelli, Al, 134, 146
Maritote, Frank, 201, 212
Martin (Megilowsky), Jules, 167, 169
Masseria, Giuseppe "Joe," 105–6, 132, 133,
134–35
murder of, 252
showdown with Maranzano, 136–38, 139,
140
Matranga, Charlie, 9, 13, 16, 17
Matrangas, 9–10, 13
Mayfield Road gang, 150, 240
Mayo, Katherine, 39–40, 42, 45
Medalie, George, 157, 165, 178
Meehan, "Dinny," 223
Mellon, Andrew, 122
Merlo, Mike, 97, 100, 118
Metropolitan Restaurant and Cafeteria
Association, 167
Miami, 154, 156, 248
Miami Beach, 245
Miami Crime Commission, 254
Miami Daily Herald, 259
Milano, Frank, 150, 152
Milano family, 149
Miro, Henry, 167, 168
Missouri, 248–49

About the Author

THOMAS REPPETTO is a former Chicago commander of detectives and has been the president of New York City's Citizens Crime Commission for more than twenty years. He is the author of *NYPD: A City and Its Police*, a *New York Times* Notable Book.